UNFOLDED

WHAT AILS INDIA'S MSME & STARTUP ECOSYSTEM?

UNFOLDED
WHAT AILS INDIA'S MSME & STARTUP ECOSYSTEM?

P Sesh Kumar
IA&AS (Retd)

THE BROWSER

Title: Unfolded: What Ails India's MSME & Startup Ecosystem?
Author: P Sesh Kumar, IA&AS (Retd)

ISBN: 978-93-49042-41-4

Published by:
JGS Enterprises Pvt Ltd
Imprint: The Browser | Fauji Days

Publisher's Address:
SCO 14-15, FF, Sector 8-C, Chandigarh 160 009

Website: thebrowser.org
Email: service@thebrowser.org

Printed in India

© Layout and Cover Design by beagles
99beagles.com

Publishers & Booksellers

Contents

Section III: Budgets, Crises, and Policy Promises

Section IV: Institutions Under the Scanner

Section V: The Road Ahead: Global Headwinds, Local Challenges

Prologue

◆◆◆

What Ails the Indian MSME Ecosystem – And Why This Book Had to Be Written

It started with a nagging thought. Every time I read a new policy note, an RBI bulletin, or one more press release declaring the MSME sector as the backbone of the Indian economy, I felt: Something isn't quite right.

The Micro, Small, and Medium Enterprises (MSMEs)—our much-vaunted 'small giants'—were being spoken about more than ever before. New schemes were being announced, portals launched, and budgets earmarked. Definitions were changed, credit lines promised, and handholding institutions established. And yet, in the same breath, came news of widespread closures, choking credit, rising NPAs (Non-Performing Assets), and a lingering sense of despair among MSME entrepreneurs. How could both be true?

It took me back to my years in the Ministry of MSME, though that was over 14 years ago. Much has changed since then, at least on paper. We've had Startup India,[1] Stand-Up

1. Startup India is a flagship initiative launched by the Government of India in January 2016 to promote entrepreneurship, innovation, and the creation of startups across the country. It offers a range of benefits, including tax exemptions, easier compliance, access to funding, and support for incubation and intellectual property protection.

India,[2] the MUDRA[3] scheme, Skill India,[4] Digital India,[5] RAMP,[6] CHAMPIONS,[7] Udyam[8] Portal, Emergency Credit Lines—the alphabet soup of initiatives is long. Some have delivered impact; others have struggled. Demonetisation

---

2. Stand-Up India is a government scheme launched in April 2016 to promote entrepreneurship among women and members of the Scheduled Castes (SC) and the Scheduled Tribes (ST) by providing bank loans ranging from ₹10 lakh to ₹1 crore. The scheme aims to facilitate job creation and inclusive economic growth by supporting greenfield enterprises in manufacturing, services, or the trading sector.

3. MUDRA (Micro Units Development and Refinance Agency) is a financial initiative launched by the Government of India in 2015 to provide collateral-free loans up to ₹10 lakh to micro and small enterprises. The loans are categorised under three products—Shishu, Kishore, and Tarun-based on the stage of growth and funding needs of the borrower.

4. Skill India is a national campaign launched by the Government of India in 2015 to train over 40 crore people in various industry-relevant skills to enhance employability and productivity. It encompasses multiple initiatives like the Pradhan Mantri Kaushal Vikas Yojana (PMKVY), aiming to bridge the gap between skill demand and supply across sectors.

5. Digital India is a flagship initiative launched by the Government of India in 2015 to transform the country into a digitally empowered society and knowledge economy. It aims to improve online infrastructure, expand Internet connectivity, and deliver government services digitally to all citizens, especially in rural and remote areas.

6. RAMP (Raising and Accelerating MSME Performance) is a World Bank-supported program launched by the Government of India in 2022 to strengthen the productivity, resilience, and competitiveness of MSMEs. With a total outlay of $808 million over five years, it aims to improve access to markets and credit, enhance policy and regulatory frameworks, and support technology upgrades and skill development.

7. CHAMPIONS (Creation and Harmonious Application of Modern Processes for Increasing the Output and National Strength) is an initiative launched by the Ministry of MSME in 2020 to help small businesses overcome challenges, enhance productivity, and become self-reliant. It functions as a technology-driven platform to provide real-time grievance redressal, support for market access, finance, raw materials, and guidance for MSME growth.

8. Udyam is the official online registration portal launched by the Ministry of MSME in 2020 for classifying and registering MSMEs in India. It provides a paperless, self-declaration-based process that enables businesses to access government schemes, credit facilities, and market support using a unique Udyam Registration Number.

came like a bolt from the blue. COVID-19 (coronavirus disease of 2019) followed as a sucker punch. In the process, India's MSME ecosystem took body blows that have still not fully healed.

What struck me was this: despite the importance of the sector—understood to be contributing over 30% to GDP (Gross Domestic Product) and employing 110 million people—very few have attempted a holistic, honest, and independent evaluation of what ails MSMEs and what genuinely helps. Reports trickle out from time to time by think tanks, professional associations, or inter-ministerial committees, but they're often narrow in scope, sometimes compromised by vested interests, and rarely stitched together into a clear narrative.

Worse still, multiple ministries target the same set of beneficiaries—finance, commerce, rural development, textiles, skill development, not to mention state governments. The result? An administrative babel. Policies overlap. Schemes duplicate. Accountability blurs. The CAG (Comptroller and Auditor General), where I once served for decades, has audited many of these interventions. But these have been piecemeal and fragmented—never a comprehensive performance audit of the ecosystem itself. It is only in November 2025 that the CAG announced it would examine 'ease of doing business' with reference to the MSMEs—though the manner, scope and extent of such audit are awaited.

Then there's the issue of finance. Public banks and financial institutions have an outsized role in the sector's health. But small entrepreneurs tell a different story—of high rejection rates, collateral nightmares, and recovery agents. Ailing MSMEs are hounded, while large corporate defaulters negotiate write-offs with impunity. It's an imbalance that rankles. It demands investigation.

So, why write this book now?

Having worked in this sector from within the system, even after retiring from government service a decade ago, my interest hasn't faded—it has deepened. I have watched policy swings, scheme rollouts, and field outcomes from both inside and outside the arena. And I've seen the disconnect—the wide, painful chasm between what's announced and what's experienced on the ground.

This book is not a white paper nor a policy sermon, but a practitioner's account, a policy analyst's inquiry, and above all, a concerned Indian's attempt to put the pieces together. To ask the inconvenient questions, spotlight what works and what doesn't, and what needs urgent fixing. Also, take into account relevant international developments, as is practicable.

If India is to truly become a $5 trillion economy, our MSME Start up sector cannot remain a slogan. It must be an engine—and a well-oiled one at that. This book is my contribution to that conversation.

Preface

Micro, Small, and Medium Enterprises—those 'small giants' of the global economy—are often spoken of in reverence but rarely understood in depth. They are where jobs begin, where families escape poverty, and where dreams take shape on shop floors and in backroom workshops. They are the heartbeat of resilience, the shock absorbers when economic tsunamis hit, and the spark of innovation in spaces where big corporates fear to tread. Yet in India, the paradox is glaring. We worship MSMEs in political speeches and policy papers, but in practice, we trip them with red tape, starve them of timely credit, and occasionally smother them with our own good intentions.

For me, this paradox became personal in 2006 when I took charge as Joint Secretary in the Ministry of MSME. I had served in several assignments by then, but nothing prepared me for the heady mix of hope and helplessness that came with this portfolio. The ministry was buzzing with reform talk. We had just enacted the MSMED (Micro, Small, and Medium Enterprises Development) Act, finally giving India's millions of small businesses a proper legal framework. We revamped the KVIC (Khadi and Village Industries Commission) Act to inject life into a sector long burdened by nostalgia rather than innovation. We even pushed through the Prime Minister's Employment Generation Programme (PMEGP)[9], merging two disparate schemes into one

9. The Prime Minister's Employment Generation Programme (PMEGP) is a credit-linked subsidy scheme launched by the Government of India in 2008 to

unified architecture. And perhaps most ambitiously, we launched the Khadi Reform and Development Programme (KRDP) with the Asian Development Bank's $150 million backing.

I remember the excitement of those days vividly—the sense that we were on the cusp of transformation. Yet, within months, I also witnessed the first cracks. Khadi Institutions (KIs) that had clamoured for support baulked at the demands of reform. KVIC, expected to lead the charge, shrank into passivity. Slowly, the momentum fizzled. For me, it was a harsh lesson: policy design can be flawless, but without execution muscle, it is just paper. That contradiction—between vision and reality—became the recurring theme of my years in the ministry.

I also learnt that small, almost invisible interventions could change lives far more than grand programmes. A tweak in subsidy disbursal, a simplification in documentation, a fair hearing for a cluster of artisans—these modest acts often did more for entrepreneurship than entire glossy policy launches. I left the ministry in 2011 with a head full of memories—some proud, some frustrating, all unforgettable.

But leaving the ministry did not mean leaving MSMEs behind. If anything, I became more fascinated. As an auditor, and later as a writer, I saw India's small enterprises not as statistics but as flesh-and-blood stories. I met entrepreneurs who mortgaged jewellery for a machine loan, only to be hounded by SARFAESI (Securitisation and Reconstruction of Financial Assets and Enforcement of Security Interest) notices when payments were delayed by a few weeks. I met artisans in Moradabad who continued to hammer away at brassware, while exporters and middlemen reaped profits. I met women in rural clusters who

---

generate self-employment opportunities through the establishment of micro enterprises in the non-farm sector. It is implemented by the Khadi and Village Industries Commission (KVIC) at the national level and provides subsidies of 15% to 35% on project costs, depending on the applicant's category and location. The scheme is open to individuals above 18 years of age and offers financial assistance for both manufacturing and service sector projects.

stitched together livelihoods with microloans that barely covered raw materials but gave them pride and independence.

It was here that the patterns revealed themselves: fragile access to finance, the asymmetry of power between small units and corporate titans, the brutality of compliance, and the chronic mismatch between what schemes promised and what beneficiaries received. The numbers looked tidy in official reports, but the lived reality was messy, chaotic, and too often, heartbreaking. There is no objective and independent third-party evaluation of outcomes from various (often overlapping) initiatives of government—only eulogy and self-congratulation. The proposed audit of ease of doing business by CAG would be keenly awaited.

This book is born of that dual vantage point—the insider who once helped craft policy and the outsider who later watched the outcomes with a mixture of admiration, exasperation, and hope. It is a narrative told in five acts, like a play where MSMEs are both protagonists and victims, and where policymakers, bankers, auditors, and entrepreneurs enter and exit with varying degrees of responsibility and blame.

In the first act, we pan the camera outward. We travel to Germany, China, Brazil, and Australia to see how their small enterprises thrive—and then hold up a mirror to India, asking why we lag behind despite decades of interventions.

The second act shifts to the glittering world of startups—our 'new economy' darlings. We unpack the Gensol-BluSmart fiasco, the unicorn hype cycles, and the reverse-flipping trend, questioning whether we are building sustainable value or simply living in valuation bubbles.

The third act is the story of shocks and slogans. Demonetisation, COVID-19, and a long parade of budgets and schemes—MUDRA, RAMP, CHAMPIONS—all tested the resilience of India's MSMEs. On dashboards, the numbers looked triumphant. On the ground, they often rang hollow. This act blends statistics with stories—of tea sellers in Darjeeling, fabricators in Tiruppur, and artisans in Moradabad—to show the gap between promise and performance. There is also India's defence MSME story—a paradox of grand design and ground-level disarray. Since 2016, a torrent of reforms—from DAP (Defence Acquisition Procedure) 2020, Make-I/II, and iDEX (Innovations for Defence Excellence) to SRIJAN (Self-Reliant Initiatives through Joint Action) and revamped offset rules—has promised to transform small enterprises into the backbone of national security. We peel away the rhetoric to reveal why 'Make in India' risks becoming 'Missed in India'. We call for a frank CAG-style audit, faster procurement, and real empowerment so that India's defence MSMEs can finally march from policy files to production floors.

The fourth act is the most searing. It takes readers into the very institutions created to nurture the sector: KVIC, NSIC (National Small Industries Corporation), the Coir Board, and even the ministry itself. Here, the narrative is less about the failure of entrepreneurs and more about the failure of the state. Tokenism, self-certified glory, bureaucratic apathy—the rot is laid bare. Yet even here, I pay tribute to the reformers who tried, against odds, to shift the system.

The final act looks outward again. It grapples with global headwinds—from Trump's punitive tariffs to China's relentless manufacturing juggernaut—and asks whether India's MSMEs can truly rise to the challenge of global competitiveness. It is not just a question of policies, but of vision, leadership, and trust.

This book, then, is not a lament, nor a conventional critique. It is a call to action—urgent, insistent, and hopeful. I remain convinced that India's small giants, if truly empowered, can deliver growth with both scale and soul. They can give us not just GDP but dignity, not just exports but employment, not just numbers but resilience.

If my years in the ministry taught me anything, it is this: change is possible, but only if we stop treating MSMEs Startups as poster children of speeches and start treating them as partners in nation-building.

That is the spirit in which this book is written.

SECTION I

◆◆◆

GLOBAL AND NATIONAL BACKDROP: SETTING THE CONTEXT

Before we dissect India's MSMEs, we travel across borders to see how other nations empower their small businesses, and then turn the mirror back on ourselves.

CHAPTER 1

Small Giants Across the World – Lessons from the USA, the UK, Germany, China, Brazil, and Australia

When it comes to building resilient economies, it is not always about the titans of industry. Sometimes, it is the small, nimble, and determined enterprises—the MSMEs or Small Business Concerns (SBCs)—that carry nations on their shoulders. They spark innovation, generate employment, and fuel exports. But across the world,[10] these small giants are defined, nurtured, and supported in vastly different ways.

What Is in a Definition? A World of Difference

Imagine three friends starting different businesses in different countries. Ravi in India opens a small garment stitching unit and invests ₹30 lakh, earning ₹1 crore annually. In India, he is a small enterprise. Emily in the UK starts a bakery with an £8 million turnover and 45 employees—she qualifies as a

---

10. We critically compare, in Chapter 25, India's ease of setting up a small business with ten other economies—China, the USA, Indonesia, Germany, Brazil, South Africa, Kenya, Singapore, the Philippines, and Australia—by mapping essence of their approvals, federal structures, administrative rationalisation, and actual experience of entrepreneurs.

small business. Chen in China runs a mobile parts unit with 250 employees—still a small firm under Chinese rules. Each is 'small', but the size and support they get depend entirely on where they live. Definitions vary, and so does the help they receive. Forward linkage is what turns a backyard enterprise into a brand.

In India, an MSME is primarily defined by its investment in plant and machinery or equipment, and its turnover. As per the revised 2020 classification, a micro enterprise is one with investment up to ₹1 crore and turnover up to ₹5 crore. Small enterprises can go up to ₹10 crore investment and ₹50 crore turnover, and medium enterprises up to ₹50 crore investment and ₹250 crore turnover. These have been further liberalized/rationalized in 2025. Chapter 8 refers.

But India is not alone in this definitional juggle. Let's jet-set across continents to see how other countries size up their small businesses.

In the United States, the Small Business Administration (SBA) doesn't go by a one-size-fits-all rule. It varies by industry, revenue, and number of employees. Typically, a business with fewer than 500 employees qualifies, but in sectors like manufacturing and wholesale, thresholds are stricter. The SBA uses the North American Industry Classification System (NAICS)[11] to calibrate its support structures.

The United Kingdom, under its Companies Act, defines a small company as one with a turnover of less than £10.2 million, a balance sheet total under £5.1 million, and fewer than 50 employees. For medium enterprises, the thresholds go

11. The NAICS is a standardised classification used by the US Small Business Administration (SBA) to categorise businesses by industry for the purpose of determining size standards and eligibility for federal programmes. Each business is assigned a specific NAICS code based on its primary economic activity, which helps assess whether it qualifies as a 'small business' under SBA guidelines.

up to £36 million turnover and 250 employees. The UK also uses terms like SMEs (Small and Medium Enterprises) more frequently than micro.

Germany, the engineering powerhouse of Europe, uses the EU (European Union) definition—fewer than 250 employees, with annual turnover not exceeding €50 million or a balance sheet total not exceeding €43 million. Yet Germany's famed 'Mittelstand'—its backbone of medium-sized, family-owned enterprises—goes beyond these metrics to represent a unique business culture of innovation and global leadership in niche areas.

France similarly uses the EU SME definition but is more aggressive in offering tax rebates, research grants, and export support. French SMEs often have under 250 employees but form 99% of the country's businesses and employ over 60% of the private workforce.

Australia goes with the Australian Bureau of Statistics' (ABS) classification: micro (1–4 employees), small (5–19 employees), medium (20–199 employees), and large (200+ employees). However, the Australian Taxation Office (ATO) defines SMEs for tax purposes as businesses with a turnover under AUD 50 million.

Brazil uses different definitions under various regimes. Under the 'Simples Nacional' tax regime, small businesses are classified based on annual revenue—up to BRL 360,000 for micro, and up to BRL 4.8 million for small. The definitions link directly to tax slabs, making compliance simpler.

Indonesia defines MSMEs through Law No. 20/2008 based on asset size and revenue. Micro enterprises have assets up to IDR 50 million and revenue up to IDR 300 million. Small and medium thresholds are IDR 500 million to IDR 10 billion in revenue, and employee counts are also considered.

China, the dragon economy, classifies the SMEs sector-wise with thresholds for revenue, assets, and employees. In manufacturing, a small enterprise employs up to 300 people; in retail, the bar is 100. The emphasis is not just on classification but on high-tech, export-oriented, and innovation-driven small firms. China also promotes 'gazelles'—fast-growing startups that show promise to become unicorns.

Not Just Definitions, But Dedicated Lifelines

Definitions are only the starting line. The real race is won—or lost—in how countries support their MSMEs across the value chain.

> Think of a tiny company making handcrafted wooden toys. In the US, that company could win a contract to supply toys to Walmart under small business procurement rules. In India, the same toy maker might struggle to get an online GST (Goods and Services Tax) registration, have no idea how to sell on Amazon, and end up relying only on local festivals. This is the gap between being part of a supply chain and simply surviving.

The United States excels in financial support through the SBA's 7(a) loan programme,[12] disaster loans, and SBIC (Small Business Investment Company) equity funds. Government contracts mandate a percentage share for small businesses, and federal agencies run targeted export promotion and training schemes. Crucially, the US ecosystem ensures backward linkages through supply chain integration with larger firms.

The UK offers generous R&D (Research and Development) tax credits, Innovate UK grants, and the British Business

---

12. The US Small Business Administration's 7(a) Loan Program is its primary and most flexible lending initiative, designed to help small businesses access financing for various purposes such as working capital, equipment purchase, or real estate acquisition. Under this program, the SBA guarantees a portion of the loan—up to 85% for loans up to $150,000 and up to 75% for larger amounts—to reduce lender risk and encourage approvals. Loan amounts can go up to $5 million, with repayment terms varying based on the use of funds, making it a popular choice for startups and growing small businesses.

Bank's loan guarantees. Digital business advisory services and enterprise zones reduce barriers to entry. Exports are incentivised through the UK Export Finance scheme.[13] SMEs are also supported by public procurement quotas.

Germany, with its KfW Bankengruppe (a government-owned development bank), provides low-interest loans, equity finance, and export credits. The hallmark, however, is its dual education and vocational training system that creates a steady supply of skilled workers for the Mittelstand. Forward linkages come through strong industry associations, innovation clusters, and export platforms.

France offers direct subsidies, zero-interest loans, and Bpifrance's financing arms for innovation. The French Tech Mission promotes tech startups, offering incubation, grants, and tax relief. There is targeted support for SMEs led by women, minorities, and those in rural areas.

Australia combines tax incentives with the Entrepreneurs' Programme, which provides expert mentoring, business diagnostics, and co-funding. Export assistance through Austrade and digital market access programmes is available, while state governments offer land and logistics support for small manufacturers.

Brazil's Simples Nacional regime is globally lauded for easing tax compliance across federal, state, and municipal levels. Small businesses can opt for a unified tax return. Funding is more fragmented, but development banks like BNDES (Brazilian Development Bank) step in for priority sectors. Brazil also uses fintech and mobile platforms to promote financial inclusion for informal enterprises.

---

13. The UK Export Finance (UKEF) scheme supports SMEs by providing government-backed loans, insurance, and guarantees to help them export goods and services. It offers products like the Export Working Capital Scheme and Bond Support Scheme, enabling SMEs to access financing when private lenders are unable or unwilling to lend due to export-related risks. UKEF works alongside commercial banks to ensure UK businesses can fulfil international contracts and compete globally with confidence.

Indonesia has a wide range of state-owned enterprises (SOEs) and ministries offering microcredit, entrepreneurship training, and subsidies. Programmes like Kredit Usaha Rakyat (KUR) provide loans with government interest subsidies. The challenge lies in the fragmentation and overlap between schemes.

China is the most aggressive in promoting MSMEs. Tax exemptions, interest subsidies, export facilitation, and digital enablement are standard. Special economic zones offer tailor-made infrastructure for small firms. More than policy, it's execution through local government units that makes the difference. China has also built an army of unicorns like ByteDance and DJI (Da Jiang Innovations), thanks to tech parks, venture capital support, and strategic IP (Intellectual Property) policies.

Let us now explore the status of the challenges that MSMEs face across the nations.

Global Voices of Distress: What MSME Surveys Reveal About Challenges Across Nations

MSMEs may differ in scale, geography, and product lines, but a common thread unites them across continents—a shared struggle against rising costs, vanishing markets, and inaccessible finance. A sweeping set of global surveys compiled in the November 2022 report by the Centre for Strategic and International Studies (CSIS) shines an unflinching light on the precise pain points that MSMEs are grappling with, from the developed corridors of the United States and Europe to the fragile economies of the Least Developed Countries[14] (LDCs), India, and Bangladesh.

14. An LDC is a nation classified by the United Nations (UN) as having the lowest indicators of socioeconomic development, based on criteria like gross national income (GNI) per capita, human assets (health and education), and economic vulnerability. These countries face severe structural impediments to sustainable development and are highly susceptible to economic and environmental shocks.

In the United States, the epicentre of free enterprise, the very heartbeat of small business is threatened not by lack of ambition but by labour shortages and inflationary pressures. A Goldman Sachs survey of 1,533 small firms across 48 US states and two territories painted a picture of rising frustration. A staggering 71% of respondents flagged the lack of qualified workers as their most critical challenge, while 63% pointed to high labour costs as a debilitating burden. Supply chain fragility (13%) and inflation (32%) formed the background noise of every business decision, with 45% of firms reporting difficulty in hiring and retaining skilled staff.

A small spice grinder in Germany sells herbs to a giant organic supermarket chain. Why? Because German law encourages big companies to source from small ones, and helps the small firm meet packaging, hygiene, and tax standards. In India, the same small spice grinder is stuck in a local mandi, selling to a middleman who pays late and takes a cut.

Another nationwide sample by Capital One involving 1,200 small enterprises (each earning below $20 million annually) found that inflation had become a pervasive concern, cited by 48% of respondents, followed by supply chain constraints (28%) and heavy taxation (26%). Even more telling was the anxiety over competition from large businesses, mentioned by one in five firms—a reminder that David still feels crushed under the heel of Goliath in the modern American economy.

The National Federation of Independent Business (NFIB) corroborated these trends with a separate survey of 2,553 firms. Here, the soaring cost of health insurance emerged as the single largest concern for 50.6% of businesses—an issue that remains uniquely American in scale. Beyond healthcare, locating qualified employees (30.5%) and tax burdens (both in terms of amount and complexity) also loomed large. What these surveys reveal is a system that allows immense entrepreneurial freedom, but also exposes small businesses to market forces with little institutional buffer, especially in periods of macroeconomic turbulence.

Now consider the LDCs, where the problems are not structural complexities but elemental deprivations. A joint survey by the UN Capital Development Fund, the International Chamber of Commerce, and other global institutions covered 2,245 SMEs across 47 LDCs. The findings were nothing short of alarming. Over 83% of firms cited a sheer lack of access to customers as their top obstacle. Nearly half (45.6%) struggled with obtaining reliable suppliers, while 24% pointed to rising input costs. The most jarring insight: only 17% mentioned access to finance, suggesting that in these economies, the very architecture of commercial exchange remains broken. There are no buyers, no suppliers, no liquidity, and, therefore, no business. In these contexts, a loan is meaningless if the enterprise cannot even find its next customer or stable source of input.

India's story lies somewhere in the middle—between overregulation and under-support. The Dun & Bradstreet survey of 250 Indian MSMEs operating with annual revenues of ₹100–300 crore revealed a consistent demand for deeper credit lines and market linkages. Fifty-nine per cent of respondents pleaded for better credit facilities, underscoring a chronic mismatch between what MSMEs need and what banks are willing to provide. Another 48% wanted marketing support, indicating that even if production problems were solved, demand stimulation and sales infrastructure were still missing. Market access (42%) and productivity improvements (37%) were also cited as key needs, alongside complaints about burdensome compliance requirements (29%). In short, Indian MSMEs don't merely suffer from funding constraints—they also feel starved of systemic recognition and policy empathy. The expansion of Udyam registration and schemes like the Emergency Credit

Line Guarantee Scheme (ECLGS) has helped, but many firms remain underserved, unregistered,and unseen.

Bangladesh, too, offers a sobering cautionary tale. According to a survey by the International Finance Corporation (IFC) of 500 MSMEs, the sector was ravaged by the pandemic and its aftermath. A jaw-dropping 91% of businesses reported declining cash flows, while 88% cited a plunge in demand. More than 86% experienced reduced working hours per week, and 78% faced difficulties in procuring inputs. Nearly two-thirds (67%) reported a drop in access to financial services—a sign that when the tide turned, banks walked away instead of stepping up. These figures illustrate how the economic architecture in many developing nations remains fragile, with external shocks swiftly translating into existential threats for small businesses.

Meanwhile, Europe—a region often held up as a model of institutional resilience—showed a different pattern of stress. A massive survey covering 16,365 MSMEs across 27 EU nations and 12 neighbouring countries revealed that administrative

> Think of your neighbourhood tailor who stitches school uniforms. She doesn't have a GST number. She doesn't pay income tax. She hires two helpers but pays them in cash. She doesn't qualify for MSME schemes because she isn't registered. She is part of India's 90% 'informal' MSME sector—visible everywhere, but invisible to policy.

burden was the biggest concern (57%), especially among firms navigating multiple regulatory layers. Payment delays haunted 35% of businesses, while access to finance (29%) and digital readiness (14%) were also problematic. Interestingly, 23% cited skills and managerial competence as gaps, suggesting that even in well-regulated environments, MSMEs crave not just funds but also capacity building.

Together, these surveys strip away the policy gloss and expose the beating hearts of small businesses—each survey, a mirror to the lived reality of entrepreneurship under stress. Whether it's an American firm struggling to pay health premiums or a Bangladeshi trader reeling from input shortages or an Indian MSME desperate for a working capital top-up, the challenges are real, varied, and intensely local.

What India can learn from this is simple but vital: no one-size-fits-all policy will do. Different countries have responded to MSME distress with a mix of demand stimulation, wage subsidies, regulatory relaxation, skill support, and financial deepening. India's policy toolkit must evolve to reflect that complexity. The future lies not in doling out templated schemes from Delhi but in listening to what the surveys say from Dhaka to Dallas, and designing policy not from ivory towers, but from the factory floors, kirana shops, and warehouse sheds that define the real economy.

India's Missed Linkages: The Elephant in the Room

India, with over 63 million MSMEs, arguably has the largest micro-enterprise ecosystem in the world. Yet, it struggles to translate numbers into sustained economic value. Most Indian MSMEs operate informally, rely on family labour, and remain excluded from formal credit, market linkages, or technology.

Schemes like MUDRA, CGTMSE,[15] PMEGP, and the Fund of Funds for Startups (FFS)[16] offer financial and

15. The Credit Guarantee Fund Trust for Micro and Small Enterprises (CGTMSE) is a scheme launched by the Government of India and SIDBI (Small Industries Development Bank of India) to provide collateral-free credit to micro and small enterprises through a credit guarantee mechanism. It assures lenders up to 75%–85% of the loan amount in case of default, thereby encouraging banks and financial institutions to lend to first-time entrepreneurs and small businesses without demanding security.

16. The Fund of Funds for Startups (FFS) is a Government of India initiative under the Startup India program, approved in June 2016 with an initial corpus of ₹10,000 crore and managed by SIDBI on behalf of DPIIT. It does not invest directly in startups; instead, it channels capital into SEBI registered Alternative Investment Funds (AIFs), which are required to invest at least twice the FFS contribution

Imagine a student trying to get a study loan. In the US, the process is mostly online and quick, based on credit score. In Brazil or Indonesia, small businesses apply the same way—digitally, with quick approval under unified national schemes.

But in India, an MSME often needs to submit physical papers, GST returns, past income, land records—and even then, the bank might say no. The process is the barrier, not the borrower.

technical support. However, unlike the US or Germany, India lacks a strong system for forward linkages, like mandated procurement, integrated vocational training, or digital marketing handholding. Subsidies are patchy and often captured by middlemen. Export readiness is low, with only 48,000 MSMEs actively engaged in exports as per 2023 data.

While India has celebrated the rise of unicorns—over 110 as of early 2024—most of them are tech-based B2C (business-to-customer) platforms, heavily funded by foreign VCs (Venture Capitalists). MSMEs in manufacturing, agro-processing, or rural crafts are largely left out of this innovation wave. There is little crossover between traditional MSMEs and India's startup ecosystem.

What Can India Learn?

First, make the definition dynamic and industry-specific. Sectoral thresholds, like in the US or China, may help with better targeting of support.

---

into eligible startups. By using a structured, multiplier-based approach, FFS is reported to have catalysed a significant increase in private funding—over ₹81,000 crore mobilised across more than 1,100 startups as of early 2025—and strengthened India's venture capital ecosystem, particularly supporting early-stage, deep-tech, and innovation-driven enterprises.

Second, streamline access to credit through unified digital platforms with real-time disbursements, like Brazil's Simples Nacional or Indonesia's KUR.

A tech startup in Bengaluru builds an app that helps people order groceries. It raises ₹50 crore from US investors and becomes a unicorn. Meanwhile, a ten-year-old paper bag unit in Tirunelveli, employing 25 women, can't get a ₹10 lakh loan.

Both are startups. One is glamorised. The other, ignored. India celebrates digital disruption but must also nourish manufacturing, services, and rural enterprises.

Third, institutionalise forward linkages. Mandate public procurement quotas for MSMEs, integrate them into PLI (Production Linked Incentive) schemes, and offer GST exemptions for B2B (business-to-business) supplies to large exporters.

Fourth, encourage mentorship and clustering. The success of Germany's Mittelstand lies in localised hubs of innovation, backed by universities, R&D, and industry chambers.

Fifth, align the MSME policy with the unicorn policy. Encourage deep-tech, high-growth potential MSMEs with innovation grants and tax holidays. Invite cross-investment from large unicorns into MSME clusters.

Finally, evaluate outcomes, not just outlays. India must move beyond loan disbursal numbers to assess job creation, productivity, and export contribution of its MSME sector.

The world has shown us what works. It is time the Indian MSME story evolved from a survival narrative to one of global leadership.

We now move over to the central issue of the book: 'The MSME ecosystem and its challenges in India'.

CHAPTER 2

◆◆◆

What Ails India's MSME Ecosystem? – Structural Weaknesses and Policy Contradictions

Abstract:

India's MSMEs form the backbone of its economy, accounting for roughly 30% of GDP and employing over 110 million people. In recent years, the government has launched numerous initiatives—from Startup India and a dedicated FFS to the Skill India Mission (with flagship scheme PMKVY) and the CGTMSE—to catalyse MSME and startup growth. This chapter critically examines these support schemes and finds significant gaps between policy intent and on-ground outcomes[17]*. Key challenges include implementation inefficiencies, limited access to formal credit (only ~14% of India's 63 million MSMEs have such access), suboptimal skill development outcomes (with only ~43% of trainees placed in jobs and even lower effective placement rates), overlapping bureaucratic jurisdictions, and questions over data reliability. Comparative insights from China's 'Little Giants' programme—which has nurtured over 14,600 high-tech small firms—and*

17. Chapter 9 discusses the reliability and objectivity of MSME statistics and suggests a critical assessment, considering the methodologies employed and the challenges inherent in data collection, especially within the informal sector.

other international best practices underscore how targeted support and skill development can yield far better results. A contrast emerges between India's broad but fragmented approach and China's focused, innovation-driven model. The chapter concludes with a Way Forward that advocates strategic, regulatory, and institutional reforms—including streamlined governance, enhanced credit and market access, integration of MSMEs into global value chains, and robust skill-training ecosystems—to revitalise India's MSME sector. The tone throughout is policy-oriented, grounded in evidence, and geared toward actionable reforms to unlock the potential of India's MSMEs.

Introduction

> Why Only 14% Get Bank Loans
>
> Think of a school student asking for a cycle loan from the bank. The bank says, 'Do you have your mark sheet, address proof, and your father's job letter?' But the student only has his school ID and says, 'I use the cycle to deliver tiffins in the neighbourhood to earn money.' The bank refuses. That's how most Indian MSMEs feel when they apply for loans—they have income, but no official paperwork.

MSMEs are widely recognised as the engine of growth and job creation in India. As of the mid-2020s, India is home to an estimated 63 million MSMEs, which are stated to contribute approximately 30% of the country's GDP and about 40% of exports. These enterprises are understood to provide livelihoods to roughly 110 million Indians, secondonlytoagriculture in terms of employment. Given their economic significance, successive governments have introduced a plethora of schemes to support MSMEs' expansion, enhance their competitiveness, and foster entrepreneurship. Major national initiatives—such as the Startup India programme (launched in 2016 to

Imagine you want to bake a cake. One person brings flour. Another brings sugar. A third adds milk. But no one knows who's supposed to mix it, bake it, or serve it. The cake never gets made. That's what happens when different ministries run similar MSME schemes without talking to each other.

promote startups and innovation), the FFS (managed by SIDBI to channel venture capital to startups), the Skill India Mission (launched in 2015 to impart market-relevant skills through programmes like PMKVY)[18], and credit facilitation schemes like Pradhan Mantri MUDRA Yojana and the CGTMSE—comprise the backbone of India's MSME support ecosystem. These schemes share ambitious goals: to ease regulatory burdens, provide funding and credit support, upgrade workforce skills, and ultimately enable MSMEs and startups to thrive.

Despite these well-intentioned efforts, India's MSME ecosystem continues to face persistent challenges that hinder its growth and global competitiveness. Many MSMEs remain micro in scale and informal in nature, struggling to scale up. Access to finance is a chronic problem—a recent report estimated a staggering $530 billion credit gap in the Indian MSME sector, with only about 14% of small businesses able to access formal credit. Skill development programmes have expanded training capacity but often fall short on quality and job placement outcomes, raising concerns about the return

18. PMKVY is the flagship skill development scheme launched in July 2015 by the Ministry of Skill Development and Entrepreneurship to provide free, industry-relevant training and certification—aligned with the National Skills Qualifications Framework—aimed at enhancing the employability of youth through Short Term Training, Recognition of Prior Learning, and specialised targeted projects. Under the program, trainees receive monetary rewards upon successful certification and placement, while accredited training centres across the country deliver standardised, outcome-based skill development.

on investment in skilling. Multiple agencies and overlapping jurisdictions lead to fragmented implementation, while data on MSME performance and scheme outcomes is sometimes unreliable or inconsistent. The net result is that, despite a robust framework of support schemes, India's MSMEs have not realised their full potential, especially when benchmarked against international peers.

Major Initiatives to Support MSMEs and Startups in India

> Imagine a cricket academy that trains 100 students every month, but only five make it to a local club.
>
> The rest go back to their schools or stop playing.
>
> Now imagine the government funding that academy year after year, without checking if the training is helping the students get selected.
>
> That's what's happening with many short-term skill programmes—lots of training, but few real jobs.

Startup India and the Fund of Funds (FFS)

The Startup India initiative, launched in 2016, marked a watershed in government support for entrepreneurship. It introduced a definition for 'startup' and a recognition process under the Department for Promotion of Industry and Internal Trade (DPIIT) to extend various benefits. Over the past several years, Startup India has led to the recognition of more than 1,00,000 startups across the country, with an average of 80 new startups gaining formal recognition each day. Notably, roughly half of these startups have originated from Tier-II and Tier-III cities, signalling a broadening of the startup movement beyond the major metros. Recognised startups enjoy incentives such as tax holidays on profits, easier compliance norms, and access

Meena learns how to do digital marketing in a two-week training program. She gets a certificate, but the only job she finds is at a sweet shop managing sales.

Her training didn't match the real-world job needs, and the sweet shop didn't care about her certificate. The system taught her something, but not what the market wanted.

to government support programmes. According to official estimates, the Startup India programme has helped generate around 4,20,000 direct jobs (an average of 11 jobs per startup) and many more indirectly. India today boasts the world's third-largest startup ecosystem by number of startups and ranks second among middle-income countries in innovation quality—reflecting the high aspirations behind this initiative.

A key component of Startup India is the Fund of Funds for Startups (FFS), a ₹10,000 crore corpus operated by SIDBI to provide growth capital. Rather than investing directly in startups, the FFS acts as a 'fund of funds', investing in SEBI (Securities and Exchange Board of India)-registered VC and alternative investment funds which, in turn, finance startups. The goal is to leverage private VC expertise and create a multiplier effect on government funding. In practice, however, the deployment of FFS funds has been gradual. As of 31 March 2022—nearly six years into the programme—SIDBI had sanctioned about ₹7,225 crore from the fund, but had disbursed only around ₹2,492 crore to VC firms. This meant only one-fourth of the corpus had actually reached startups via intermediaries by that date. While the sanctioned amount indicates a strong commitment (over 70% of the corpus approved for allocation), the slower disbursement reflects the time taken for VC funds to draw capital and invest in portfolio companies. It also points to the stringent selection and due diligence processes in place—important for quality control, but potentially delaying much-needed capital for startups. In response to evolving needs, the government has periodically adjusted the focus of FFS (for instance, prioritising new-age sectors like AI (Artificial Intelligence) and manufacturing in recent allocations). Moreover, recognising the continued funding crunch, especially in the early stages, Budget 2025 announced an additional ₹10,000 crore to supplement the FFS. The FFS has thus been a novel experiment in public venture funding, showing some success but also underlining that accessing capital remains a leading challenge for Indian startups—particularly those outside the top tier that attract private VC investment on their own.

Skill India Mission and PMKVY

A vibrant MSME sector requires not just entrepreneurs and credit, but also a skilled workforce. The Skill India Mission was launched in 2015 to impart skills to millions of youth and make them employable, thereby meeting industry needs (including those of MSMEs) and promoting self-employment. The flagship of this mission is the PMKVY, which offers free

> In Germany, Rakesh (if he were German) would go to school in the morning and work part-time in a bakery as an apprentice. By the time he finishes school, he's already job-ready.
>
> In India, Rakesh finishes college and then starts searching for a job without any real-world skills. This is why Germany's MSMEs are productive—they train while people learn.

short-term skill training courses through accredited training partners across the country. Since its inception, PMKVY (along with associated schemes like Jan Shikshan Sansthans and ITIs (Industrial Training Institutes)) has enrolled a massive number of candidates. According to official data, from 2015 to the end of 2024, over 16 million (1.6 crore) individuals have received some form of skill training or orientation under PMKVY.

This scale is unprecedented, reflecting the government's commitment to addressing India's skills gap in a demographic dividend era.

However, the ultimate measure of a skill programme's success is gainful employment of its trainees—and here PMKVY's outcomes have been underwhelming. The Ministry of Skill Development reports an overall placement rate of about 43% for certified trainees under PMKVY (across its first three phases, 2015–2022). In other words, less than half of those who complete a short-term training course are able to secure a job placement. Moreover, few independent assessments suggest that even this figure may be inflated, given the laxness of outcome tracking and potential biases in the reported data. One detailed analysis found that while official reports claimed a 54% placement rate for PMKVY, the actual verified placement rate was only around 22%, implying that many 'placed' candidates might not have remained in jobs or the placements were of questionable quality. Indeed, the placement rate plummeted to the single digits in later phases of PMKVY: Phase 2.0 (2016–2020) saw only ~20% placement by some counts, and Phase 3.0 (2020–2021) reached as low as ~6%. Such outcomes are clearly far below expectations, raising concerns over the efficacy of the short-term skilling model. A parliamentary answer in early 2023 acknowledged that across PMKVY 1.0, 2.0, and 3.0, out of about 7.1 million trained, only 2.4 million (34%) were confirmed placed—and even this likely counts any form of employment, including informal and short-term jobs.

Several factors contribute to these inadequate placement outcomes. The training courses under PMKVY are often very short in duration (sometimes just a few weeks or even days), which limits the depth of skill imparted. Many courses emphasise quantity over quality, partly driven by targets and funding structure. There have been instances of mismatches between training and industry demand, resulting in certified candidates not being hired. Additionally, monitoring of training centres has been a challenge, leading to variability in quality and even cases of misuse (e.g., reports of ghost candidates or exaggerated placement claims in some centres). To its credit, the government has taken steps in the latest PMKVY 4.0 to address some of these issues—for example, focusing on new-age skills (such as AI, robotics, and green jobs), mandating On-the-Job Training components, and launching a digital Skill India portal to connect trainees with employers. Yet, the structural issue remains that short-term skilling without strong employer linkages yields limited employment traction. The Skill India Mission's mixed record thus reflects an implementation inefficiency: enormous resources and efforts have been put into training, but the translation into sustainable livelihoods has been weaker than anticipated. This gap directly affects the MSME ecosystem, as MSMEs both contribute trainees (many skilling programme entrants are educated unemployed youth who might otherwise start micro enterprises) and are potential employers if skilled talent is available.

Credit Access and the Credit Guarantee Scheme (CGTMSE)

Access to finance is routinely cited as the most pressing constraint on MSMEs in India. Recognising this, the government and RBI (Reserve Bank of India) have introduced various channels of credit support—from priority sector lending mandates for banks, to specialised institutions like SIDBI, to innovative fintech-based lending solutions. Among government schemes, a cornerstone is the CGTMSE, which provides collateral-free loans to MSMEs by assuring lenders against default risks. Under CGTMSE, loans up to a certain limit (recently increased to ₹5 crore from the earlier ₹2 crore) are guaranteed, so that banks/NBFCs (Non-Banking Financial Companies) can lend to small businesses without collateral, the guarantee covering a significant portion of any loan losses. This scheme, operational since 2000 (and revamped in 2023), has grown to become one of the largest credit guarantee programmes globally. In 2023, the scheme was revamped with a fresh infusion of corpus and more liberal terms—guarantee coverage was enhanced, fees reduced, and claim procedures simplified—to encourage lenders to utilise it fully for boosting credit flow to MSMEs.

The impact of the credit guarantee mechanism is evident from recent data. In the calendar year 2024 alone, CGTMSE approved nearly 2 million (19.9 lakh) guarantees for MSME loans, amounting to a total credit coverage of ₹2.44 lakh crore (≈ $30 billion). This represents a sharp increase in uptake, aided by the post-revamp push. It indicates that a large number of micro and small enterprises received collateral-free loans with government backing in that year. In addition to CGTMSE, micro enterprises have benefited from the MUDRA loan scheme (which offers unsecured loans up to ₹10 lakh through banks and MFIs (Microfinance Institutions)). Since 2015, over 37 crore MUDRA loans have been sanctioned, though mostly of very small ticket sizes (average loan under ₹50,000), largely to micro-entrepreneurs, reflecting more of a livelihood credit programme than growth capital.

Despite these schemes, credit access remains grossly inadequate relative to needs. The vast majority of India's MSMEs are informal micro units that lack documented financial statements or collateral, making banks hesitant to lend. Even among formal MSMEs, many avoid borrowing due to cumbersome procedures or fear of debt. As noted earlier, only about 14% of Indian MSMEs currently access formal credit—meaning over 85% rely on self-finance or informal sources. The financing gap for Indian MSMEs is estimated at roughly $330–530 billion,[19] indicating that existing schemes (including

19. Relevant also to Chapters 10, 12, and 13.

credit guarantees) have a long way to go. For instance, while ₹2.4 lakh crore in guarantees in one year is significant, the total addressable credit gap is on the order of ₹20–30 lakh crore. Moreover, many micro enterprises remain unaware of schemes like CGTMSE, or face difficulties in application; conversely, some banks remain cautious and impose their own criteria (such as insisting on collateral despite the guarantee, or not extending loans to first-time borrowers).

Another financial challenge is the problem of delayed payments to MSMEs, especially by large corporate buyers and government departments. Chronic payment delays strain MSME liquidity and often force them to seek working capital loans (if they can) or to downsize operations. The government has mandated payment to MSMEs within 45 days and set up online complaint platforms (MSME Samadhaan), but enforcement is weak. This issue, while beyond the scope of support 'schemes' per se, is a critical aspect of the ecosystem that nullifies the benefits of credit schemes if not addressed. In summary, India's MSME financing initiatives, including credit guarantees and refinance schemes, are well-conceived and have yielded some positive outcomes, but the reach and scale are still insufficient. Substantial segments of the MSME sector remain financially excluded or underfunded, highlighting the implementation gap between policy and practice in credit delivery.

Other Support Schemes and Institutional Framework

In addition to the flagship programmes above, numerous other schemes target specific aspects of MSME promotion. For example, the PMEGP provides subsidies for micro-enterprise creation in rural and small towns, and the CLCSS (Credit Linked Capital Subsidy Scheme) subsidises technology upgrades in manufacturing MSMEs. The Atal Innovation

Mission and Atal Incubation Centres were established to nurture startups and innovation hubs, complementing Startup India. The Ministry of MSME runs cluster development programmes to improve infrastructure and common facilities for MSME clusters, and has schemes for skill upgradation, tooling, and quality certification for traditional industries. There are also targeted initiatives like Stand-Up India (to promote entrepreneurship among women and disadvantaged groups through bank loans) and various state-level MSME policies.

On the skilling front, beyond PMKVY, the government launched the National Apprenticeship Promotion Scheme (NAPS) in 2016 to incentivise firms to engage apprentices (sharing stipend costs). However, apprenticeship uptake in India remains very low—just about half a million apprentices in a workforce of 500+ million—implying that MSMEs too are not significantly using apprenticeships as a talent pipeline. The Skill India ecosystem includes the ITIs and polytechnics under the formal system, but their integration with MSME needs has room for improvement.

The institutional landscape itself is crowded. The MSME sector's development cuts across multiple ministries and levels of government. The Ministry of MSME handles many schemes (credit guarantee, cluster development, khadi, etc.), while the Ministry of Skill Development and Entrepreneurship (MSDE) handles skill training and apprenticeship, and DPIIT (Ministry of Commerce) oversees Startup India and related investment funds. In addition, state governments have their own MSME and startup promotion policies, and various departments (e.g. rural development, textiles) run programmes that overlap with MSME development. This fragmentation means that a single MSME owner may have to interface with multiple agencies to avail different benefits—for instance, training from one scheme, credit from another, marketing support from yet another—each with separate paperwork and criteria. While bodies like MSME Development Institutes and single-window portals exist to help navigate these, the coordination challenges remain. Overlapping mandates can also lead to duplication of efforts and suboptimal use of resources (for example, two departments running similar skilling programmes or multiple agencies offering parallel credit schemes), which is a recurring issue identified by oversight agencies.

In summary, India has no shortage of schemes or institutions aimed at helping MSMEs. The policy support framework is expansive and has steadily evolved, especially in the last decade, to address finance, technology, skill, and infrastructure gaps. However, the effectiveness of this support ecosystem is undermined by several systemic ailments, which are discussed next. The experiences of these schemes reveal a pattern: significant ambition and investment on paper, but inconsistent execution and impact on the ground. This dichotomy is at the heart of 'what ails' the MSME ecosystem in India.

Key Challenges and Implementation Gaps

Despite the array of initiatives, India's MSME ecosystem continues to be afflicted by structural challenges that limit the success of support schemes. Key issues include:

Limited Access to Formal Credit

Financial exclusion of MSMEs remains pervasive. The majority of micro and small units still cannot easily secure bank credit, relying instead on personal funds or informal lenders. As noted, only about 14% of India's MSMEs have access to formal credit. This stems from factors on both the demand and supply sides. On the demand side, many entrepreneurs lack collateral or credit histories or are deterred by complex loan procedures. On the supply side, formal lenders perceive MSMEs as high-risk due to information asymmetry (opaque financials and a lack of credit scores) and often require collateral or extensive documentation that micros cannot provide. Government schemes, like CGTMSE, aimed to bridge this gap by guaranteeing loans, but banks' utilisation of such schemes was initially modest. Even with recent upticks, a large credit gap (estimated at $330–$530 billion) persists. Consequently, MSMEs face high costs of capital or invest suboptimal amounts, constraining their growth. In many cases, credit is available only for short-term working capital but not for long-term expansion, affecting modernisation efforts. Venture capital and equity financing options exist only for a tiny sliver of high-growth startups, leaving typical small businesses dependent on debt financing. The net effect is that well-intended schemes like MUDRA or interest subventions have not yet achieved a game-changing expansion of credit outreach. This chronic credit crunch stymies MSME operations and makes them vulnerable to shocks.

Implementation Inefficiencies in Schemes

Many MSME schemes suffer from a gap between design and delivery. Implementation bottlenecks range from procedural delays to capacity constraints and leakages. For instance, the FFS took considerable time to deploy money on the ground, delaying support to startups. In some subsidy-based schemes (like capital investment subsidies or cluster grants), cumbersome approval processes and coordination failures between central and state agencies have led to under-utilisation of allocated funds. In the Skill India programmes, quality control has been a major inefficiency—a proliferation of training centres occurred rapidly, but oversight could not keep up, resulting in variable training quality. Placement tracking systems were initially weak, causing unreliable reporting. The government's own data shows large drop-offs between the numbers trained and the numbers placed, indicating that many trainings did not translate into jobs, effectively an inefficient use of resources. In credit schemes, the experience has been that if public sector banks are not proactively driven, they meet priority sector lending targets via safest bets (such as loans to well-established small firms or through NBFCs[20]) rather than reaching new micro-borrowers, thereby diluting the additionality of schemes like CGTMSE. Bureaucratic red tape and lack of last-mile connectivity also plague implementation. MSMEs in smaller towns often are not aware of all the benefits or face hurdles in claiming them (e.g., complex online application portals and slow response times). There have been cases of funds remaining unspent at year-end under MSME ministry schemes, pointing to execution shortfalls. These inefficiencies mean that the impact per rupee spent is lower than it could be, and the objectives of schemes are only partially achieved.

Inadequate Skill and Placement Outcomes

As discussed in the PMKVY analysis, a critical challenge is the poor linkage between skill training and employment. While millions are being trained, the absorption into the labour market is weak. Surveys have found that a significant proportion of youth who underwent short-term skilling under government programmes remained unemployed or took up unrelated work afterwards. This outcome suggests issues in curriculum relevance, assessment, and industry engagement. Employers often report that many certified candidates still lack the practical skills or the soft skills needed in the workplace. On the other hand, trainees sometimes find the jobs on offer

---

20. In the Indian context, an NBFC is a financial institution registered under the Companies Act, 2013 (or 1956) that provides banking-like services, such as loans, credit facilities, leasing, and investments, but does not hold a banking license. Regulated by the RBI, NBFCs cannot accept demand deposits like banks, but they play a crucial role in financial inclusion by serving sectors and borrowers often underserved by traditional banks.

(e.g., entry-level positions in sales or services) unattractive or too low-paying, leading to attrition. The net result is a paradox: employers cite skill shortages, yet many formally trained candidates are without jobs. This points to a mismatch that the current skilling ecosystem has not solved. It also indicates that India's approach of short, centralised training programmes might need reform—possibly a greater emphasis on on-site apprenticeships or longer dual-training models (as international best practice shows). The inadequate placement outcomes are not just a social issue, but also an economic one: it means MSMEs do not get the skilled labour force they need to improve productivity, and the youth bulge isn't translating into productive human capital as intended.

Overlapping Jurisdictions and Fragmented Support

The multiplicity of agencies and schemes has led to overlapping bureaucratic jurisdictions, causing confusion and inefficiency. For example, an entrepreneur looking for support with a new business idea might approach Startup India for recognition, SIDBI for venture funding, the MSME Ministry for a capital subsidy, and the state government for local incentives—each with its own criteria and paperwork. There is no single unified interface for an MSME to access all relevant schemes seamlessly (though efforts like the Udyam portal and Champions portal are steps in that direction). Different ministries sometimes run parallel programmes targeting similar outcomes. A case in point: the Ministry of Labour's vocational training programmes vs MSDE's skill programmes vs state skill missions—without robust coordination, they risk duplicating efforts or setting different standards. Inter-departmental silos can also mean important issues fall through the cracks. For example, MSME export promotion might be handled by the commerce ministry, while MSME technology upgradation might be handled by another, without a unified strategy to make MSMEs globally competitive. Furthermore, certain regulatory domains affecting MSMEs (like labour laws, taxation, or land clearance) are controlled by other ministries or state governments, at times working at cross-purposes with MSME growth objectives. An overlapping issue is that of definition and data alignment: until recently, different agencies had varying definitions of MSMEs (though now a unified investment/turnover-based definition is adopted). Fragmentation leads to inconsistent data collection—the MSME Ministry's figures on the number of units and employment differ from those of NSSO (National Sample Survey Office) surveys or those inferred from GST registrants, etc., complicating planning. Overall, the lack of a cohesive, 'whole-of-government' approach means even well-designed schemes do not add up to a coherent push; instead, they operate in silos, limiting systemic impact.

Data Reliability and Transparency Issues

A less visible but significant ailment in the MSME ecosystem is the poor quality of data and information on which policies are based and outcomes are measured. For instance, the oft-quoted statistic of '63 million MSMEs employing 110 million people' comes from the last comprehensive MSME survey (NSSO, 2015). The business landscape has changed since then, yet a new census is overdue. While the Udyam Registration portal (launched in 2020) has registered about 5.7 crore enterprises by the end of 2024, questions remain on the duplication or accuracy of some self-reported data (the Udyam figures suggest MSME employment of over 240 million, which is dramatically higher than previous estimates, indicating possible inconsistencies or over-reporting). Reliable data on MSME performance, finance, and jobs is hard to come by. This hampers effective policymaking and makes it difficult to evaluate which schemes are working. Moreover, as seen with

PMKVY's placement statistics, official reporting sometimes paints a rosier picture than independent evaluations. Until recently, there was limited third-party evaluation of MSME schemes. The absence of rigorous monitoring and evaluation (M&E) frameworks means that feedback loops to improve schemes are weak. Data fragmentation is another issue—information on MSME credit may sit with the RBI and banks, while information on skilling outcomes is with MSDE, and neither may be linked to specific enterprises to see a holistic impact. Transparency is improving with measures like public dashboards (e.g., the MSME Samadhaan portal shows delayed payment cases, and the Startup India portal shows recognised startups, etc.), but many schemes still report only input metrics (number of loans given, people trained) rather than outcomes (businesses sustained, income generated). Without credible data, it becomes difficult to diagnose problems and press for accountability. For example, if a scheme claims 90% success, but the ground reality is different, policymakers might continue it without any modifications. This is why independent assessments, like those by researchers or CAG audits, are crucial; some have revealed issues such as inflated placement numbers or funds lying idle. Going forward, improving data reliability—through better enterprise surveys, integrating databases (GST, Udyam, EPFO (Employees' Provident Fund Organisation), etc.), and transparent reporting—will be key to addressing the other challenges effectively.

In summary, the ailments of India's MSME ecosystem are multifaceted. They include the tangible (credit and infrastructure deficits, skill gaps) and the systemic (governance fragmentation, weak implementation and feedback). As analyst Harrison Blackwell observes in his assessment of India's MSME landscape, despite numerous reforms and schemes, 'India's 63 million small businesses struggle' to thrive due to these enduring challenges, especially when compared to countries like China, which have taken a more focused approach. The next section delves into that comparison, drawing lessons from how other nations have bolstered their small enterprises and what India can learn from them.

Comparative Insights: China's 'Little Giants' Programme and International Best Practices

To gain perspective on India's MSME difficulties, it is instructive to compare with international experiences—notably, China's successful nurturing of its MSMEs as exemplified by the 'Little Giants' programme. China and India have comparable scales in terms of population and even the number of SMEs, but their trajectories in supporting these enterprises diverge in important ways. While India's approach has been broad-based—attempting to uplift the entire spectrum of MSMEs (most of which are micro units) through widespread schemes—China has, in recent years, pursued a more targeted strategy, focusing on high-potential SMEs that can drive innovation and industrial upgrading.

China's 'Little Giants' – Targeting High-Tech SMEs

Amid the US-China tech competition and a drive for self-reliance, China launched an initiative to identify and turbocharge its most innovative small and medium enterprises. Branded as 'Little Giants', these are government-certified, high-tech SMEs that specialise in niche sectors, possess advanced technologies, or fill critical gaps in supply chains. China's Ministry of Industry and Information Technology (MIIT) set clear criteria for qualifying as a 'Little Giant': for example, a company must have annual revenues between 100–400 million yuan (roughly $15–60 million), healthy growth and profitability, a high proportion of staff in R&D (usually >15%), and a significant number of patents or proprietary technologies. The 14th Five-Year Plan (2021–2025) explicitly set a target to cultivate 10,000 such 'Little Giant' firms by 2025. Remarkably, China has already surpassed that goal ahead of schedule—by the end of 2024, it had recognised about 14,600 Little Giant enterprises across the nation. These firms operate in strategic industries such as artificial intelligence, semiconductors, biotechnology, advanced materials, and industrial machinery. According to Chinese media, around 5,000 of them are in cutting-edge technology fields, like AI, aerospace, and commercial drones.

What sets the Little Giants programme apart is the comprehensive and coordinated support system underpinning it. Beijing has developed a tiered cultivation mechanism: promising SMEs are first recognised at city or provincial levels as 'specialised and innovative' enterprises, and the best of them are elevated to the national Little Giant status. This creates a pipeline and competitive process, ensuring that firms continue to strive for innovation. Once on the Little Giant roster, these companies receive a bonanza of state support: targeted tax breaks, R&D grants and subsidies, subsidised loans from state banks, priority access to equity financing (e.g., special SME boards in stock exchanges), and facilitation in obtaining necessary licenses or certifications. They are also often plugged into networks with large state-owned or leading private enterprises—as suppliers or partners—effectively integrating them into major supply chains. Provinces and cities have their own incentive packages (for instance, some local governments offer cash rewards for each patent filed or for each export market entered by a Little Giant). The state also fosters linkages between these SMEs and research institutions or universities to encourage the commercialisation of innovation. Importantly, the designation is periodically reviewed (usually a three-year term), and firms must continue performing to retain the benefits—preventing complacency and ensuring support is performance-linked.

The early outcomes of this approach are evident. Many Little Giant firms have grown rapidly, and some have become leaders in their niche. According to one account, the average R&D investment of these firms is about 7% of their revenue, and each holds an average of 22 patents—numbers far above a typical small firm. They contribute substantially to China's innovation drive; indeed, SMEs in China now account for 70% of the country's technological innovation outputs and around 80% of urban employment. The programme's success is not just in fostering individual firms but in strengthening entire supply chains: for example, a Little Giant producing a critical electronic component can help multiple larger manufacturers reduce dependence on imports. By mid-2023, China had also identified a broader cohort of 'Little Giant' candidates—over 98,000 'specialised and new' SMEs at the provincial level ready to move up—ensuring a continuous funnel. In essence, China has created an 'accelerator state' where the government actively scouts, validates, and accelerates the growth of its small enterprises as a matter of industrial strategy. This is a stark contrast to India, where support is spread thin across millions of tiny units, and few mechanisms exist to systematically pick winners or provide tailored support to high-growth-potential firms.

International Best Practices in MSME Support and Skill Development

Beyond China, other countries offer useful models for MSME promotion and skill building:

- **Germany's Mittelstand and Dual Training:** Germany is renowned for its Mittelstand—a network of highly productive small and medium manufacturers, often family-owned, that are global niche champions. A key pillar of their success is Germany's dual apprenticeship system for skills. About half of German youth enter apprenticeships straight out of school, splitting time between classroom instruction and on-the-job training. This ensures a steady supply of technically skilled workers for SMEs and large firms alike, and is credited with Germany's low youth unemployment and world-class craftsmanship. German SMEs also benefit from dense industry clusters, technology extension services, and export facilitation by institutions like chambers of commerce. The culture of long-term investment in employee skills and incremental innovation is deeply ingrained in the Mittelstand model—something Indian MSMEs struggle with due to resource constraints.

- **United States – SBA**: The US supports small businesses through the SBA, which runs programmes providing government-backed loan guarantees (somewhat akin to CGTMSE but with different execution), direct lending during crises, as well as advisory services and federal procurement set-asides for small businesses. The SBA's 7(a) loan guarantee programme, for instance, has been instrumental in enabling SMEs to get bank loans, with the government guaranteeing up to 85% of the loan value. The US also has a vibrant private venture capital and angel investment ecosystem that funds startups (with relatively limited direct government intervention aside from R&D grants like SBIR (Small Business Innovation Research)). However, what stands out is the SBA's integrated approach—combining credit facilitation, mentorship (through Small Business Development Centers), and market access support—under one roof, making it easier for small firms to navigate.
- **East Asian Economies (Japan, South Korea, Taiwan)**: These countries have historically employed a mix of protection and promotion for SMEs. Japan has long-running credit guarantee corporations in each prefecture that collectively guarantee a large portion of SME loans, along with policy banks that cater to small enterprise finance. It also has specialised SME agencies and programmes to help SMEs upgrade technology and quality (e.g., Japan's stringent quality standards indirectly force SMEs to improve to stay in supply chains). South Korea, similar to China,

identified 'strong small companies' and provided them targeted support to become global exporters. Taiwan fostered SME supplier networks that plugged into its giant tech companies (like TSMC (Taiwan Semiconductor Manufacturing Company)), ensuring SMEs could benefit from large firms' success. A common thread is the integration of SMEs into industrial policy—rather than treating them solely as beneficiaries of welfare or social schemes, these countries viewed SMEs as critical cogs in economic strategy and tailored support accordingly.

- **Singapore's Skills Development:** Singapore, a much smaller economy, nonetheless offers lessons in continuously upskilling the workforce. Its SkillsFuture programme gives every citizen credits to pursue certified courses throughout their career, keeping the labour force adaptable. For vocational training, Singapore involves industry heavily in curriculum design and mandates internships. This demand-driven approach results in very low mismatch—something India aspires to with recent efforts to involve industry in Skill India course design.

In comparing these global practices to India, a few key contrasts emerge. India's MSME support has a strong element of social policy (job creation, inclusion, poverty alleviation), which means efforts are spread across quantity—training millions and giving loans to millions of micro units—whereas countries like China or Germany focus more on quality and productivity, even if that means concentrating resources on a smaller subset of firms or workers. India's challenge is unique due to the sheer size of the informal micro-enterprise sector; yet, the international examples suggest that greater focus and integration of support could yield better results. Rather than hundreds of disparate schemes, a more consolidated approach that identifies different tiers of MSMEs (such as survival micro units vs growth-oriented small firms) and addresses their specific needs might be more effective.

India vs China: A Comparative Snapshot

To highlight the differences between India's MSME ecosystem and China's SME/Little Giant ecosystem,

Table 1 compares some key parameters and approaches.

Table 1: Key parameters of India and China.

Aspect	India (MSME Ecosystem)	China (SME 'Little Giants' Programme)
Number of MSMEs/ SMEs	~63 million MSMEs (broadly defined, mostly micro units).	~14,600 'Little Giant' SMEs (national-level) by 2024; ~98,000 specialised SMEs at the provincial level.
Contribution to GDP	~30% of GDP (and ~40% of exports).	~60% of GDP, ~50% of tax revenue (SMEs overall); Little Giants are drivers in strategic sectors.
Employment Share	~110 million employees (≈25% of the workforce).	~80% of urban employment via SMEs. Little Giants contribute significantly to high-tech job growth.
Focus of Support	Broad-based schemes for credit (e.g. MUDRA), skilling (PMKVY), infrastructure, etc., targeting inclusivity and mass access.	Highly targeted support to selected high-tech SMEs ('specialised, innovative' firms) to become global niche leaders.
Primary Government Agencies	Multiple: Ministry of MSME, MSDE (Skill Development), DPIIT (Startup India), plus state governments—coordination challenges.	Centralised under MIIT with local governments' cooperation—tiered identification and support structure.
Credit Access	Only ~14% of MSMEs have formal credit; ~$530 billion credit gap. Credit schemes exist (CGTMSE, etc.), but outreach is limited.	Aggressive financial support: state banks directed to lend to SMEs, dedicated SME boards for equity financing. Tens of billions of yuan funnelled into SME loans and venture funds.

Aspect	India (MSME Ecosystem)	China (SME 'Little Giants' Programme)
Innovation & R&D	Low R&D investment by typical MSMEs; few patents (innovation driven mostly by large firms or startups).	High emphasis on innovation: Little Giants spend ~7% of revenue on R&D on average, hold ~22 patents each. SMEs account for ~70% of tech innovation output.
Skill Development Model	Largely short-term training schemes (e.g. 3-month courses); weak apprenticeship uptake; <50% placement from skilling.	Strong vocational system integrated with industry; millions of apprenticeships; SMEs collaborate with universities. Focus on continuous skill upgrading in firms.
Integration in Supply Chains	Many MSMEs operate as informal, standalone units or local suppliers; linkage programmes (cluster development, vendor development) exist, but have limited reach.	SMEs are tightly integrated as suppliers to large enterprises (often mandated or facilitated by government); Little Giants fill critical supply chain gaps for big industries.
Policy Orientation	MSMEs are seen partly as engines for inclusive growth and job creation at the base of the pyramid—hence widespread small interventions.	SMEs are seen as engines of innovation and self-reliance in high-tech domains—hence heavy investment in select firms to become future champions.

Sources: Indian MSME data from MSME Ministry and IFC; Credit gap from Avendus; Chinese data from SCMP (South China Morning Post), MERICS (Mercator Institute of China Studies), Global Times.

This comparison underscores why India's MSMEs struggle while China's thrive, echoing Harrison Blackwell's assessment. India's approach, though inclusive, has resulted in shallow penetration of benefits—many enterprises have been touched, but few have been transformed. China's approach, though exclusive to a subset, has achieved depth, creating globally competitive firms out of small enterprises. Of course, the contexts differ: China's industrial policy framework and financial firepower are different from India's democratic, market-driven setup. India cannot and need not replicate China wholesale, but it can certainly draw lessons.

Notably, India has begun some similar moves—for instance, the MSME Ministry's new 'Champion MSME' scheme aims to identify and support high-growth MSMEs, and PLI schemes in sectors encourage localisation that could benefit SMEs as suppliers. The challenge is to implement these in a way that complements the broad-based support.

International best practices also suggest the importance of industry involvement and accountability. Germany's vocational training works because companies co-invest in apprentices and curricula. In India, increasing industry partnership in skill training (through initiatives like Apprenticeship 2.0 or incentivising MSMEs to hire trainees) could improve outcomes. Similarly, credit support must be coupled with making lenders accountable for reaching targets (as was done with priority sector norms historically).

The comparative perspective highlights both the shortcomings in India's current MSME support structure and the potential pathways to reform. The next section outlines a concrete way forward, recommending strategic, regulatory, and institutional changes to address 'what ails' the MSME ecosystem, informed by these insights.

Conclusion

India's MSME ecosystem stands at a crossroads. On the one hand, never before have small businesses and startups enjoyed so much attention in policy discourse, with a multitude of schemes attempting to bolster every aspect from funding to skills to infrastructure. On paper, India has constructed an expansive support edifice for MSMEs that rivals that of any other large economy. Yet on the other hand, the on-ground reality for many MSMEs remains challenging. This analysis reveals a sobering picture: despite notable successes at the margins, India's MSME and startup schemes have not fully delivered on their promise, due to a confluence of implementation gaps and structural issues.

Major initiatives like Startup India have certainly catalysed entrepreneurial activity, but the impact is uneven—a few thousand high-growth startups flourished (mostly in technology and urban centres), whereas the vast base of traditional small businesses saw relatively little change. Skill India managed to mobilise and train millions of youth, an achievement in itself, but fell short in translating those numbers into quality employment, leaving industries still complaining of skill shortages and many trainees empty-handed. Credit schemes and loan guarantees expanded the flow of credit somewhat, yet the fundamental issue of MSMEs being under-financed and financially fragile persists. The economic shock of the COVID-19 pandemic, for instance, hit small businesses disproportionately hard, revealing their limited buffers and access to emergency capital. Meanwhile, the proliferation of programmes has led to a complex bureaucratic maze that an ordinary entrepreneur struggles to navigate. In short, the intended benefits often diffuse before reaching the beneficiaries in full measure.

Our comparative look at China's Little Giants and other global models drives home the point that India needs to reimagine its MSME strategy. The Chinese example illustrates the power of targeted support and integrated policy execution—something that India's fragmented approach has not achieved. Of course, India operates in a different political-economic context; policies must be adapted to Indian conditions. Nevertheless, certain principles seem universally applicable: the importance of nurturing firms that can innovate and compete, the value of investing in human capital through rigorous training systems, and the need for a responsive financial ecosystem that actively includes small enterprises.

Encouragingly, the issues identified are not intractable. They are policy and governance challenges, which can be overcome with sustained commitment and smart design. Overlapping schemes can be consolidated or better coordinated. Data systems can be improved in this digital age to accurately track outcomes. Credit flows can be enhanced by leveraging technology (e.g., fintech platforms that use GST data for credit scoring) alongside reforms in banking. The government has shown agility in the past—for example, quickly tweaking GST rules when small businesses faced hardship, or rolling out emergency credit lines during COVID. A similar resolve now needs to be applied to long-standing structural issues.

In conclusion, India's MSME ecosystem is a sleeping giant of its own—full of potential but weighed down by old burdens. If 'what ails' it can be treated through purposeful reforms, the MSME sector could truly become the dynamo for inclusive and innovation-led growth.

Way Forward

Addressing the ailments of India's MSME ecosystem requires bold and coordinated action on multiple fronts. This section outlines a strategic, regulatory, and institutional reform agenda to revitalise the MSME and startup landscape. Most of what follows have been targeted for many years by both the Union and State governments but perhaps without required concerted action as is required. The recommendations focus on improving the effectiveness of support schemes, enhancing the business environment for MSMEs, and drawing on global best practices to create an ecosystem where small businesses can thrive and grow into tomorrow's giants.

Strategic Interventions for MSME Growth

1. **Segmented and Targeted Support:** India should adopt a more segmented approach to MSME policy. Not all 63

million MSMEs have the same needs or growth potential. The government can stratify the sector (for example: nano enterprises/self-employed, traditional micro/small businesses, and high-growth innovative firms) and devise targeted programmes for each. High-potential MSMEs—those with scalability or export potential—could be identified through a transparent mechanism (akin to a localised 'Little Giant' selection) and provided tailored assistance (e.g., facilitated credit, mentoring, technology adoption support). This does not mean abandoning broader support, but rather focusing additional resources where returns are likely highest. For the vast micro enterprise base, the focus can be on formalisation, basic technology upgrades (such as digital payments, accounting), and gradual scaling; for the dynamic minority, on fast-tracking growth and integration into global value chains.

2. **Cluster Development and Infrastructure:** Building on the cluster development programmes, a more intensive push is needed to develop MSME clusters as centres of excellence. World over, clusters (like Italy's industrial districts or China's manufacturing hubs) have shown that colocation and specialisation yield competitiveness. India should expand common facility centres, testing labs, and design centres in major MSME clusters (textiles, leather, auto-components, etc.), with private sector participation. Strengthening industrial infrastructure—reliable power, logistics, plug-and-play factory shells—in these clusters will attract investments and enable existing MSMEs to operate more efficiently. Linking clusters to the 'Make in India' and PLI schemes can ensure MSMEs become suppliers to the large industries being promoted. A strategic thrust could be on export-oriented MSME clusters, providing them with marketing support (through e-commerce integration, trade fairs, and branding initiatives) to penetrate global markets.

3. **Technology Upgradation and Digitalisation:** To avoid MSMEs stagnating with outdated methods, a mission-mode programme for technology upgradation is required. This could involve expanding the CLCSS with larger outlays and creating Technology Support Centres that provide technical consulting to MSMEs. Partnerships with organisations like the Quality Council, IITs (Indian Institutes of Technology), and NITs (National Institutes of Technology) can help transfer knowledge on process improvement, automation, and innovation. Additionally, leveraging the ongoing digital revolution is key—promoting digital platforms for MSMEs in areas such as e-commerce (to reach wider markets), fintech (for easier loans and invoice financing), and cloud computing (affordable IT solutions). The government can incentivise MSMEs to adopt digital tools by offering tax rebates or subsidies for software, much like it did for adopting digital payments post-demonetisation. A digitally empowered MSME can better compete, access credit (since digital transactions build financial history), and integrate with formal supply chains.

4. **Market Linkages and Procurement:** Ensuring stable markets for MSME products is crucial. The government should strengthen MSME procurement mandates—currently, central ministries and PSUs are mandated to source at least 25% of their requirements from MSMEs (with sub-targets for women, SC/ST entrepreneurs). Compliance with this should be strictly monitored and enforced, potentially raising the quota over time if absorption is good. Also, large private corporations could be encouraged or required (via corporate social responsibility or ESG (Environmental, Social, and Governance) norms) to include MSMEs in their supply chains and to pay them on time. Timely payment enforcement deserves special mention: implement stringent penalties for late payment to MSMEs by any buyer (including government departments), perhaps by mandating interest payments beyond 45 days. The TReDS

(Trade Receivables Discounting System) platform, which allows MSME invoices to be auctioned to financiers for early payment, should be made mandatory for all large buyers—this will greatly ease working capital woes. By guaranteeing markets and fair payment, MSMEs will have the confidence and cash flow to invest in growth.

Regulatory Reforms for Ease of Doing Business

1. **Simplify Compliance and Reduce Regulatory Burden:** Despite improvements, many MSMEs find regulatory compliance (registrations, filings, inspections) overwhelming, especially when transitioning from informal to formal. A radical simplification can be game-changing. For instance, implement a 'Single Window MSME Compliance System'—one interface where an MSME can manage all mandatory filings (GST, PF (Provident Fund)/ESI (Employee State Insurance), labour returns, etc.) instead of dealing with multiple systems. Moreover, build on the notion of 'ease of doing business for small businesses' by exempting or simplifying certain regulations for firms below a size threshold. The government has already increased the employee limits for labour laws applicability; it can further streamline by introducing self-certification and third-party audit regimes for low-risk compliance areas. The cost (monetary and time) of compliance for a small unit should be drastically cut. A move towards the decriminalisation of business offences (already initiated for companies law) should encompass minor compliance lapses of MSMEs—replacing penalties or imprisonment with warning and education for first-time unintentional errors.

2. **Reform Taxation Procedures:** The introduction of GST was a major step benefiting MSMEs by unifying the market, but many micro firms still find it complex. Continued simplification of GST returns, especially for the smaller turnover

slabs (such as the composition scheme), will help. Additionally, the income tax regime for proprietorships and partnerships (most MSMEs) could be simplified with presumptive taxation limits raised further, so that more small businesses don't need detailed bookkeeping to comply. Reducing the burden of random audits and inspections under tax and other laws will also create a more trust-based environment. States and local bodies should also streamline licensing (for example, a single annual trade license covering various local permissions, with a green channel for renewals). A harmonisation of the myriad state-level permissions into a centralised MSME license could be explored through consensus in GST Council-like bodies.

3. **Strengthen Credit and Financial Reforms:** Policy reforms to improve access to credit dovetail with strategic initiatives. One key regulatory change could be to operationalise cash flow-based lending norms—RBI can push banks to adopt cash-flow assessment (using GST data and bank statements) rather than asset-based assessment for MSME loans. Additionally, expanding the scope of credit guarantee programmes and making them more attractive: for example, increasing the guarantee cover percentage to reduce banks' risk further, and streamlining claim settlement so banks have confidence to lend to riskier profiles. Introducing a credit guarantee for slightly larger SMEs (medium enterprises up to ₹50 crore loans) could also encourage banks to fund SME expansions. Another area is factoring and invoice financing—implementation of the amended Factoring Act can bring more players to provide receivables finance to MSMEs. On fintech, regulators should enable account aggregator frameworks and alternative data usage to flourish, which can materially increase lending to thin-file MSMEs. Lastly, encourage venture capital and private equity into the MSME space by easing norms for SME listings (the SME exchange platforms) and perhaps providing tax incentives for investing in MSME equity or venture debt. A

vibrant MSME financing market needs both debt and equity; policy can catalyse both.

4. **Legal and Structural Reforms:** Some deeper reforms will also aid MSMEs indirectly. Land and real estate reforms that make it easier and cheaper for MSMEs to acquire or lease space for operations (e.g., developing more industrial estates with transparent allocation) would remove a big entry barrier. Similarly, continued labour law reforms that allow flexibility in hiring (with social security nets) will encourage MSMEs to expand their workforce without fear of future rigidities. Enforcing contracts is a systemic issue in India. Setting up fast-track courts or arbitration mechanisms for commercial disputes up to a certain value (say ₹1 crore) can help MSMEs resolve issues without expensive, time-consuming litigation. Simplifying insolvency procedures for proprietorships and partnerships (perhaps through out-of-court resolution schemes) would also be beneficial, as the current insolvency law mainly caters to companies, giving honest entrepreneurs a second chance rather than trapping them in debt. In essence, the regulatory environment should be reformed with a 'small-first' principle—designing rules from the viewpoint of the smallest player, which will likely end up helping larger ones too.

Institutional and Governance Reforms

1. **Improved Coordination – 'Whole of Government' Approach:** To eliminate overlapping jurisdictions, India could establish a National MSME Council chaired by the Prime Minister or a senior minister, with representation from all relevant ministries (MSME, Finance, Commerce, Skill, Labour, etc.) and key states. This body would oversee the MSME strategy holistically, ensure synergy among schemes, and monitor progress. At an operational level, consolidating schemes, where feasible, under one umbrella could reduce fragmentation—for instance, merging various skill

training initiatives across ministries into one unified programme with common standards (even if delivered by multiple agencies). The creation of the MSME Ministry's Champions portal to address grievances is a good step; this can be expanded to a full MSME single window for scheme applications, where technology routes each application to the right scheme automatically. Essentially, the institutional silo walls must be broken. One radical idea is to merge the Ministry of MSME and the Ministry of Skill Development (since their objectives are intertwined for enterprise and employment development).

2. **Capacity Building at the Grassroots:** Often, the weakest link is local implementation. Strengthening MSME Development Institutes (MDIs) and District Industries Centres (DICs) with adequate staffing, training, and digital tools would provide MSMEs with a reliable touchpoint for navigating government support. These local bodies should be empowered to act as facilitators/consultants to MSMEs, helping them prepare loan applications, connect to mentors, or form cooperatives/producer companies. A programme to empanel professional MSME mentors or business development service providers (subsidised by the government) could help improve MSME capabilities in marketing, accounting, etc. The institutional ecosystem should also include stronger industry associations for MSMEs—the government can encourage cluster-level associations and support them to run common facilities or training centres.

3. **Monitoring, Evaluation, and Data Systems:** A major institutional reform is to embed robust M&E in every MSME scheme. Setting clear outcome metrics (not just outputs) and publishing quarterly/annual progress in a transparent manner will increase accountability. Wherever possible, independent third-party evaluations (by academic institutions or reputed agencies) should be commissioned—for example, evaluating PMKVY outcomes or the impact of credit guarantees on actual

firm growth—and the findings used to recalibrate programmes. On data, creating an integrated MSME data platform that merges information from Udyam registrations, GST filings, bank credit data, and employment records (while ensuring privacy) can provide a dynamic picture of the sector. This would help in identifying stress (e.g., if GST filings drop for many units, it may signal distress) and targeting interventions. The upcoming MSME Census should be executed with tech-enabled surveys for accuracy. Reliable data will also help address the trust deficit: if banks can access authenticated financial data of MSMEs (through account aggregators), they may lend more willingly; similarly, if MSMEs can see market intelligence (prices, demand trends), they can plan better. Government portals should evolve from being merely application portals to rich information dashboards for MSMEs, sharing insights and opportunities.

4. **Fostering Entrepreneurship and Innovation Culture:** Finally, beyond specific schemes, India needs to cultivate a stronger culture of entrepreneurship and innovation at the MSME level. This involves education and societal attitudes. The government can work with educational institutions to introduce modules on entrepreneurship and vocational skills in high school or college curricula, so that more youth consider entrepreneurship (and are prepared for it). Expanding initiatives like Startup India down to the grassroots (e.g., innovation competitions in every district or innovation hubs in tier-2 cities) will help discover and nurture local entrepreneurs. Innovation within traditional MSMEs should be encouraged through challenges and awards (for example, a national MSME innovation prize). Public-private partnerships can set up maker spaces and incubators in smaller towns where potential entrepreneurs can experiment at low cost. Over time, this will replenish the MSME sector with more dynamic, resilient entrepreneurs who can adapt to changes and drive growth. Policymakers should also maintain an advocacy stance—

championing the cause of MSMEs in all forums—ensuring that big business interests do not overshadow the 'little guys'. A vibrant MSME sector is in everyone's interest as it leads to broad-based development.

In implementing these recommendations, it is important to adopt a consultative and iterative approach. Policymakers should continue to engage MSME stakeholders—business owners, industry associations, experts—in refining reforms. Some reforms may face resistance (for instance, tightening payment enforcement might be resisted by large corporates); political will and stakeholder consensus-building will be key. Furthermore, given the diversity of India, state governments should be encouraged (and incentivised) to compete and innovate in MSME policy—much like they did under the ease of doing business rankings. One state's successful experiment (say, a one-stop clearance for MSMEs or a mentorship scheme) can then be replicated elsewhere.

Ultimately, curing 'what ails' India's MSME ecosystem is not an overnight task—it is a continuous process of policy learning and improvement. The COVID-19 crisis showed that when pushed, the system can respond with agility (witness the ₹3 lakh crore Emergency Credit Line Guarantee during the pandemic, which saved many MSMEs). The lessons learned in those exigencies, if applied in normal times, can greatly strengthen the MSME support framework. With the reforms above, India can aim not just to have the world's most numerous MSMEs, but to transform a significant number of them into competitive, innovative, and sustainable enterprises that drive the next chapter of India's growth story.

References:

1. Aftab, A. (27 June 2024). Small Business, Big Impact: Empowering Women SMEs for Success. International Finance Corporation (IFC).

2. Press Information Bureau. (26 March 2025). 1,60,33,081 candidates have been trained/oriented under the PMKVY scheme from 2015 to 2024 [Press Release, Ministry of Skill Development & Entrepreneurship].

3. Press Information Bureau. (30 December 2024). Year-End Review 2024 – Ministry of MSME: Key Initiatives and Achievements [Press Release, Ministry of MSME].

4. SIDBI (Small Industries Development Bank of India). (2022). Annual Report 2021–22: Fund of Funds for Startups (FFS) Section.

5. Lukmaan IAS. (28 February 2025). Startup India – Schemes and Programmes (Blog).

6. Khan, S. (28 January 2025). 'Affordable credit, timely payments: MSMEs' Key Budget Demands.' The Economic Times.

7. Sharma, H, & Mehrotra, S. (13 October 2023). 'Skill development in India: The facts behind the figures.' India Development Review.

8. Jennings, R. (3 December 2024). 'China's strategic "Little Giant" firms quickly rise to 14,600, surpass 2025 goal.' South China Morning Post.

9. Mercator Institute for China Studies (MERICS). (2023, 3 August 2023). 'Accelerator state: How China fosters "Little Giant" companies' (Report).

10. Mujeeb, S. (8 August 2024). 'China Is Betting Big on Its "Little Giants".' The Diplomat.

11. Expatrio. (n.d.). 'German dual apprenticeship system.' (Web article).

12. Harrison Blackwell (Info Safari). (2023). 'Why India's MSMEs Struggle While China's Thrive' [Video]. YouTube.

CHAPTER 3

◆◆◆

Twin Engines of Growth: MSMEs and Startups – Parallel Tracks, Convergence, and Collisions

Abstract:

India's economic growth narrative increasingly revolves around two vital yet structurally different pillars—the MSME ecosystem and the startup ecosystem. While both contribute to employment, innovation, and entrepreneurship, they operate in distinct spheres of governance, access to finance, regulatory frameworks, and growth trajectories. This chapter unpacks the fundamental differences between these ecosystems, highlights areas of overlap, and offers vivid everyday examples to illustrate their interaction. It also explores how policy and institutional structures are beginning to align these once-parallel tracks to unlock their combined potential. As India aspires to become a $10 trillion economy, harmonising the energy of startups with the resilience of MSMEs could be the game-changing synergy the country needs.

India's economic landscape today is often depicted as a tug-of-war between tradition and disruption, between legacy businesses and digital unicorns, between the dusty shop floor and the cloud server. This tug-of-war plays out through two powerful and overlapping yet distinctly different ecosystems—the MSME ecosystem and the startup ecosystem. Both are courted by policymakers, cheered by politicians, and wooed by investors, but they travel two vastly different tracks even as they occasionally intersect.

To grasp the differences and overlaps, imagine a bustling bazaar in Kanpur and a sleek co-working space in Bengaluru. In the Kanpur alleyway sits Ramesh, running a leather unit employing 25 workers, supplying belts and wallets to traders across India. His business is registered as a small enterprise under Udyam and is eligible for a collateral-free loan under the CGTMSE scheme. Two thousand kilometres away, in the air-conditioned startup accelerator of Bengaluru, Mehak and Aarav pitch their AI-powered supply chain platform to a group of angel investors. Their startup has no factory, no labour-intensive operations, but it has a pitch deck, patents, and Series A ambitions. Both are entrepreneurs. Both create jobs. But their worlds are structurally and philosophically different.

The MSME ecosystem in India is considered the bedrock of employment generation. It is traditional, deeply embedded in local economies, and spread across manufacturing, services, and trade. These enterprises—numbering over 6.3 crore—range from small repair shops and family-run garment units to component manufacturers in automotive clusters like Rajkot and Tiruppur. Their growth is mostly incremental. They borrow from cooperative banks or NBFCs, rely on decades-old relationships, and navigate bureaucratic paperwork with dogged persistence. Government support is structured through schemes like PMEGP, MUDRA loans, Credit Linked Capital Subsidy, and public procurement reservations. Their problems are equally grounded—delayed payments, inadequate technology adoption, stiff compliance norms, and vulnerability to macroeconomic shocks like demonetisation or COVID lockdowns.

The startup ecosystem, in contrast, is a child of liberalisation, digitisation, and globalisation. Startups don't just aim to make a profit—they aim to scale, disrupt, and innovate. They are born not in industrial sheds but on Google Docs and GitHub repositories. From fintech apps to health-tech platforms, from agri-tech and ed-tech analytics to ed-tech delivery models, Indian startups aim to solve problems using new-age technologies. They often begin with an idea and grow with the backing of venture capital, not bank loans. Their mentors are not bank managers but accelerators, angel networks, and pitch competitions. Government schemes like Startup India, FFS, startup accelerators of MeitY (Ministry of Electronics and Information Technology), and SIDBI VC have supported this surge. Startups are unencumbered by legacy, but their mortality rate is high—over 90% fail in the first five years. They are not constrained by geography; their clients may be in Berlin, their tech stack in San Francisco, and their founders in Pune.

Yet, the dichotomy is not absolute. The two ecosystems overlap, blur, and sometimes merge. Picture a traditional MSME making auto parts in Pune that gradually adopts IoT (Internet of Things)-based production scheduling developed by a nearby startup. Or consider a small dairy cooperative in Gujarat that uses a startup's blockchain tech to trace milk quality across the chain. Increasingly, startups are acting as digital enablers for MSMEs, offering ERP (Enterprise Resource Planning) solutions, logistics tech, or payment gateways tailored for small businesses.

Conversely, many startups, especially D2C (direct-to-consumer) brands in fashion, wellness, and packaged food, eventually mature into MSMEs in scale and structure. After the initial funding and product-market fit phase, they need to manage inventory, comply with GST filings, and ensure labour law compliance, just like any MSME. The moment Mehak and Aarav's AI startup starts hiring more than 50 employees and clocks crores in turnover, they enter the MSME zone for statutory recognition and financial schemes.

There is also institutional and policy-level overlap. The Ministry of MSME, once focused solely on the traditional sector, now finds itself engaging with new-age MSMEs with startup DNA. Simultaneously, the DPIIT, under the Ministry of Commerce, spearheads Startup India and handles regulatory easing for them, creating a dual-governance structure. SIDBI, for instance, supports both MSMEs through traditional lending and startups via equity-based investments. Schemes like RAMP and the Udyam Assist Platform (UAP) are slowly nudging small businesses toward digital transformation, often facilitated by startup innovations.

But tensions remain. MSMEs often feel left behind in the glamour race. They complain that startups get media limelight, policy buzzwords, and investor attention, while MSMEs struggle to get paid on time or access simple credit. On the other hand, startups argue that, despite rhetoric, the ease of doing business remains a mirage, with tax notices, angel tax issues, and regulatory bottlenecks pulling them down.

What India needs is convergence without confusion. The future lies in creating a continuum, where startups don't view MSMEs as outdated relics, and MSMEs don't view startups as urban toys. The government's challenge is to design policies that build bridges between innovation and execution, between those who dream of the next big thing and those who build it brick by brick.

Imagine if Startup India and MSME India were not two parallel trains on separate tracks but coaches on the same train—one accelerating the engine of innovation, the other stabilising the bogie of execution. That train could very well be India's vehicle to become a $10 trillion economy.

In the end, Ramesh in Kanpur and Mehak in Bengaluru are not rivals. They are co-travellers on India's economic highway. One brings scale, the other brings disruption. One brings rootedness, the other brings flight. Both are needed. Both must thrive. The bridge between them is not just policy. It is collaboration, mutual respect, and a shared vision of inclusive growth.

Conclusion

In India's grand story of economic transformation, MSMEs and startups are not competing characters but complementary protagonists. One represents legacy and livelihood, the other stands for disruption and innovation. MSMEs are the quiet workhorses powering India's manufacturing, services, and retail sectors, rooted deeply in geography and community. Startups, on the other hand, are agile explorers, leaping across sectors and borders with a laptop, a codebase, and a dream. Yet their destinies are increasingly intertwined. Startups offer MSMEs the tools to digitise, grow, and compete globally. MSMEs offer startups real-world problems to solve and platforms to scale innovation. The government, meanwhile, must stop treating them as siloed categories and start crafting integrated policy interventions. For India to leapfrog into the league of developed nations, the question is not whether MSMEs or startups are more important, but how fast and effectively they can work together. Ramesh's machine shop and Mehak's AI dashboard may seem worlds apart, but when aligned, they form the true engine of India's inclusive, job-rich, innovation-led growth.

References:

1. Ministry of MSME Annual Report 2023–24, Government of India, https://msme.gov.in

2. Startup India Progress Report 2023, DPIIT, Ministry of Commerce and Industry, https://www.startupindia.gov.in

3. 'Udyam Registration Data' – MSME Dashboard, https://udyamregistration.gov.in

4. Reserve Bank of India Report on MSME Credit Flow, March 2024, https://rbi.org.in

5. NASSCOM Start-up Ecosystem Report 2023, https://nasscom.in

6. Economic Survey of India 2023–24, Chapter on Industry and Services, Ministry of Finance.

7. SIDBI Annual Report 2023–24, including Fund of Funds for Startups and CGTMSE data.

8. Press Information Bureau Releases on RAMP and PMEGP, 2022–24.

9. Interviews and case studies published in The Hindu BusinessLine, YourStory, and Financial Express (2022–2024).

SECTION II

◆◆◆

STARTUP DREAMS AND NIGHTMARES

The glitter of unicorns hides cracks in the startup story. This section unpacks hype, hubris, and heartbreak—and what they mean for India's growth narrative.

CHAPTER 4

◆◆◆

The Gensol-BluSmart Debacle – A Cautionary Case Study

Abstract:

The Gensol-BluSmart episode is not merely a cautionary tale for equity investors—it is a full-blown morality play on the dangers of unchecked ambition, regulatory loopholes, and systemic complacency. What began as a modest SME listing in 2019 with 96% promoter holding culminated in near-zero promoter equity by 2025, leaving in its wake a trail of misleading disclosures, phantom electric vehicle (EV) orders, fictitious financial documents, and a plant with barely any manufacturing activity. This narrative dissects how the scam unfolded, the regulatory failures (SEBI,[21] Audit Committees, Independent Directors, Statutory Auditors, and the CAG—yes, the CAG too) that enabled it, and the profound lessons it offers to India's capital markets. Let us explore how an ambitious startup leveraged the green energy narrative to mislead investors and regulators alike—until the music stopped.

---

21. The SEBI is the regulatory authority established in 1988 and given statutory powers in 1992 to oversee and regulate the securities market in India. Its primary role is to protect investor interests, ensure fair and transparent market practices, and regulate intermediaries like stock exchanges, brokers, mutual funds, and credit rating agencies.

A Green Beginning: The Rise of Gensol Engineering and the EV Promise

Imagine a student telling everyone he has '30 job offers'.

But when asked, he admits they're just 'verbal promises' from relatives, with no offer letters or salaries. That's what Gensol did with its EV orders—told the market it had 30,000 pre-orders, but they were just empty MOUs (Memorandums of Understanding) with no contracts, payments, or delivery plans.

Gensol Engineering burst onto the public stage in September 2019 with a modest ₹18 crore SME IPO (Initial Public Offering). It was not a head-turner—just 1.3 times subscribed—but it quietly laid the groundwork for a future replete with promise. The promoters, Anmol and Puneet Jaggi, held an overwhelming 96% stake, which was reduced to just over 70% after listing. That dilution seemed normal. But what followed was anything but.

Over the next few years, Gensol rode the clean energy wave and the EV euphoria, sweeping India's markets. In July 2023, the company graduated to the mainboard, gaining access to broader investor pools and increased liquidity. Simultaneously, its subsidiary, BluSmart, grew in public visibility as a green cab aggregator powered by Gensol's EV fleet. Beneath this eco-friendly image, however, lay layers of deception waiting to be peeled.

A friend owes ₹500 to the school canteen.

He convinces another friend to 'buy' his lunchbox for ₹500, but they never exchange money. A week later, the friend asks for the lunchbox back. Gensol's deal with Refex was like that—an illusionary transfer of EVs in exchange for loan liabilities, later reversed.

The Investigation Unravels: From Pre-Orders to Phantom Plants

SEBI's investigations began in June 2024, prompted by whistleblower complaints alleging price manipulation and fund diversion. What followed was a revelation of corporate deceit with cinematic audacity.

On 28 January 2025, Gensol told the stock exchanges that it had received pre-orders for 30,000 EVs at the Bharat Mobility Global Expo. The news lifted expectations, but upon probing, the company admitted those were merely non-binding MOUs with nine entities, for 29,000 cars. No payment terms. No delivery schedules. No guarantees. Just a wishful handshake dressed up as a committed order book.

> Suppose your school says it has built a new science lab.
>
> You go there and find one table, two stools, and no microscope. The electricity bill is barely ₹200. That's how Gensol's Pune EV plant was—a showroom of dreams, but no real work happening

An on-ground visit by an NSE (National Stock Exchange) official to Gensol's so-called manufacturing plant in Chakan, Pune, sealed the suspicions. The facility was eerily quiet. Just two to three labourers were seen, and electricity bills showed laughably low consumption—₹1.57 lakh in December 2024, implying negligible industrial activity. The EV dream began to dissolve into the fumes of corporate fiction.

A House of Cards: Strategic Deals, Dubious Subsidiaries, and Debt Shenanigans

The rot did not stop at fake pre-orders. In mid-January 2025, Gensol announced a 'strategic tie-up' with Refex for the transfer of 2,997 EVs in exchange for Refex assuming ₹315 crore of Gensol's loan liabilities. Just two months later, the deal was scrapped. In February, a fresh claim was made—Gensol had inked a ₹350 crore non-binding term sheet to sell its US subsidiary Scorpius Trackers, which was incorporated just six months earlier. When SEBI asked for a valuation basis, Gensol had no explanation.

> Your parents give you ₹10,000 to buy ten books for a class library. You only buy seven books worth ₹7,000, but tell them you bought all ten. Gensol did something similar—claimed to buy 6,400 EVs with government loans but actually bought fewer, with ₹262 crore unaccounted for

This was not just poor governance—it was outright obfuscation. Rating agencies ICRA (Investment Information and Credit Rating Agency) and CARE (Credit Analysis and Research), smelling smoke, downgraded Gensol's credit facilities to 'D' on 3 and 4 March 2025, citing delays in loan servicing. The company responded with defiance, but soon SEBI would expose forged documents submitted to lenders IREDA[22] and PFC[23] to mask loan defaults.

IREDA and PFC had loaned ₹977.75 crore to Gensol, including ₹663.89 crore for the purchase of 6,400 EVs. When probed, Gensol admitted that it had bought only 4,704 EVs, costing ₹567.73 crore. That left ₹262.13 crore missing. The

22. The Indian Renewable Energy Development Agency (IREDA) is a government-owned financial institution under the Ministry of New and Renewable Energy (MNRE), established in 1987 to promote, develop, and extend financial support for renewable energy and energy efficiency projects in India. It provides loans, refinancing, and other financial products to projects in solar, wind, hydro, biomass, and energy conservation sectors to accelerate the country's transition to clean energy.

23. Power Finance Corporation (PFC) is a Government of India-owned NBFC established in 1986 under the Ministry of Power to provide funding and financial services for the power sector. It plays a key role in financing generation, transmission, distribution, and renewable energy projects across India, supporting both public and private sector initiatives.

scam had moved beyond fibs into the realm of suspected fund siphoning.

> A class monitor is supposed to check if students are cheating in exams, but he's busy texting on his phone. Statutory auditors and even the CAG (for PSU lenders) failed to detect fake letters, missing assets, and cooked-up numbers.

At the heart of the scandal lies a three-pronged deception strategy.

First came inflated and misleading disclosures—non-binding MoUs were passed off as firm orders to boost share prices. Second, there were fake documents—'Conduct Letters' falsely attributed to IREDA and PFC to mask debt defaults. Third, the company engineered liquidity by steadily offloading promoter holdings to unsuspecting retail and institutional investors riding the EV hype.

By the time SEBI stepped in with an interim order banning the Jaggi brothers from holding key positions in listed companies, the promoters had almost completely exited their equity positions, leaving investors holding a story that no longer held up to scrutiny.

The Regulatory Blind Spots: What Didn't Happen, But Should Have

Despite years of falsehoods, regulatory red flags failed to flutter early enough.

Where were the stock exchanges when Gensol made its exaggerated announcements? Why did the NSE's surveillance mechanism not trigger alerts based on price and volume spikes following such disclosures?

Why were rating agencies reliant solely on documents provided by Gensol, without verifying directly with IREDA and PFC?

Why were auditors (the CAG is the Government auditor, as both IREDA and PFC are Central Public Sector Enterprises, and it conducts supplementary audit of the statutory auditors) and independent directors silent despite glaring discrepancies in procurement costs, financial statements, and capital deployment?

The SEBI action came only after a formal complaint was filed, suggesting a reactive—not proactive—regulatory posture.

The Lessons: What Stakeholders Must Learn from the Gensol Collapse

For investors, the lesson is brutal but clear—do not trust glossy green narratives without hard facts. ESG and EV-themed stocks need more scrutiny, not less.

For promoters, Gensol is a reminder that stock markets are not piggy banks to be milked. The paper trail will eventually lead to the truth, and when it does, consequences are inevitable.

A student starts a group project, builds hype, then leaves midway after taking all the credit. The rest of the group gets blamed for the mess. Gensol's promoters sold most of their shares before SEBI acted, leaving investors with a collapsing company and worthless dreams.

For auditors (including the CAG), CRAs (Credit Rating Agencies), and exchanges, it is time to stop rubber-stamping disclosures and start demanding granular evidence. The financial system cannot run on trust alone—it must be built on verification.

And for SEBI, the wake-up call is urgent. This was a fraud hidden in plain sight, built over years. Surveillance systems must evolve to spot deception masked as growth—especially in high-buzz, low-regulation domains like EVs, green energy, and startups.

Conclusion: When the Green Turns Grey

Gensol's unravelling is not just a story of regulatory failure—it is yet another warning shot to India's capital markets. In the chase for growth and valuations, the system failed to catch a runaway narrative built on air. What's worse, the promoters got away by selling their stake to an unsuspecting public under the guise of success. SEBI's actions, though decisive in the end, came after most of the damage was done.

The hope is that this debacle serves as a watershed moment, where investor diligence, regulatory foresight, and institutional accountability converge to build a market less vulnerable to charm and more loyal to truth.

We now move to examining the challenges of the startup ecosystem in India.

CHAPTER 5

The Flawed Foundations of India's Startup Ecosystem – Soonicorns, Hype, and Fragile Structures

Abstract:

India's startup ecosystem is a paradoxical tapestry of exhilarating growth and exasperating hurdles. This chapter dissects what ails the startup ecosystem in India by exploring its systemic challenges, from a high failure rate of ventures and stifling bureaucracy to infrastructural bottlenecks, talent gaps, and an innovation deficit, while also spotlighting the burgeoning strengths that promise a brighter future. We delve into the dramatic rise-and-fall stories of Indian startups (PepperTap, Dazo, TinyOwl,

Imagine your school's canteen suddenly becomes a sensation after adding momos and bubble tea. Every student wants in. But within three months, the excitement dies down. Orders drop. The owner hadn't saved enough money or thought of new menus. Eventually, the shop shuts down. That's what happened with many food delivery startups like TinyOwl and Dazo—popular for a while, but unprepared for the long game.

and more) and examine how red tape, complex taxes, power outages, skill shortages, and legal inefficiencies have often conspired against entrepreneurial success. Yet, amid these challenges, the narrative is far from grim: government initiatives and policy shifts are gradually easing burdens, and a new generation of startups is thriving. Backed by supportive reforms, record digital adoption, global investor interest, and success stories like Zerodha, BYJU'S, and Freshworks, India's startup landscape is evolving. This racy, analytical chapter presents a two-sided chronicle, lamenting the systemic 'ailments' that plague Indian startups while celebrating the emerging strengths that make the ecosystem more resilient. The goal is to provide a comprehensive, data-driven, and metaphor-rich account for policy-savvy readers on how India's startup story is one of both cautionary tales and triumphant breakthroughs.

Introduction

On a sweltering Bangalore afternoon, a young founder in a co-working hub hits 'refresh' on her pitch deck as the lights flicker from yet another power surge. In that brief blackout, she reflects on the rollercoaster of building a startup in India—a journey equally defined by audacious dreams and archaic obstacles. Her food delivery venture shares the same city that birthed billion-dollar unicorns, yet she's haunted by the ghost stories of failed predecessors. Not long ago, ventures like Peppertap and TinyOwl enjoyed euphoric heights before crashing suddenly, reminding everyone that in India's startup arena, survival is far from guaranteed. Indeed, India has seen over 1,20,000 startups registered in the last decade, making it the world's third-largest startup ecosystem. But behind the unicorn headlines lies a sobering statistic: up to 90% of Indian startups fail within the first five years. Such odds turn entrepreneurship into high drama—a race where founders must outrun systemic challenges as much as market competitors.

Systemic Challenges Facing Indian Startups

High Failure Rates and the Tales of Fallen Startups

India's startup landscape is littered with cautionary tales, with failure rates among the highest in the world. A landmark study by the IBM Institute for Business Value found that over 90% of Indian startups collapse within five years. The primary culprit wasn't a shortage of capital or ambition, but a lack of innovation—too many startups were mere copycats of Western business models. VCs grew wary as 77% of them felt that Indian startups lacked unique value propositions, triggering a funding pullback that pruned many ventures. The fallout was stark: since 2015, at least 1,503 startups have shut down in India, often because replicating someone else's idea without local innovation proved unsustainable.

The year 2016 became emblematic of this shakeout. What had been a fever-pitch startup boom (with three to four new startups launching every day in 2015) suddenly morphed into a bust. The second quarter of 2016 saw mass layoffs and an epidemic of shutdowns. Food-tech was hit particularly hard—startups like TinyOwl, Dazo, and ZuperMeal, once darlings of India's tech press, abruptly shuttered. TinyOwl, a food-ordering app founded in 2014, burned through cash and by May 2016 had to close operations in all but one city, after laying off over 600 employees. PepperTap, a hyperlocal grocery delivery startup, famously fell to fierce competition; it couldn't keep pace with deep-pocketed rivals, Grofers and BigBasket, who raised substantially more funding and squeezed PepperTap out of the market. These rise-and-fall sagas underscore a brutal truth: while starting up in India is easy, staying up is hard. Lack of product-market fit, unsustainable cash burn, and an overreliance on trends (food delivery was 'hot' until it wasn't) all contributed to a high mortality rate. Each failure story—be it the sudden shutdown of Dazo that stunned its users or the slow death of once-promising e-commerce players—

served as a reality check that entrepreneurial enthusiasm must be tempered with business fundamentals and adaptability. In essence, the graveyard of Indian startups has taught today's founders that innovation and resilience are not optional; they are prerequisites for survival in this ecosystem.

Say you want to open a lemonade stall outside your home. But instead of just mixing juice and selling it, you're asked to fill 10 forms, get 3 signatures, pay tax upfront, and wait two weeks for permission. That's how starting a business often feels in India: lots of paperwork, approvals, and delays-even for simple ideas.

Bureaucracy, Taxation, and Regulatory Red Tape

If launching a startup is a leap of faith, doing so in India can sometimes feel like leaping in shackles. Despite high-profile campaigns like 'Startup India' promising a new era of ease, many entrepreneurs report that the bureaucratic and regulatory hurdles remain daunting. The process of registering a company, securing permits, and complying with innumerable regulations can sap a young venture's energy. As one frustrated founder put it in an open letter to the government, 'I will not talk about how challenging it was to open an entity in India. I am going to talk about what a messed up system I deal with every day.' Strong words—backed by real struggles. Founders often grapple with endless paperwork, approvals, and

You build a cool mobile app in English, but when your cousin from a village tries it, he doesn't understand it. He prefers using apps in Hindi or his local language. That's what startups face when trying to reach rural markets-language, affordability, and digital literacy are big barriers.

'signatures in triplicate' that hark back to India's 'License Raj' days. While Startup India was intended to slash red tape, in practice, many startups still face complex procedures and delays that strangle their agility.

Taxation has been another perennial thorn. Until recently, India's infamous 'angel tax' cast a long shadow over startup investments. Introduced in 2012 to curb money laundering, this tax treated capital raised above a startup's 'fair market value' as income, taxable at over 30%. For years, it was a nightmare for nascent startups—an unpredictable levy that could hit founders simply for raising funds at a healthy valuation. The impact was chilling: many investors hesitated to fund Indian startups, or forced ventures to incorporate abroad to escape this tax. Relief came only after sustained lobbying: in 2019, the government exempted DPIIT-registered startups from angel tax, and by 2023, extended relief to certain foreign investors. Finally, in July 2024, the angel tax was abolished for all classes of investors, removing what investors called a 'major irritant' that had caused 'angst and anguish among angel investors and founders for 12 years'. The move was celebrated as eliminating a significant barrier to early-stage funding.

Tax complexity doesn't end there. The roll-out of a nationwide GST in 2017, while economically transformative, initially confounded startups with frequently changing rules and compliance burdens. Many small firms lacked the resources for dedicated tax teams and struggled with the transition to digital tax filing, invoice matching, and multi-state registrations. Employee Stock Option Plans (ESOPs) too became a double-edged sword: a

> Imagine you want to become a YouTuber or app developer, but your parents insist you study engineering or write civil service exams. They worry that if you 'fail', you'll be ruined. That fear of risk has kept many brilliant people from becoming startup founders in India.

crucial tool to attract talent but taxed in a manner that often hurt employees. Until 2020, employees had to pay income tax on ESOPs at the time of exercise (when they buy the shares), even if they hadn't sold them—meaning they could face hefty tax bills on paper gains. A 2020 reform deferred this taxation for certain DPIIT-recognised startups (up to five years or until shares are sold), a welcome step, yet many argue that ESOP taxation in India remains among the harshest, and further rationalisation is needed.

The smartest students in your class get into top global universities—and don't return. Instead of building new companies here, they work in the US or Europe. India loses its brightest minds who might have started groundbreaking startups at home.

Beyond taxes, the regulatory environment can be painfully Kafkaesque. Compliance requirements—from labour laws to data localisation rules—often come with overlapping authorities and unclear guidelines. Bureaucratic red tape frequently kills speed and innovation; for example, obtaining just the right approvals to import high-end equipment or electronics can be slow and costly. One US-based Indian founder noted that importing laptops for his engineering team in India was a saga: high customs duties on essential tech like MacBooks effectively act as a 'productivity tax' on Indian professionals, and shipping devices between Indian cities could inexplicably take over 30 days. Such delays are more than minor irritants—they are growth inhibitors in a field where speed is life. The

Your neighbourhood tuition teacher starts uploading videos online. Suddenly, lakhs of students watch her lessons, and she builds a full business out of it. That's similar to what happened with BYJU'S—started small, went digital, and then scaled globally.

government acknowledges these issues: in 2025, the commerce minister even set up a special Startup India helpline to allow entrepreneurs to report harassment or bribery by officials and to suggest regulatory fixes. That such a helpline is needed speaks volumes about the persistence of red tape and petty corruption. Indeed, founders often swap war stories of having to pay 'speed money' or endure interminable waits for things as basic as utility connections, construction permits for office space, or export documentation. These bureaucratic hurdles can drain startups of precious time and capital, forcing them to focus on form-filling and court petitions instead of innovation and scaling. In summary, while India's ease-of-doing-business rankings have improved on paper, the on-ground reality for startups is that bureaucracy and regulatory burden still pose serious challenges.

Infrastructure Bottlenecks: Power, Connectivity, and Logistics

The infrastructure underlying India's startup ecosystem often creaks under the weight of its aspirations. It's hard to build a twenty-first-century tech company on twentieth-century foundations, and Indian entrepreneurs often find themselves stymied by gaps in basic infrastructure—be it electricity, Internet, or transport logistics. Power outages, for instance, remain distressingly common in many Indian cities (including major tech hubs). A city like Bengaluru, dubbed the 'Silicon Valley of India', endures routine blackouts that force startups to invest in backup generators and UPS (Uninterruptible Power Supply) systems just to keep servers running and data safe. The situation can be worse in smaller cities and towns: unreliable power supply can disrupt operations, damage hardware, and inflate costs (via fuel for generators)—an unwelcome 'tax' on doing business that startups in developed countries rarely worry about. These disruptions steal focus and productivity; as one entrepreneur quipped, 'In India, you sometimes spend more time worrying about the power staying on than your product roadmap.'

Digital infrastructure, the lifeblood of modern startups, is another mixed bag. On one hand, India's telecom revolution (turbocharged by affordable data from Jio and others) has led to over 750 million active Internet users and an Internet penetration of about 52% of the population by 2024. On the other hand, this connected India has a flip side: the country also leads the world in Internet shutdowns imposed by authorities. In 2022 alone, India implemented 84 Internet shutdowns—the highest number of any country. For context, that was more than 3.5 times the shutdowns in war-torn Ukraine that year. The reasons range from curbing misinformation and preventing exam cheating to controlling protests, but the economic consequences are severe. Startups in regions under Internet blackout effectively go dark, unable to serve customers or coordinate teams. Frequent shutdowns, sometimes lasting days or even months (as happened in Kashmir with a 552-day blackout, the longest ever), undermine India's 'Digital India' vision. It's a poignant policy contradiction: even as the Prime Minister evangelises a billion connected Indians driving innovation, local authorities routinely pull the plug on connectivity at the slightest hint of unrest. The result is lost business, shaken user confidence, and a lingering unpredictability that makes planning difficult for startups, especially those offering real-time services or relying on cloud connectivity. Aside from deliberate shutdowns, network quality can be patchy. Urban areas enjoy 4G (and now 5G in pockets) speeds, but many rural and semi-urban regions still struggle with slow, inconsistent Internet. 'Last mile' connectivity issues mean a fintech app or e-commerce service might work flawlessly in Mumbai but sputter in a small town due to bandwidth constraints. The urban-rural digital divide thus remains a barrier to truly scaling digital startups across India.

Logistics and physical connectivity present yet another hurdle. India's sheer size and diversity mean reaching customers nationwide is a formidable challenge. Startups in e-commerce, for example, have had to master the art of deliveries in a country with over 6,00,000 villages and often poor road connectivity to many of them. While things have improved with new highways and dedicated freight corridors, the cost of logistics in India has historically been around 14% of GDP—far higher than the global average of ~8%. This indicates systemic inefficiencies: slow transit times, bureaucratic checkpoints for goods, and losses due to pilferage or damage. For startups, high logistics costs squeeze margins, and slow delivery times can alienate customers. Consider a small craft producer selling via an online marketplace—shipping a product from a village in, say, Uttar Pradesh to a customer in Karnataka might involve delays and high courier fees, making it hard to compete on price and reliability. Additionally, infrastructure bottlenecks in transportation—congested ports, outdated rail freight systems, and traffic-choked city roads—can blunt the competitive edge of Indian startups trying to implement fast, on-demand services. A food delivery or ride-sharing startup in a metro must navigate not just literal potholes but a lack of reliable address systems and traffic jams that add uncertainty to every trip.

In summary, while Indian entrepreneurs have proven adept at 'jugaad' (frugal innovation) to workaround infrastructure issues, these bottlenecks undeniably slow down the ecosystem's momentum. The government has been investing heavily in infrastructure—new power plants, fibre optic networks, smarter logistics via projects like Bharatmala and Dedicated Freight Corridors, etc.—and these efforts are gradually bearing fruit. However, until such improvements are widespread, India's startups must continue building in an environment where the basic foundations can't be taken for granted. This challenge, arguably more than capital or ideas, often separates those who merely launch startups from those who successfully scale them.

Talent Shortages, Education Gaps, and Low R&D Spending

India produces over a million engineers and graduates each year, but amidst this sea of degrees, startups often struggle to find the specialised talent they need. It's a perplexing paradox: plenty of people, yet a shortage of skills. The crux lies in the quality and relevance of education. Many Indian graduates enter the job market without the practical skills or creative problem-solving experience that startups thrive on. In fact, industry surveys have frequently found that a majority of Indian engineering graduates are not immediately employable in their core domains without significant additional training. As a result, startups face a 'talent gap' in cutting-edge fields—whether it's a dearth of experienced product managers who can build user-centric apps or a lack of data scientists and AI specialists crucial for tech-driven ventures. A 2023 PwC (PricewaterhouseCoopers) report highlighted that 77% of Indian CEOs cited skill shortages as a major barrier to growth, up sharply from 64% just a few years prior. This indicates that, at the highest levels, business leaders see the talent crunch worsening, especially in emerging technologies like AI, machine learning, and cybersecurity. In other words, despite India's huge workforce, the supply of industry-ready, innovation-ready human capital is not keeping pace with the digital ambitions of its startups.

Part of the challenge is an education system that historically emphasised rote learning over creativity. This has begun to change with new policies and a growing emphasis on skill-based training, but cultural shifts take time. Moreover, advanced research talent—like PhDs in biotech, semiconductor design experts, or seasoned deep-tech researchers—is relatively scarce in India's talent pool. The country's low expenditure on R&D aggravates this. India spends only around 0.7% of its GDP on R&D, one of the lowest ratios among major economies.

For perspective, China spends about 2.4%, the US 3.5%, and tiny Israel about 5% of its GDP on R&D. This under-investment has persisted for years—in fact, India's R&D spending actually declined from 0.8% to 0.7% of GDP over the decade up to 2018. The implications are significant: fewer cutting-edge projects at universities, limited industry-academia collaboration, and a smaller pipeline of innovations and highly trained researchers who can fuel startup breakthroughs. Low R&D spending is both a cause and effect of the talent issue—without enough funding, labs don't flourish and high-potential scientists leave for better opportunities abroad, which leads to fewer innovations, reinforcing perceptions that India is better at outsourcing than inventing.

Another facet is the leadership deficit in startups. India's modern startup boom is barely 15 years old, meaning there are relatively few seasoned entrepreneurs with multiple company-scaleups under their belt. In Silicon Valley, a failed startup is considered a valuable learning experience, and serial founders are common; in India, the ecosystem is still minting its first generation of serial entrepreneurs. This translates to a scarcity of mentors and experienced C-suite talent (e.g. CTOs (Chief Technology Officers) who have scaled a tech platform to millions of users, or CFOs (Chief Financial Officers) who have navigated an IPO) available to guide new startups. In a way, the ecosystem is 'learning on the job', with fewer guardrails. Many founders are young and brimming with energy, but they may falter in strategy or execution, where experience counts. Brain-drain compounds this leadership gap. For decades, India's best and brightest tech minds often emigrated—to Silicon Valley, to research hubs in Europe, or to global corporates—seeking better research facilities, higher pay, or simply a different lifestyle. The trend is so notable that today, approximately one-third of Silicon Valley's engineers are of Indian origin, and by some estimates, 11% of Fortune 500 companies are led by CEOs (Chief Executive Officers) born in India. While that is a point of pride, it represents a loss of talent that could have been building enterprises in India. Encouragingly, a nascent 'reverse brain drain' is underway, with some successful Indians abroad returning to start ventures at home, but it's only a trickle relative to the vast diaspora.

Moreover, gaps in India's education system—especially primary and secondary schooling in large parts of the country—mean that a significant portion of the population isn't adequately prepared for the knowledge economy. Literacy rates and basic digital skills lag in rural areas, and although India boasts IITs and IIMs (Indian Institutes of Management) (elite engineering and management institutes) that are world-class, access to quality education for the masses remains uneven. Startups not only need coders and MBAs (Masters of Business Administration); they also need skilled technicians, design thinkers, salespeople who understand modern consumers, and workers who can operate advanced machinery. The paucity of vocational training and polytechnic education has left many manufacturing or hardware-oriented startups lamenting the difficulty of hiring competent technicians.

In sum, talent is the oxygen of startups, and in India, that oxygen can be thin. The country is addressing this by pushing initiatives in skilling (such as Skill India missions, coding bootcamps, and AI/machine learning specialised courses), and by courting diaspora experts to return. But until the educational reforms take root and R&D investment increases, Indian startups will need to invest extra in training employees, partnering with global experts, or even acqui-hiring niche talent from abroad. Despite the huge population advantage, human capital remains a critical chokepoint.

Intellectual Property and Legal Inefficiencies

In the realm of IP and legal systems, Indian startups often find themselves navigating an obstacle course that can sap their innovative spirit. The process of securing and defending IP rights in India has historically been slow and cumbersome. For a startup with a novel invention or a proprietary technology, obtaining a patent can take years—often longer than the relevant market window for that technology. The Indian Patent Office, despite recent improvements, has had a notorious backlog. Until a few years ago, it was not uncommon for patent applications to languish five to seven years before grant, by which time a fast-moving tech startup might already be obsolete or have been copied by others. Comparatively, patent regimes in the US or Europe, while not lightning-fast, at least have more predictable timelines. The slow pace in India has a chilling effect: some startups either don't bother to file (sacrificing protection) or file in jurisdictions like the US first, incurring higher costs.

Moreover, enforcing IP rights through the legal system can be an ordeal. If a startup discovers that its code has been pirated or its design infringed by a competitor, getting injunctions or damages awarded through Indian courts can be daunting. India's courts are overwhelmed: as of recent counts, tens of millions of cases are pending, and civil suits (like IP disputes) move glacially. In 2017, India ranked 172nd out of 190 countries in enforcing contracts, with an average of nearly four years required to resolve a commercial dispute. In many instances, by the time a judgment arrives, the market context has changed or the infringer has moved on. This legal delay essentially means that for a startup, 'winning' a lawsuit might still feel like losing, given the time and resources drained. The Economic Survey of India has highlighted how such delays in courts are not just a legal issue but also an economic one, causing stalled projects and reduced investment as businesses lose confidence in timely dispute resolution.

Contract enforcement issues hit startups particularly hard in areas like payments (chasing defaulting clients), partnerships gone sour, or employee disputes. The cost of litigation is also high—on average, about 30% of the claim value can be spent on legal fees by the time a contract dispute is resolved. For a cash-strapped startup, this often means justice is unaffordable. So startups either resort to arbitration (if included in contracts) or, more often, just swallow losses and move on, which can encourage a culture where contracts are not taken as seriously as they should be.

Another facet of the legal inefficiency is regulatory inconsistency and complexity in areas like IP. For example, the process for patenting software or algorithms in India is still somewhat unclear, given India's IP laws traditionally didn't recognise software 'as such' as patentable. This creates uncertainty for software startups on whether their innovations can be patented domestically. Similarly, data protection and privacy laws are evolving (India's Personal Data Protection law is relatively new), and startups must stay nimble to comply with changing rules. Legal inefficiency also crops up in things like winding down a failed startup—ironically, it can be easier to start a company than to close one in India. Until the Insolvency and Bankruptcy Code (IBC) was introduced in 2016, there was virtually no straightforward path for quick exits of failed businesses, leaving founders stuck with shell companies and lingering compliances. The IBC has improved matters, but small startups still struggle to navigate it due to cost and complexity, meaning failures can't even 'fail fast' cleanly.

IP culture is also at a nascent stage. While India has improved its international ranking in the Global Innovation Index (moving up from the 80s a decade ago to around the 40s today), the number of patents filed and trademarks registered by Indian companies still trails global leaders by a huge margin. For instance, China filed about 1.4 million patent applications in 2019 (43% of the world's total), whereas India's filings were a tiny fraction of that. One positive sign is that international patent filings by India have been growing at double-digit rates, indicating that Indian startups and companies are becoming more IP-conscious and globally oriented. However, converting those applications into granted patents and then into commercialised products is another leap.

From a startup founder's perspective, the legal and IP environment often shapes strategic choices: 'Should I base my HQ (headquarters) or R&D centre in a country with stronger IP protection?' or 'Do I limit my business model because enforcing my contracts at scale will be too risky here?' These are hard questions. The government, to its credit, has taken steps like modernising IP offices, hiring more patent examiners, setting up commercial courts and alternative dispute resolution mechanisms, and digitising legal processes. Yet, change is gradual. Until then, legal inefficiency remains an ailment that can undercut the confidence of entrepreneurs. It subtly incentivises operating in the grey (e.g., using informal agreements) or focusing on services over products (since services rely less on patents). For India to truly become an innovation hub, a swift and fair legal system is as crucial as code and capital. And while it's getting better, the clock speed of the courts still lags far behind the clock speed of startups.

Market Barriers: The Urban-Rural Divide and Consumer Readiness

Indian startups not only battle internal challenges but also face market-specific barriers that can hamper growth. One of the most significant is the urban-rural digital divide. India lives in 'many centuries at once'—its mega-cities buzz with 4G smartphones and food-delivery drones on the horizon, while in many villages, reliable Internet and digital literacy are still catching up. This divide means that a product that takes off in affluent urban pockets might find little traction beyond them. For startups aiming for scale, the limited access to technology and lower purchasing power in rural India can be a growth limiter. While more than half of India's Internet users are now in rural areas (roughly 488 million rural Internet users projected by 2024), the penetration rate in rural India is still significantly lower than in cities. Many rural users also access the Internet via shared devices or limited data plans, which influences their online behaviour. For instance, an ed-tech startup creating English-learning apps found that urban uptake was great, but rural users needed vernacular language support and more offline functionality due to patchy connectivity. In short, what works in Mumbai may not work in Mandla (a small town) without adaptation. Bridging this urban-rural gap requires extra effort—tailoring products to local languages, educating consumers about the product's value (sometimes from scratch), and dealing with distribution challenges in remote areas. Startups face a classic catch-22: the 'next billion' users in India are in smaller towns and villages, but reaching them profitably and effectively is hard.

Consumer readiness is another nuanced barrier. The Indian market can be paradoxical—cost-sensitive yet attracted to quality, traditional in habits yet curious for new services. Startups offering novel solutions sometimes find that consumers need time and trust to change their habits. For example, early e-commerce companies had to overcome a cultural trust deficit in online shopping. Consumers worried about fraud and preferred cash transactions, which led Indian e-commerce to innovate cash-on-delivery (CoD) payment modes. CoD solved one problem but created another—higher returns and logistical costs. It took years, demonetisation, and the rise of UPI for digital payments to gain broader acceptance beyond early adopters. Even today, a segment of customers remains wary of pre-paying online. Similarly, ride-sharing companies had to teach customers the concept of hailing rides via an app and sitting in a stranger's car—concepts that met initial scepticism. Lack of consumer readiness can thus slow down the adoption curve, forcing startups to expend resources on customer education and trust-building.

Socio-economic diversity also means market segmentation is extreme. India has a booming middle class, but also hundreds of millions of low-income consumers for whom many products are simply unaffordable or low-priority. A subscription service that might work in a Western market at $10/month needs a different pricing model to attract users in India's smaller cities, perhaps as low as $2/month or ad-supported freemium models. Startups in fintech that offer, say, personal finance management tools find that only a thin slice of Indians invest in stocks or mutual funds; the majority are not financially included to that extent. So the addressable market for certain advanced products can be much smaller than headline population figures suggest. On the flip side, the mass market that does exist often has to be reached via trusted intermediaries or influencers—for example, farmers may trust an agri-tech app more if it's recommended by a local cooperative or a well-known NGO (Non-Governmental Organisation). Thus, distribution and marketing require a feet-on-the-ground approach in many cases, which can be resource-intensive.

Another barrier is the payments and infrastructure readiness of consumers. Until the mid-2010s, credit card penetration in India was minuscule—only around 3–5% of people had a credit card. This meant startups that relied on recurring payments or online billing had to engineer alternatives. The advent of UPI (Unified Payments Interface) (discussed later) solved a chunk of this, but earlier, many startups built cash collection or invoice systems because the consumer market was not uniformly online or banked. Even today, only about 5% of Indians are credit card users, so certain models (like credit-based fintech or subscription commerce) need creative localisation. Consumer behaviour rooted in tradition is another consideration—for example, grocery shopping in India has been a daily fresh produce affair at local markets for centuries; convincing households to order veggies via an app and trust the quality was an uphill battle that is only now seeing broad acceptance via services like BigBasket or FreshToHome.

Lastly, cultural and language diversity adds complexity. India has 22 official languages and dozens of dialects. A startup can't assume English—or even Hindi—will suffice for all communication. A Kannada-speaking user in Bangalore and a Bengali-speaking user in Kolkata interact with technology differently. Localisation of products into multiple languages and cultural contexts becomes important to tap the full market, but it's something even many larger startups didn't prioritise in their early years, to their detriment. Now, voice interfaces and vernacular support are being added, but it's a corrective measure.

In essence, Indian startups face a market that is huge but fragmented, enthusiastic but cautious. The onus is often on the startup to mould itself to the market's readiness, rather than expecting the market to neatly fit the startup's offering. Those who understand the local consumer psyche, are patient in educating the market, and innovate around price and distribution, manage to unlock India's enormous demand; those who don't, often scale a tall wall of initial user resistance. Over time, as digital literacy improves and younger, tech-savvy generations constitute a larger share of consumers, these barriers will decrease. But until then, navigating the intricacies of the Indian market is akin to solving a Rubik's Cube—it requires strategy, adaptation, and sometimes a bit of trial and error to get all sides aligned.

An Innovation Deficit? Copycat Culture and Creative Conundrums

For years, a critique levelled at Indian startups was that of an 'innovation deficit'—the perception (and, to an extent, reality) that many were building clones of successful Western or Chinese startups rather than original products or breakthrough technologies. Food delivery, ride-hailing, e-commerce, and home services—playbooks from developed markets—were often simply localised and executed in India. To be fair, localisation itself required innovation in operations and pricing (India's startups had to invent solutions like cash-on-delivery, two-wheeler rides, or sachet-sized pricing). Yet, the core business models were rarely invented from scratch in India. This fostered a copycat culture: entrepreneurs and investors both felt safer emulating concepts that had been validated elsewhere. The downside was a relatively low emphasis on deep R&D or out-of-the-box ideas. By 2017, the narrative hit headlines with IBM's (International Business Machines) aforementioned study indicating a lack of pioneering innovation as a top reason for startup failures. When 77% of VCs say Indian startups aren't offering unique business models, it's a stark call-out that too many companies were chasing the same taxi app or food delivery idea with nothing distinctive to offer. The result? A crowd of lookalikes burning cash for market share in red ocean markets, rather than creating blue oceans of their own.

This innovation shortfall is also reflected in global indices and research output. Historically, India underperformed on the Global Innovation Index (GII), languishing in the 80s ranks in the mid-2010s. (It has improved significantly since, reaching the 40s by the mid-2020s, which we'll discuss at length.) The number of patents filed domestically by Indian entities was low relative to the size of the economy—a symptom of companies not pushing the technological frontier. Additionally, corporate R&D spending in India is concentrated in a few sectors (like pharmaceuticals or automotive) and in large firms (like Tata or Reliance), with startups contributing only a sliver. There have been fewer breakthrough products 'invented in India' that achieved global renown, which in turn affects the ecosystem's confidence in chasing moonshots.

However, it's important to note that the innovation deficit is not due to a lack of creativity or intellect among Indians—evidenced by the fact that Indian-origin innovators thrive in Silicon Valley and global academia—but often due to systemic factors: risk aversion in funding, less developed research infrastructure, and a market that historically rewarded speed and scale over uniqueness. For much of the 2010s, investors were pouring money into 'proven models'—the focus was on execution in a large market, not necessarily on inventing something completely novel. Consequently, hundreds of me-too startups emerged in each hot sector. Inevitably, most failed or consolidated, because only a couple could realistically win in each space, and none had an IP edge to separate them from the pack. It was essentially a marketing and fundraising battle rather than an innovation battle, which is a costly game.

This scenario led to commentary that India excels at jugaad (frugal improvisation) but not so much at fundamental innovation. For instance, in the crucial area of product design and hardware, India lagged behind. The country became a software outsourcing hub but not a product powerhouse. An oft-cited statistic was how many patents companies like IBM or Samsung were filing in India (often via their R&D centres) versus Indian startups themselves. Even in software, Indian companies were seen as service providers rather than creators of globally dominant software products (though this has begun to change with the SaaS (Software as a Service) wave). Innovation culture needs an ecosystem: research institutions, VC willing to fund R&D, legal protections for IP, a market for advanced products, and celebrated role models of innovators. Many of those pieces were undercooked in India for a long time.

There were also contradictions in policy, affecting innovation. For example, until recently, public funding for startups and research was limited, and the bureaucratic processes to get grants were discouraging. Importantly, India's education system rarely encouraged risk-taking or questioning the status quo—the very traits that drive innovation. A generation of Indians was reared on the ambition of landing a stable IT (Information Technology) job, rather than starting a garage startup to change the world. That mindset has been shifting in the past few years (with more hackathons, startup weekends, and inclusion of entrepreneurship in curricula), but cultural changes lag behind entrepreneurial success stories.

That said, calling it a pure deficit might now be an outdated notion. By the mid-2020s, signs show a closing gap: The GII ranks India around 40th (having leapt up from 81st in 2015 to 39th in 2024), indicating a rapid improvement in the innovation ecosystem. Indian startups have started filing more patents, and some are actually innovating world-first solutions in areas like digital payments (the UPI story), space tech (witness startups building small satellite launchers), and affordable healthcare devices. We'll explore these silver linings soon. However, in the context of challenges, the earlier copycat era and its hangover did slow the emergence of truly disruptive startups from India. The ecosystem had to learn that while First-to-India might bring short-term wins, being First-to-World is what cements long-term leadership. The encouraging news is that many in India's startup community have recognised this ailment and are working to cure it by fostering originality, investing in R&D, and celebrating innovation as much as valuation.

Sociopolitical Issues: Leadership, Brain Drain, and Policy Paradoxes

No analysis of India's startup ecosystem would be complete without examining the broader sociopolitical undercurrents that influence it. One challenge is a certain leadership void in fostering entrepreneurship at the societal level. India, for decades after independence, followed a socialist-inspired model that valued large public-sector enterprises and stable careers (civil service, engineering, medicine) over business creation. Entrepreneurship didn't figure as a national priority until recently. Consequently, unlike the US or Israel, where entrepreneurial culture runs deep, India didn't have as many home-grown entrepreneurial icons to inspire the next generation (apart from a few IT services stalwarts in the 1980s and 1990s). This meant a mindset gap: risk-taking, accepting failure as a stepping stone, and thinking big were not part of the collective psyche for a long time. The sociopolitical narrative only shifted in the last decade, with the government itself starting to tout startups as engines of job creation and innovation. Even so, many startup founders lament a lingering 'safety-first' mentality among both talent and regulators. For example, a talented engineer might still prefer a cushy job at Infosys or Google India than to join a volatile startup, partly because our social fabric traditionally prizes job security. Leadership in this context isn't just about individuals, but thought leadership—who sets the narrative for youth. That narrative in India is in flux, tilting towards entrepreneurship, but not uniformly across the country.

Brain drain, touched upon earlier, is another sociopolitical phenomenon with a direct impact. For years, some of the best minds graduating from India's IITs and IIMs ended up in Silicon Valley or on Wall Street. This exodus included potential startup founders and key team players. While it's impossible to quantify the 'lost startups' because of brain drain, one can surmise that many innovations happened abroad with Indian talent that, in an alternate scenario, could have been Indian companies. The tide has started to turn, with more global Indians looking back home due to India's growth story and perhaps US immigration hurdles, but it's a gradual change. In the meantime, the leadership deficit manifests in fewer globally experienced mentors on the ground. It's telling that several of India's current unicorn founders have had either overseas education or work stints that broadened their perspective. As more such people reintegrate into the Indian scene, the leadership gap will shrink. However, historically, the brain drain siphoned off the very people who might have accelerated the maturation of India's startup ecosystem.

Then there are policy contradictions and political risks that often baffle startup stakeholders. Governments at both the central and state levels announce grand initiatives (Startup India, Digital India, Make in India, etc.), which generate excitement. But on the flip side, other arms of the government might enforce rules that counteract these goals. One example: even as the government talks about boosting startups and innovation, the tax authorities were (until recently) slapping angel tax notices or retroactive GST demands that spooked founders. Similarly, there have been instances where protectionist impulses (e.g., sudden bans on certain e-commerce discounts or stringent data localisation mandates) created turbulence for startups trying to operate in a predictable regulatory environment. A standout paradox is the aforementioned Internet shutdowns—promoting a trillion-dollar digital economy while frequently shutting off the Internet is certainly a conflicting stance. Another example is inconsistent policymaking in sectors like fintech or crypto: one day, crypto exchanges found themselves flourishing, another day, a central bank circular virtually cut them off from the banking system (a decision later overturned by the Supreme Court). Startups thrive in stable policy environments, and India's can sometimes feel like shifting sands due to bureaucracy or political calculations.

Corruption, a long-standing issue in India's business environment, also seeps into the startup space occasionally. While tech startups may face it less directly than, say, construction companies (since many operate online), any startup dealing with government procurement, licenses, or public sector clients can encounter the expectation of bribes or favouritism. This erodes the level playing field—a well-connected entrepreneur might secure deals that a scrappier but honest competitor cannot. The government's push towards transparency (through digitisation of processes, e-tendering, etc.) is mitigating some of this, but anecdotal evidence suggests paying 'speed money' is still sometimes the secret to moving files faster. This is an affront to meritocratic ideals and can disillusion principled founders or foreign investors.

Finally, the societal safety net and bankruptcy stigma deserve mention. In Silicon Valley, failing in a startup is almost a badge of honour; in India, business failure traditionally carried social stigma and financial ruin (since there wasn't much of a safety net or bankruptcy protection historically). That's sociopolitical context—families might discourage entrepreneurship because a failure could mean debt and disgrace. This too has been changing, as high-profile failures are seen as opportunities for learning rather than sources of shame, but it's a subtle cultural shift in progress. Notably, the introduction of the personal bankruptcy law and the evolution of insolvency codes are providing ways for honest business failures to wind up without lifelong liability, which is crucial for encouraging risk-taking.

In summary, the sociopolitical climate in India has been a mix of encouraging winds and rough crosscurrents. On one hand, there's a newfound admiration for entrepreneurs (the word 'startup' is now part of common parlance, and even small-town parents are getting used to their kids choosing startups over PSU jobs). On the other hand, vestiges of the old mindset and systemic friction remain. The leadership and talent diaspora is slowly reversing course to enrich the local ecosystem. Policy intentions are aligning more with policy outcomes, though some contradictions persist. For Indian startups to truly soar, the sociopolitical context must consistently champion innovation, reward risk, and provide a stable platform.

Strengths and Achievements

Government Initiatives and Support: A New Policy Ecosystem

Despite the challenges, the Indian government, in recent years, has emerged as a proactive supporter of the startup ecosystem, rolling out policies and programmes that are starting to bear fruit. The flagship Startup India initiative, launched in January 2016, marked a turning point in official attitude—from scepticism to full-throated encouragement of entrepreneurship. Under Startup India, a slew of incentives were offered: easier company incorporation, self-certification for labour and environmental laws, income-tax holidays for the first three profitable years, and the creation of startup 'hub' cells to handhold new ventures. A tangible outcome has been the recognition of startups by DPIIT. From essentially zero before 2016, as of mid-2024, over 1,40,000 entities have been officially recognised as startups by DPIIT. This recognition isn't merely symbolic; it entitles startups to various benefits and signals a cultural shift where calling your new company a 'startup' is a badge of honour rather than a suspect endeavour. The explosion from a few hundred startups pre-2016 to 1.40 lakh (140k) recognised startups by 2024 is astonishing—it illustrates both the pent-up entrepreneurial energy and the enabling effect of government validation. These startups are spread across diverse industries and, importantly, across geography: while hubs like Maharashtra, Karnataka, and Delhi lead in numbers, thousands of recognised startups are coming from Uttar Pradesh, Gujarat, and beyond, indicating a broad-based movement.

To address the perennial funding gap at the early stages, the government launched the FFS, managed by the SIDBI. This fund doesn't invest in startups directly but rather in venture capital funds (AIFs (Alternative Investment Fund)), which, in turn, invest in startups, thus catalysing private capital. By mid-2024, FFS had deployed over ₹3,300 crore (about $450 million) through such AIFs, supporting hundreds of startups indirectly. Furthermore, the Startup India Seed Fund Scheme was introduced, earmarking ₹945 crore (about $120 million) to provide seed grants to early-stage startups via incubators. By mid-2024, nearly ₹90 crore had already been disbursed to startups under this scheme (with more in the pipeline). These numbers may not be Silicon Valley-scale, but they represent a crucial seeding mechanism in a country where angel investor networks are still growing. Complementing this, the government set up a Credit Guarantee Scheme for Startups to encourage banks and NBFCs to lend to startups by guaranteeing a portion of the loan. While uptake has been modest (around ₹150+ crore in loans guaranteed by mid-2024), it is an important piece of the puzzle for non-dilutive funding.

Perhaps one of the most lauded government moves has been Simplifying Regulatory Compliance. Efforts such as reducing the number of touchpoints for starting a business, enabling online single-form registrations, and integrating systems like the Ministry of Corporate Affairs portal have cut down the time and pain to incorporate. India jumped in the World Bank's Ease of Doing Business rankings from 142 in 2014 to 63 in 2019, with particular improvements in areas like starting a business and resolving insolvency (though enforcing contracts remains weak). Abolishing the angel tax in 2024 (as detailed earlier) removed a long-standing thorn. There have also been tax tweaks beneficial to startups, such as lowering corporate tax rates for small companies and easing ESOP taxation for employees of DPIIT-recognised startups (tax can be deferred by five years). Moreover, programmes like the Atal Innovation Mission (AIM) under the NITI (National Institution for Transforming India) Aayog have nurtured innovation from the ground up by establishing over 1,000 Atal Tinkering Labs in schools and dozens of Atal Incubation Centres across India. AIM has been creating a pipeline of young innovators and providing incubation support, which, in turn, feeds the startup ecosystem with ready talent and ideas.

Government support is also evident in sector-specific policies. For instance, in fintech, the introduction of UPI by the NPCI (National Payments Corporation of India) (with regulatory blessings) provided a world-class digital payments infrastructure on which countless fintech startups have built solutions. In biotechnology, the Biotechnology Industry Research Assistance Council (BIRAC) (a government arm) has funded many biostartups through grants. The space sector, once the monopoly of ISRO (Indian Space Research Organisation), has been opened to private startups with a new Spacecom policy and the creation of IN-SPACe (Indian National Space Promotion and Authorisation Centre) to facilitate private participation—already leading to a few space-tech startups launching satellites. State governments, too, have joined the bandwagon: almost every Indian state now has its own startup policy or cell, offering local incentives like subsidised incubation space, seed funds, and mentorship programmes. Karnataka's Elevate programme, Kerala's Startup Mission with a focus on grassroots innovation, and Telangana's T-Hub incubator (which is one of the largest in the world) are noteworthy examples of local governments embracing startups to drive economic growth.

Data from NITI Aayog[24] and other official sources show that these efforts are paying off in employment as well. DPIIT-registered startups have reported creating over 1.2 million jobs directly by 2023. That's significant in a country where job creation is a top priority. Each startup job is estimated to create three to four indirect jobs, suggesting that the overall impact is much larger. The narrative of startups being just a metro phenomenon is also changing, as 45% of recognised startups emerged from Tier II and III cities (as per Startup India data). This decentralisation is partly thanks to state policies and

24. NITI Aayog is the policy think tank of the Government of India, established in 2015 to replace the Planning Commission and promote cooperative federalism through structured support to states. It provides strategic and technical advice on economic, social, and developmental policies, and drives innovation, digital transformation, and evidence-based policymaking across sectors

improved Internet connectivity, which allow entrepreneurs to build companies in smaller cities where costs are lower and competition for talent is less fierce.

In summary, the government's role has transitioned from bystander to facilitator. There is a policy ecosystem now conducive to startups: from funding support and tax breaks to infrastructure like incubators and innovation labs. Red tape hasn't vanished, but layers have been peeled off. And importantly, the government is listening—the formation of dedicated platforms for startup feedback (like the Startup India portal, or regular meetings between industry groups and policymakers) means many policies are increasingly being designed or tweaked in consultation with startup stakeholders. While historically one might have said Indian entrepreneurs succeeded in spite of the government, today it is fair to say many are succeeding in part because of it. The partnership is far from perfect, but it's a strength that simply did not exist a decade ago.

Let us now discuss some success stories of startups in India.

Homegrown Success Stories: Unicorns[25] and Beyond

Nothing breeds success like success. Over the past few years, India has produced a constellation of high-profile startup successes that serve as beacons for the ecosystem. These success stories are not just feel-good narratives; they have tangible effects, instilling confidence in founders, attracting global investor capital, and creating a pool of experienced talent (and even wealthy angel investors) for the next generation of

25. A unicorn is a privately held startup company valued at $1 billion or more, typically in the technology or innovation-driven sectors. The term was coined to signify the rarity of such ventures, and unicorns often achieve rapid growth through disruptive business models and venture capital backing.

startups. By 2023, India became home to over 100 unicorns (startups valued over $1 billion), making it the third-largest such base in the world. This is a meteoric rise from just one unicorn in 2011. Each unicorn carries its own story of triumph over odds.

Take Flipkart, often touted as the pioneer. Founded in 2007 out of an apartment in Bengaluru by two ex-Amazon employees, Flipkart began as an online bookstore and grew into India's e-commerce titan. Its journey had all the makings of an epic—it ignited India's e-commerce boom, navigated logistical nightmares to ship goods across the country, survived aggressive onslaught by Amazon's entry, and ultimately got acquired by Walmart in 2018 for a stunning $16 billion. Flipkart's success (and investors' payday) arguably opened the floodgates of capital for Indian startups circa 2014–15.

Now consider Zerodha, a startup that breaks many conventions. Zerodha, a bootstrapped online brokerage firm started in 2010, never took a rupee of external funding and yet became India's largest stock trading platform by volume. In an industry dominated by legacy banks and brokers, Zerodha's discount brokerage model, savvy use of technology, and customer-centricity paid off. By FY2024, Zerodha was reporting astonishing numbers—₹8,320 crore in revenue with ₹4,700 crore in profit, effectively making it one of the most profitable 'startups' in the country. Its valuation is hard to pinpoint (since it hasn't raised funds), but it is widely regarded as a unicorn by virtue of its market position. Zerodha's success is a beacon showing that Indian startups can achieve scale and profitability, and that patient, sustainable growth can win the race.

Another homegrown champion is BYJU'S, the ed-tech juggernaut. What began in 2011 as a passionate teacher's tutoring classes evolved into a global online education company with tens of millions of users. BYJU'S leveraged India's massive student population and smartphone penetration to deliver animated, gamified lessons in everything from math to coding. Its meteoric rise saw it hit a valuation of $22 billion by 2022, making it, at that time, the world's most valuable ed-tech company. It acquired multiple companies domestically and abroad (including the popular coding-for-kids platform WhiteHat Jr and US-based Osmo) to expand its offerings. BYJU'S proved that Indian startups can lead in sectors beyond pure tech—like education—on a global stage, attracting investments from the likes of Tencent, Sequoia, and even sovereign wealth funds. (It's worth noting that BYJU'S has faced its share of growing pains recently, but its rise remains emblematic of India's potential to create decacorns. Chapter 7 examines BYJU'S story exclusively)

Then there's Freshworks, a SaaS provider born in Chennai. Freshworks' story is particularly inspiring because it shows that an Indian company can build software products for the world and achieve a Silicon Valley-style exit. Founded in 2010, Freshworks makes customer engagement and CRM (Customer Relationship Management) software, competing with giants like Salesforce. In 2021, Freshworks went public on the Nasdaq—raising $1.03 billion in its IPO and achieving a market capitalisation of over $10 billion on listing day. It was a watershed moment: the first Indian SaaS unicorn to IPO on a US exchange, validating the 'build from India, sell globally' model. Freshworks' success has paved the way for a wave of Indian SaaS startups aiming for similar global success. Its founder, Girish Mathrubootham, has become a mentor and angel investor to many budding SaaS companies, exemplifying the virtuous cycle of success breeding success.

Other notable successes abound across sectors: Ola in ride-sharing gave Uber a run for its money in India and expanded to international markets; Paytm, which started as a mobile recharge platform, rode the digital payments wave to become a fintech super-app and even launched a record-breaking IPO (though its post-IPO journey has been bumpy); OYO Rooms reimagined the hotel industry with an asset-light aggregation model, becoming a global name in budget hospitality. Udaan showed innovation in B2B commerce, and Nykaa became a rare profitable unicorn, achieving a successful IPO in the beauty e-commerce space. Each of these has demonstrated that Indian startups can scale to unicorn status and also provide exits, which is crucial for the health of the ecosystem.

These success stories have had ripple effects. Global investor interest in India surged as the success rate improved. By 2021, venture funding in Indian startups hit an all-time high (over $38 billion in that year alone, according to industry reports), indicating that the world saw India not just as a place where startups launch, but where they succeed and return capital. The presence of unicorns and notable exits (like Flipkart-Walmart, or several IPOs) gave confidence to investors that India's promise translates to reality. This, in turn, means more capital is available to current and future startups—a virtuous funding cycle.

Moreover, the alumni of successful startups often become the next-gen founders. The early Flipkart team has seeded multiple new startups (Ola's co-founder was an early employee, for instance). Paytm's and Ola's former executives branched out to start ventures in fintech and cloud kitchens. This recycling of talent and capital from one wave to the next strengthens the ecosystem's resilience and know-how.

From a cultural standpoint, having homegrown icons like Zerodha's Nithin Kamath, BYJU'S Raveendran, or Freshworks' Girish has shattered the mental barrier that only Silicon Valley creates big tech companies. Young entrepreneurs in India now have relatable role models—people who studied and worked in India, understood the local context, and still achieved global scale. This does wonders in stoking ambition. It's not uncommon now to hear a startup founder in Bangalore declare they want to be the 'Freshworks of cybersecurity' or the 'Zerodha of personal finance'—shorthand for dominating a niche through product excellence.

In summary, the successes achieved by Indian startups form the bedrock of the ecosystem's confidence. They are proof points that, despite all odds, companies can start in India and become world-class. These stories mitigate the fear of failure that once loomed large; they also serve as case studies for best practices. While challenges persist, these success stories have given the ecosystem a strong spine. The conversation has shifted from 'Can India produce a billion-dollar startup?' to 'How many more and in what sectors?'—a testament to how far the ecosystem has come in a short time.

Digital Revolution: Fintech, SaaS, and Tech for Good

One of India's greatest strengths in recent years has been its embrace of digital transformation at a population scale, creating fertile ground for startups, especially in fintech, online services, and deep-tech domains. The country's rapid digitisation is often described as going from zero to 60 in record time, especially after 2016, when a confluence of factors (cheap smartphones, affordable data, demonetisation nudging digital payments, and government digital initiatives) converged. As a result, India today is a global leader in certain digital domains, offering startups a platform and market unavailable in many other countries.

Fintech is a shining example. The crown jewel here is UPI—a government-backed real-time payment system that has revolutionised how Indians transact. UPI essentially turned every smartphone into a debit card, enabling instant, free bank-to-bank transfers with just a virtual address. The growth has been staggering. By 2023, India was accounting for almost 50% of the world's real-time digital payments volume. UPI saw 117.6 billion transactions in 2023 alone, an adoption curve unseen anywhere else. For fintech startups, this has been a goldmine. It lowered the barriers for customers to adopt digital wallets, lending apps, investment platforms, etc., because the payment rails were so smooth and ubiquitous. Startups like PhonePe, Paytm, and BharatPe capitalised on UPI to build large user bases. Meanwhile, the government's push for financial inclusion (Jan Dhan accounts, Aadhaar biometric ID for KYC (Know Your Customer)) brought hundreds of millions into the formal banking system, expanding the market for fintech services. As a result, India's fintech sector today boasts dozens of unicorns and innovative models—from Razorpay in payment gateways to Zerodha in stockbroking, to Pine Labs in merchant payments, to Cred, which turns credit card bill payments into a gamified experience. Global investors have taken notice; some of the largest investments in 2020–21 went into Indian fintech, betting that the combination of a huge unbanked population and cutting-edge digital infrastructure will produce multibillion-dollar outcomes.

Another area of strength is SaaS, where Indian startups have quietly and steadily built a formidable presence on the global stage. Freed from the constraints of the domestic market, SaaS companies in India leverage the country's large pool of skilled software engineers to build products for enterprises worldwide. Successes like Freshworks (customer engagement software) proved the model. Now, there's a wave of SaaS firms, such as Zoho (which, though older and always private, is a giant in SaaS), Icertis (contract management software, a unicorn), Postman (API (Application Programming Interface) development platform, also a unicorn), and Chargebee (subscription billing software), among many others. Indian SaaS revenue was about $13 billion in 2022 and is forecasted to reach $30 billion by 2025, capturing around 8–9% of the global SaaS market. This is a remarkable share, given that a decade ago it was negligible. The SaaS boom is fueled by a few factors: cost arbitrage (Indian startups can price competitively), a global market accessible from day one, and the experience many founders gained working in or with Silicon Valley companies. It's increasingly common to hear of SaaS startups founded by alumni of IITs who have worked in big tech abroad and returned to Chennai or Bangalore to start a company targeting a niche pain point globally. The B2B focus also insulates these startups from the vagaries of the local consumer market and regulatory issues. SaaS has thus become a pillar of strength—it brings in foreign revenue, demonstrates product innovation, and creates highly skilled jobs.

India is also seeing a rise in greentech and sustainability-focused startups, aligning with global trends and the country's own environmental challenges. Entrepreneurs are tackling issues like renewable energy, electric mobility, waste management, and agri-tech with innovative approaches. For instance, Ola Electric, spun out of ride-hailing firm Ola, is now one of the leading electric scooter manufacturers, having raised huge funding rounds to build EV supply chains in India. QuantumScape, a Silicon Valley battery startup, might hog the limelight, but back home, startups are working on battery swapping, solar energy optimisation, and affordable electric tractors for farmers. The government's aggressive targets for renewable energy (450 GW by 2030) and electric vehicle adoption (aiming for 30% of vehicles by 2030) mean greentech startups have a supportive policy environment and large future markets. In agriculture, companies like DeHaat and Ninjacart are using tech to streamline farm supply chains, benefiting farmers and reducing waste. There's also a burgeoning climate-tech investment scene—with $5 billion invested in 2022 in Indian climate tech startups—reflecting that solving India's environmental problems can create hugely scalable businesses.

Another digital strength is the rise of tech-for-good and social innovation via startups. India's unique social needs (in education, healthcare, and finance) mean that startups which solve these can achieve scale and impact. Edtech, beyond BYJU'S, has seen players like Unacademy, Vedantu, and upGrad democratising learning and skill development online for millions, including in smaller towns. Health-tech startups like Practo, PharmEasy, and 1mg brought healthcare access and medicine delivery online, a trend accelerated by the pandemic. We are also seeing deep-tech research startups emerging—in areas like biotech (e.g., serum-free culture media for cell therapy by startups like Cellestial), aerospace (e.g., Bellatrix Aerospace working on electric propulsion, Pixxel launching earth observation microsatellites), and AI (with many AI startups applying machine learning to Indian language processing, or healthcare diagnostics, etc.). The government's creation of centres of excellence in AI and robotics, coupled with the large tech talent, is likely to produce some globally significant deep-tech companies from India in the coming decade.

Digitisation has also unlocked the potential of Tier II and III cities both as markets and bases of operation. With remote work becoming more accepted post-Covid, many startups are comfortable setting up teams in places like Jaipur, Coimbatore, Chandigarh, etc. This helps them tap local talent that may not want to relocate to expensive metros, and it spreads the innovation culture. The story of emerging startup hubs is real: Pune and Hyderabad have long been tech centres, but now even Kochi, Indore, Bhubaneswar, and others are making their mark, often with state-backed incubators and local angel networks. The WEF (World Economic Forum) noted that the concentration is still high in a few cities, but the gap is narrowing.

Finally, an often overlooked strength is frugal innovation—the ability of Indian startups to develop cost-effective solutions that can be scaled in other developing markets. Terms like 'Indovation' (Indian innovation) or 'Gandhian engineering' have been used to describe breakthrough products like low-cost ECG (electrocardiogram) machines, $3,000 cars (Tata Nano), or affordable point-of-care diagnostic devices. Startups are carrying that torch by creating products that serve billions affordably, which positions them well to expand to Africa, Southeast Asia, and Latin America. For example, fintech solutions for microloans or agri-market linkages in India can be exported to similar economies. This South-South opportunity is a strength that Indian startups uniquely possess—understanding and building for the next six billion people, not just the top one billion.

In sum, the digital revolution in India has given its startups an incredible launchpad: world-leading payment infrastructure, massive online consumer base, government tech stacks (like Aadhaar, UPI, DigiLocker) that are open for innovation, and a growing legion of engineers and data scientists. Fintech and SaaS are two areas where India is indisputably on the global startup map now. Greentech, ed-tech, healthtech, and deep-tech are fast catching up. This breadth of sectors doing well suggests that the ecosystem is not one-dimensional; it's diversifying and maturing. The strength here is not just in individual unicorns, but in the robust digital rails and talent that allow new startups to ride out with speed. A founder today can build a fintech app and know that even a kirana shop owner can pay or be paid digitally—that ubiquity is a huge strength. It is telling that other countries are studying India's digital public goods (like UPI, Aadhaar) to replicate them—a reverse of the copycat trend. The narrative is slowly shifting to India exporting innovation models. All these augur well for Indian startups as they script the next chapters of growth.

Funding and Global Investor Confidence

Another pillar of India's startup strength has become the robust funding environment and global investor confidence that has developed, especially in the latter half of the 2010s and early 2020s. There was a time when Indian startups struggled to raise seed capital, and venture capital was dominated by a handful of domestic players. But today, India is one of the hottest destinations for venture capital, second only to perhaps the US and China. This inflow of capital is both a result of demonstrated successes and a cause for future successes, creating a self-reinforcing cycle.

Consider the funding boom of 2021: Indian startups raised an estimated $35–38 billion in venture funding in that single year—more than the cumulative amount of some previous five-year periods. This boom resulted in the birth of over 40 new unicorns in 2021 alone. While funding can ebb and flow (2022–2023 saw a correction, or 'funding winter', globally, which also affected India with a ~24% drop in H1 2024 vs H1 2023 in PE/VC investments), the overall trajectory remains upward. Global funds—from SoftBank to Sequoia, Tiger Global, Accel, and more—have entrenched operations in India, scouting for deals. Newer entrants like Falcon Edge (now rebranded as Chimera), DST Global, and even sovereign funds like Qatar Investment Authority or Canada's CDPQ, have written big checks to Indian startups. When an ecosystem draws capital from such diverse, deep-pocketed sources, it's a sign of trust in the long-term potential.

One of the key factors driving this confidence is the realisation that India's large market can produce outsized returns if tapped well. With hundreds of millions of young consumers and enterprises modernising, a startup that cracks the code can scale revenue dramatically. Investors saw that with Flipkart's exit, with Paytm's user growth, and with the rapid revenue climb of companies like Swiggy or BYJU'S. So the earlier scepticism ('Will Indians pay for online services?') has been replaced with FOMO (fear of missing out) ('We need to get in on the India growth story'). There was a period around 2015–16 when comparisons were drawn that India was 'where China was ten years ago' in terms of Internet and GDP per capita, suggesting a similar boom could happen. That narrative attracted many global investors who had missed out on China's tech boom.

Another positive shift is the evolution of India's investor ecosystem itself. A decade ago, a startup's funding options were limited: a few angel networks, maybe Series A from Indian arms of VC firms if you're lucky, and beyond that, not much domestic growth capital (hence many companies would flip to US incorporation). Now, there's a full stack: incubators and accelerators seeding ideas (Y Combinator has taken dozens of Indian startups, and we have local ones like CIIE (Centre for Innovation, Incubation, and Entrepreneurship) at IIM-A (IIM Ahmedabad), Axilor, etc.), a thriving angel investor community (fuelled by successful founders and high-net-worth individuals who see startups as an asset class), dedicated seed funds and micro-VCs, and large India-focused VC funds that raise billions from LPs (Limited Partners) abroad to deploy in India. Even for later stages, the advent of growth equity and private equity in tech (like Prosus, TPG (Textile Paper Green), Temasek, etc.) means companies can raise $100 million+ rounds in India without going public prematurely. All these create a runway where a company can be nurtured from idea to IPO within India's funding environment.

Speaking of IPOs, the exit landscape has improved, further boosting confidence. For years, the lack of IPOs or big acquisitions in India was a sore point (investors worried about how they'd exit their investments). That changed when the likes of Zomato, Paytm, Nykaa, Delhivery, and PolicyBazaar went public in 2021–22, raising billions and debuting at strong valuations. Nykaa, notably, was profitable and showed that public markets would reward well-run tech businesses. These IPOs have created liquidity for investors and employees, proving that Indian public markets are receptive to tech startups (with some caveats, as volatility followed, but the doors are open now). Additionally, big-ticket acquisitions like Walmart-Flipkart (2018), Reliance's spree of acquiring startups in 2019–20, and strategic plays like BYJU'S acquiring Aakash (a traditional tutoring giant) for nearly $1 billion, have provided alternate exit routes. In 2023, the report shows that India had the second-largest number of unicorns and tech IPOs in the world, underscoring that exits are happening. This exit momentum gives global investors the assurance that investing in India is not a one-way street; there is yield at the end of the tunnel.

Another strength now is the increasing interest of non-traditional and strategic investors. For example, Google launched a $10 billion India digitisation fund; Facebook (Meta) and Google both invested in Jio Platforms (Reliance's digital arm) in 2020, which indirectly boosts the startup ecosystem as Jio works with many startups. Large hedge funds and crossover funds, like Tiger and Coatue, have included Indian startups in their global portfolio. Furthermore, Indian startups are now expanding abroad (Oyo to Southeast Asia, Zomato to the Middle East, Freshworks globally, etc.), catching the eye of international investors who see them as regional champions, not just local players.

It's also noteworthy that domestic institutional capital is slowly coming. Indian banks, insurance companies, and mutual funds have traditionally stayed away from startup equity; however, initiatives are underway to channel some of the large domestic savings into venture (for instance, SIDBI's funds, NITI Aayog pushing for insurance companies to invest in AIFs, etc.). While still small, as Indian capital markets deepen, local institutional money could become a big pillar for startups, making the ecosystem less reliant on foreign capital over the very long term. Meanwhile, family offices of industrialists (Ambani, Premji, Tata Trusts, etc.) have started actively investing in tech startups as well, adding to the capital pool.

Global investor confidence also stems from macro considerations. India's economy is now the fifth-largest in the world and is expected to be the third-largest in the next decade. Stable GDP growth and a large demographic dividend make it one of the few big growth stories at a time when China's allure has tempered due to regulatory crackdowns and other geopolitical issues. This has led many to call India the 'last big open frontier' for consumer Internet growth. In essence, some global capital is reallocating from China to India for diversification and opportunity, which is a strategic tailwind for Indian startups.

All this funding influx and confidence doesn't just sit in bank accounts; it translates to ground capabilities—startups can hire better talent, expand to new markets, invest in R&D, and acquire smaller companies using this capital. It's a strength that greases the wheels of the whole ecosystem.

However, it's worth adding a nuance: responsible use of this capital is crucial. 2021's exuberance led to some overvaluation and perhaps reckless spending (as seen in the corrections and layoffs of 2022–23). The maturing ecosystem is learning to calibrate growth with sustainable unit economics—and the fact that investors are now nudging companies towards profitability (Zomato, for example, got much investor pressure to cut losses) is a healthy sign. It indicates a maturation where capital will still flow, but with discipline, which ultimately makes the ecosystem stronger.

In summary, the capital and investor landscape for Indian startups is robust and largely optimistic. The country has firmly shed the image of 'high-risk, low-return'; it's now often viewed as 'high-growth, potentially high-return' with manageable risk due to structural reforms. With over $100 billion poured into Indian startups in the last few years and more dry powder waiting, funding is no longer the constraining factor it once was. This abundance of capital, combined with improved exits and global interest, forms a backbone of strength that supports startups as they tackle ambitious goals.

Emerging Startup Hubs: Beyond the Metros

For long, India's startup action was concentrated in a few metropolitan clusters—the triad of Bangalore, Delhi NCR,[26]

26. NCR stands for National Capital Region, which is a coordinated planning region centred around Delhi, encompassing nearby districts from Haryana, Uttar

and Mumbai accounted for the lion's share of startups and funding. While these cities remain dominant, a heartening strength of the ecosystem now is the rise of emerging startup hubs beyond the usual suspects. The democratisation of entrepreneurship across different regions and cities in India means more talent is being tapped and more localised problems are being solved. This not only expands the pipeline of startups but also helps reduce brain drain from small cities to big cities (since people can build or join startups closer to home) and spreads economic growth.

Consider Hyderabad and Chennai—often counted just after the top three. Hyderabad has fostered a robust startup culture with strong government backing (the state of Telangana's T-Hub incubator is a marquee initiative) and a legacy of IT services, providing a skilled workforce. It's home to unicorns like Zenoti (salon software) and has strengths in areas like blockchain (thanks to proactive policies). Chennai, with its deep engineering talent pool, has become an SaaS hotbed (Freshworks, Zoho, Chargebee, and many more are Chennai-based or have roots there). Both cities also offer slightly lower costs of living and doing business, which startups appreciate.

Beyond these, Pune has emerged as a notable hub, especially in enterprise tech, automotive tech (given the auto manufacturing around it), and education-tech (Pune has a massive student population). Pune startups, like FirstCry (now a unicorn in baby products e-commerce) and Druva (cloud data protection, another unicorn), show the city's mettle. Ahmedabad and the broader state of Gujarat are seeing a startup push, aligning with the state's trading and business-oriented culture. Gujarat has had success in fintech (e.g.,

---

Pradesh, and Rajasthan to manage urban expansion and infrastructure development collectively. It was established under the National Capital Region Planning Board Act, 1985, to promote balanced regional development and reduce pressure on Delhi's core.

Lendingkart) and is encouraging agri-tech and manufacturing startups with policy support.

Kolkata and the Eastern region had lagged, but even there, green shoots are visible—with startups focusing on industries like tea, jute, or logistics, which resonate with the region's strengths, and accelerators like NASSCOM (National Association of Software and Service Companies) 10k starting programmes. Northeast India, often off the main economic map, is getting attention too via dedicated incubators and events to integrate its talented youth (especially in IT and design) into the startup mainstream.

One of the biggest stories is the rise of Tier II city hubs: Jaipur, Indore, Kochi, Coimbatore, Bhubaneswar, Chandigarh, Lucknow—to name a few. Jaipur, for example, has produced CarDekho (a major auto portal turned unicorn) and has a growing ecosystem, thanks to some entrepreneurs choosing to base there. Indore boasted India's cleanest city tag and is developing an IT and startup scene (the success of automation startup Impetus, and food delivery startup Box8, which started in Indore, are cases in point). Kochi in Kerala has leveraged high literacy and the Kerala Startup Mission's support to host ventures in sectors like marine tech and biotech (Kerala even saw a startup, Genrobotics, which built sewer-cleaning robots to eliminate manual scavenging—a very local problem with a tech solution that could scale globally).

Government data indeed shows that nearly 45% of DPIIT-recognised startups are now coming from beyond the top metro cities. That means the concentration, while present, is easing. This diversification is a strength because it signals that the ecosystem is not limited to a few privileged urban pockets; it is tapping into the vast reservoir of talent and ideas across the nation. Local problems get local innovators—e.g., a farmer's son in a village starting an agri-tech platform for nearby farms, or a doctor in a small town creating a telemedicine solution for rural patients. These are innovations that a Bengaluru coder might not conceive of, but someone on the ground in those regions would. Thus, entrepreneurship is addressing a wider array of issues, making the overall startup output more relevant to India's needs.

The creation of state-run incubators and funds has been instrumental here. Practically every state now has incubators, often linked with engineering colleges or state industries departments, which provide seed funding, mentorship, and sometimes government as the first customer (UP's Startup Policy, Rajasthan's iStart programme, etc., are examples). NITI Aayog's India Innovation Index even ranks states on their startup ecosystem and innovation capabilities, spurring a healthy competitive spirit among states to improve their standings. Karnataka and Maharashtra might lead, but states like Kerala and Telangana rank high, given their proactive measures. Even smaller states like Himachal or Goa are trying niche approaches (tourism-tech in Goa, for instance).

Apart from geography, we also see hubs of specialised innovation—like a 'Drone Valley' emerging in Haryana after the government chose sites there for drone testing and manufacturing, or biotech clusters in Bangalore and Hyderabad due to the presence of research institutes. Such clustering helps create centres of excellence and networks of specialised talent, which is another layer of strength.

This spread of startup activity also means that the benefits of the startup boom (jobs, wealth creation, solutions) are reaching more Indians. It can mitigate the regional inequality by fostering new industries in places that need them. For example, a startup in a Tier II city can significantly boost the local economy and inspire more entrepreneurship around. Success stories from smaller cities are particularly powerful in changing mindsets. When a CarDekho or FirstCry makes it big out of Jaipur or Pune, suddenly students and professionals there realise that they don't have to move to Bangalore to succeed—they can do it right at home.

Internationally, this broad base might remind observers of how tech ecosystems in large countries mature: the US eventually developed hubs in Seattle, Austin, Boston, etc., beyond Silicon Valley; China saw activity beyond Beijing/Shanghai to Shenzhen, Hangzhou, etc. India seems to be following that path, which indicates maturity.

That said, the top cities still attract the bulk of venture capital—infrastructure, mentor network, and investor presence are still tilted. But that's slowly changing too; many VCs do nationwide scouting tours now, and some are setting up offices in second cities or at least establishing 'mentor networks'. The pandemic's normalisation of remote pitching means a founder in Kochi can Zoom with a Mumbai investor without stigma. It's levelling the field gradually.

In summary, the Indian startup ecosystem's strength today lies in its distributed nature. Entrepreneurship is no longer an exclusive metropolitan phenomenon; it has become a national movement. Emerging hubs bring their own flavour and specialisation, enriching the tapestry of Indian startups. This ensures that the next billion-dollar company might very well come from a city like Coimbatore or Nagpur, and it means that the ecosystem is tapping into the full range of India's human capital.

Conclusion

The story of India's startup ecosystem is one of dramatic dualities—a tale where daunting challenges meet burgeoning strengths, where setbacks are as prominent as successes. In this chapter, we journeyed through that story, peeling back the layers of what ails the startup ecosystem in India even as we celebrated what energises it. On one side of the ledger, we saw the tragedies and trials: sky-high failure rates that remind us how many dreams don't make it, a quagmire of bureaucracy and red tape that can snare even the nimblest innovators, infrastructural inadequacies that turn everyday operations into stress tests, and talent and innovation gaps that have at times slowed India's sprint towards the forefront of technology. These systemic challenges—the 'ailments' in our narrative—are very real. They manifest in the cautionary tales of Dazo or TinyOwl shutting down overnight, in the exasperation of founders dealing with tax inspectors or power outages, in the frustration of seeing a brilliant idea copied thrice over in the market, and in the exodus of a bright engineer to foreign shores for a lack of local opportunities. Each challenge is a call to action for policymakers, educators, and industry leaders to continue the work of reform and support. The chapter made it evident that for every inspiring unicorn, there are countless unfunded or unrealised ventures that need an ecosystem's empathy and support to flourish.

Yet, on the other side, we encountered the triumphs and turnarounds that give India's startup saga its racy optimism. The Indian startup ecosystem today stands far stronger, more mature, and more inclusive than it was a decade ago. Government interventions have moved the needle—from eliminating pernicious hurdles like the angel tax to fostering a culture of innovation via Startup India and state missions. Successful startups have shattered glass ceilings, proving that Indian companies can innovate, scale, and create immense value both at home and globally. We discussed how fintech innovations, like UPI, are making India a case study for the world, how the country's unicorn count (now in the triple digits) is cementing its place as a top-three startup hub globally, and how even the GII now acknowledges India's leap forward. Perhaps most heartening is the socio-cultural shift: entrepreneurship is no longer a fringe pursuit but a mainstream aspiration. The proverbial Indian middle-class parent is now as proud of a startup-founder child as of a doctor or civil servant. That's a sea change—an indicator that the risk-taking, the acceptance of failure, and the celebration of creativity are entering the Indian ethos.

For a globally aware readership, the Indian startup ecosystem presents a study in contrasts but also a blueprint of emerging market innovation. It teaches that context is king: one cannot transplant Silicon Valley models wholesale without adapting to local realities (be it through cash-on-delivery or frugal engineering). It also illustrates a kind of resilience—Indian startups have thrived in conditions that are arguably more challenging than those faced by peers in many other countries. This resilience, born of necessity, could well be India's competitive advantage in the long run. Founders who cut their teeth navigating India's complexities might be especially adept at expanding to other developing markets, bringing solutions to the next billion users elsewhere.

As we conclude, it's clear that the narrative of Indian startups is still being written, with new chapters unfolding every day. On the policy front, continued reforms in taxation, improvements in contract enforcement, investments in infrastructure, and an education overhaul for skill development are key to healing the remaining 'ailments'. On the industry front, the push towards original innovation (in AI, deep-tech, and beyond) will determine if India can transition from being a great executor to a great inventor on the world stage. There are encouraging signs: increased R&D spending by private players, more patents filed, and even sectors like defence and space being opened for startup innovation.

In the grand arc of history, one could say India's startup ecosystem is in its adolescence—past the childhood where it needed constant care, but still a little awkward and rough-edged as it matures. Adolescence comes with growing pains (the failures, the bubbles, the regulatory snafus), yet it's also the phase of rapid learning and growth spurts. The next decade will likely see India iron out many of the issues that currently ail it. The bureaucracy will hopefully continue to thin out and become more entrepreneur-friendly, digital infrastructure will reach every corner, and talent will be more future-ready, given the interventions now in play. If the 2010s were about establishing the startup movement in India, the 2020s might well be about globalising it and coming into full bloom.

The Indian startup ecosystem can be likened to a Bollywood drama—replete with unexpected twists, larger-than-life ambitions, formidable villains (of the systemic kind), comic relief (some jugaad innovations bring a smile), and ultimately a narrative arc bending towards hope and success. From the tragedies of premature shutdowns to the comedies of bureaucratic absurdities, and finally to the triumphs of world-beating innovations, India's startup story is as racy and riveting as they come. And like any good story, it leaves us with a resonant lesson: that adversity and advantage often go hand in hand. It's this dialectic—of challenge and strength—that makes India one of the most exciting startup ecosystems on the planet. The stage is set for even bigger things, and the world is watching closely as India transforms its ailments into achievements, one startup at a time.

References:

1. Moneycontrol News. (9 July 2018). 90% Indian startups fail within 5 years of inception: Study. Moneycontrol.

2. David, S. (17 December 2016). 10 startups that shut down in 2016. The Economic Times.

3. IBM Institute for Business Value & Oxford Economics. (2017). Entrepreneurial India (as reported in Moneycontrol and News18).

4. Reuters. (23 July 2024). India scraps 'angel tax'; startup investors rejoice. Reuters News.

5. Anand, JC. (21 July 2022). India's R&D spends amongst the lowest in the world: NITI Aayog study. The Economic Times.

6. Muneer, M. (28 February 2025). India's skill gap crisis: Plenty of

graduates, not enough leaders for emerging tech. The Economic Times (Opinion).

7. Business Today. (8 April 2025). 'Corrupt IAS are in the way': Indian-American founder rips into bureaucracy in letter to Piyush Goyal. BusinessToday India.

8. Khalid, J. (2024, 13 September 2024). India's Internet blackouts have big consequences for its economy. Fast Company.

9. Trading Economics/World Bank. (2019). Time required to enforce a contract – India (1445 days). (Original data from World Bank Doing Business Report).

10. GS SCORE. (2021). Contract Enforcement in India. (Ease of Doing Business 2017 data cited).

11. BarelyOpinionated.com. (2023). Indian talents in the US: the brain drain dilemma. (Statistics on Indian-born CEOs and engineers).

12. Press Information Bureau (PIB), Government of India. (2024). Over 1.40 lakh recognized Startups in the country as on June 30, 2024. (Minister's reply in Rajya Sabha).

13. ETCFO Desk/PTI. (27 July 2024). DPIIT recognises 1.40 lakh entities as startups as on June 30. The Economic Times – CFO.

14. Reuters. (22 September 2021). Salesforce rival Freshworks raises $1.03 bln in US IPO, valued at $10.13 bln. Reuters News.

15. The Times of India. (16 January 2024). National Startup Day 2025: Mapping India's unicorn journey over the past two decades. The Economic Times/Times Internet.

16. World Economic Forum (Sahasranamam, S. and Kuppusamy, A.). (5 December 2024). 4 emerging trends from India's booming entrepreneur ecosystem. WEF Agenda.

17. ACI Worldwide and Prime Minister's Office (India). (2024). India tops the world in digital payments with 48% global share. (As referenced in the PIB release and the RBI report)

18. Bain & Company. (2022). India SaaS Report 2022: Indian SaaS to reach $30 billion revenue by 2025. (Key findings referenced)

19. Inc42 Media. (2024). Unicorn Club Of 2024: 6 Startups Crossed $1 Bn Valuation Mark; India at 118 Unicorns. Inc42 (Startup news site).

20. NASSCOM and Zinnov. (2021). Indian Tech Start-up Ecosystem Report. (Statistics on funding and unicorn additions in 2021). [Data cited generally in text, no direct quote].

21. Press Information Bureau (PIB), Government of India. (2023). UPI: Revolutionising Digital Payments in India. (UPI usage statistics)

22. Bloomberg/Fortune India. (28 August 2023). Zerodha's FY24 profit zooms 62% to ₹4,700 cr; revenue up 21%. Fortune India.

23. Global Innovation Index (WIPO). (2024). Global Innovation Index 2024: India's ranking. World Intellectual Property Organization.

24. PwC India. (2023). Winning Today's Race While Running Tomorrow's – 26th CEO Survey: India Insights. (Skills shortage data)

25. Startup India, DPIIT. (2023). Startup India Prarambh & State Startup Rankings 2022. (Data on Tier II/III startup share and jobs created)

CHAPTER 6

◆◆◆

Reverse Flipping – Why Startups Abroad Are Returning to India

Abstract:

As India's capital markets soar and the startup ecosystem matures, a growing number of Indian-origin tech startups originally domiciled in Delaware or Singapore are seeking to return to Indian soil. This phenomenon, known as the 'reverse flip', has accelerated with increasing investor confidence and favourable IPO conditions in India. Yet, the path home is not without hurdles. From regulatory bottlenecks and FDI (Foreign Direct Investment) barriers to complex taxation on share swaps and limited eligibility for fast-track mergers, startups encounter a labyrinth of compliance and legal issues. This comprehensive chapter critically examines each challenge flagged by the Startup Policy Forum (SPF) and evaluates the government's partial reforms, offering suggestions for a more seamless and growth-oriented redomiciliation policy.

The New Gold Rush: Coming Home to India

Over the past decade, India-born startups eagerly set up shop in Delaware, Singapore, and the Cayman Islands, lured by relaxed regulations, investor familiarity, and dollar-denominated capital pools. But the tide is turning. With India's stock exchanges gaining depth, retail and institutional participation exploding, and tech IPOs like Zomato and Nykaa commanding sky-high valuations, founders now see value—not vanity—in making India their legal and operational home.

The SPF, representing over 50 Indian-origin technology firms, has struck the right chord by demanding the creation of a dedicated 'Ease of Reverse Flip Taskforce' to smoothen the redomiciliation process. While about 80% of the regulatory snarls have reportedly been untangled by the government, the remaining 20% contain the hardest knots. Let us dissect them.

Fast-Track Mergers: A Half-Open Door

One of the most visible pain points is the limited scope of fast-track mergers under Indian company law. This mechanism—intended to expedite corporate restructuring—only applies when a wholly owned Indian subsidiary is merging with its foreign parent. Most startups, however, are structured with angel investors, VCs, ESOP pools, and employee trusts, all of which invalidate the 'wholly owned' prerequisite.

This results in a forced detour through the National Company Law Tribunal (NCLT)[27], where the queue is long, hearings uncertain, and timelines unpredictable. A typical NCLT-driven merger or reverse flip can take over a year and includes public stakeholder notices, regulatory nods, and judicial vetting. For startups planning time-sensitive IPOs, such delays can be fatal.

---

27. The NCLT is a quasi-judicial authority in India that adjudicates matters related to company law, including insolvency proceedings under the Insolvency and Bankruptcy Code (IBC), mergers, demergers, and oppression or mismanagement of companies. For MSMEs and other businesses, NCLT plays a crucial role in enabling time-bound debt resolution and corporate restructuring, offering a legal pathway for revival or orderly exit in case of financial distress.

Recommendation: Amend the fast-track merger eligibility criteria to include startups with minority or institutional shareholders—subject to simplified safeguards—to enable wider access to expedited approvals.

NCLT: The Procedural Bermuda Triangle

While the government amended the Companies Rules in 2024 to exempt mergers between a foreign parent and its wholly owned Indian subsidiary from NCLT scrutiny, the benefit is limited. Startups with layered structures, convertible instruments, or existing non-controlling foreign investors continue to fall through the cracks. Once again, complex compliance, prolonged timelines, and opaque processes dominate.

Moreover, the NCLT lacks sector-specific expertise and follows general corporate law processes. Its one-size-fits-all approach makes it ill-suited for nuanced, tech-driven startups that operate under dynamic funding models. The result? Young founders, many under 35, are forced to engage expensive legal counsel and wait in procedural limbo.

Recommendation: Establish a special bench or fast-track mechanism within the NCLT to deal with startup redomiciliation cases, staffed by members with startup and capital market expertise.

FDI[28] Restrictions: Security vs Scalability

Since April 2020, any direct or indirect FDI from countries sharing a land border with India—including China—requires

---

28. FDI refers to investment by a foreign entity—individual, company, or government—directly into the equity or operations of an Indian business, including MSMEs, with the intent of establishing lasting interest and control. In the context of MSMEs, FDI can bring in much-needed capital, technology, and global market access, especially in sectors like manufacturing, textiles, and food processing, subject to sectoral caps and regulatory approvals.

prior government approval. While aimed at shielding strategic sectors, this policy has led to a deadlock for startups that earlier raised funds from Chinese VCs or Southeast Asian funds with indirect Chinese exposure.

The problem magnifies during reverse flips, where startups may need to issue new shares or restructure cap tables. These otherwise routine steps now fall under the FDI approval radar, often taking months to clear—if at all. The resulting uncertainty dissuades founders from pursuing redomiciliation despite strategic interest.

Recommendation: Create a whitelist for FDI approvals in cases of reverse flips involving non-strategic sectors, like e-commerce, fintech, or ed-tech, where the originating investments were made pre-2020 and have no control rights.

Taxation Tangles: The Capital Gains Trap

India's tax laws treat share swaps during a reverse flip as capital asset transfers, triggering capital gains tax. This is in sharp contrast to jurisdictions like Singapore and the US, where restructuring within group entities can often be tax-neutral. Even when Indian tax law permits tax-neutral inbound mergers, the conditions are stringent and subject to regulatory interpretation.

The capital gains treatment disincentivises reverse flips. In some cases, founders and early investors have to absorb significant tax liabilities just to comply with a structural reorganisation—hardly a welcome home gesture.

Recommendation: Issue a CBDT[29] circular exempting qualifying share swaps involved in reverse flips from capital

---

29. The Central Board of Direct Taxes (CBDT) is the apex policy-making body under the Department of Revenue, Ministry of Finance, responsible for administering direct tax laws in India, including income tax and corporate tax. It formulates tax policies, oversees enforcement through the Income Tax Department, and plays a key role in curbing tax evasion, resolving disputes, and ensuring tax compliance across individuals and businesses.

gains tax, provided the startups meet specified IPO-linked compliance benchmarks.

The Playbook and the Path Ahead

Recognising the complexity, the SPF is working with legal and tax advisors to publish a Reverse Flip Playbook. This initiative should be welcomed as a move toward self-regulation and market maturity. But a playbook is no substitute for policy reform.

India's startup ecosystem is at an inflexion point. The return of high-growth, billion-dollar startups could catalyse domestic employment, increase tax collections, and deepen capital markets. But unless the redomiciliation runway is cleared of regulatory potholes, many founders will continue to operate Indian businesses from foreign addresses, raising capital abroad and creating wealth offshore.

Conclusion: Bridging the Last Mile with Policy Courage

India has made significant progress in easing the reverse flip journey, but it remains a work in progress. Regulatory willpower, backed by startup-friendly tax and FDI reform, can make India not only the world's largest startup base but also its most founder-friendly jurisdiction. The 'Ease of Doing Business' slogan must now evolve into the 'Ease of Coming Home' mission.

References:

1. YourStory, 'SPF proposes taskforce to streamline reverse flips', 21 April 2025. https://yourstory.com/2025/04/spf-proposes-taskforce-streamline-reverse-flips-startups-seeking-faster-route-home

2. Companies (Compromises, Arrangements and Amalgamations) Rules, 2016; amended 2024

3. FDI Policy, Department for Promotion of Industry and Internal Trade (DPIIT), April 2020 update.

4. Income Tax Act, 1961: Sections 47, 49, and Rule 15C on tax-neutral mergers.

CHAPTER 7

◆◆◆

The Unicorn Mirage – Bursting the Valuation Bubble Through the BYJU'S Story

India's startup ecosystem has long been projected as a dazzling symbol of innovation-led growth. From NITI[30] Aayog to state governments, and from Davos panels to budget speeches, there has been no dearth of official celebration of India's rise as the third-largest startup ecosystem in the world. Amitabh Kant's[31] op-ed in The Indian Express continues this optimistic tone, mapping out India's transformation from a fledgling startup hub in 2014 to a unicorn-producing machine in just

---

30. NITI Aayog is the premier policy think tank of the Government of India, established in 2015 to replace the Planning Commission, with a mandate to drive sustainable development through cooperative federalism and evidence-based policymaking. It acts as a catalyst for economic reforms by providing strategic inputs, fostering innovation, and coordinating with states on national development priorities, including initiatives for MSMEs, health, education, and digital infrastructure.

31. Amitabh Kant is an Indian bureaucrat and member of the 1980-batch Indian Administrative Service (IAS), who served as the Chief Executive Officer of NITI Aayog from February 2016 until June 2022 and later as India's Sherpa to the G20 from July 2022 to June 2025. He is widely recognised for spearheading major national initiatives such as Make in India, Startup India, and the Incredible India campaign, along with championing reforms aimed at improving ease of doing business and accelerating India's socio-economic transformation.

under a decade. Yet, beneath the surface of impressive statistics and institutional cheerleading lies a more sobering reality—a reality that demands deeper interrogation, one that has often been glossed over in official narratives.

> Imagine you buy a house just because it looks beautiful from outside. Everyone says it's worth crores. But once you move in, you realise that the plumbing leaks, the wiring is faulty, and the foundation is weak.
>
> That's what happened with BYJU'S. Investors rushed in based on flashy valuations, but ignored governance failures. When the cracks surfaced—misreporting, lawsuits, poor management—the house collapsed.

The piece rightly acknowledges India's meteoric expansion in terms of recognised startups—over 1,30,000 as of 2024, a staggering rise from around 4,500 in 2015. Funding volumes, too, have grown 15-fold during this period. Yet, it is precisely this explosive growth that has triggered systemic issues in quality, sustainability, and accountability—issues that rarely find space in celebratory op-eds. For instance, Kant speaks of $12 billion invested in Indian startups in 2023 alone, with 75% of this capital coming from international sources. But what he doesn't tell us is that many of these capital inflows

> Say you start a café just because your cousin's café in Mumbai became a hit. You copy his model exactly—same menu, same décor—but forget that your town doesn't have the same customers or coffee culture.
>
> That's how 'me-too' startups grow. Many Indian startups replicate Western ideas (ride-sharing, grocery apps, ed-tech) without adapting to Indian realities. Without genuine innovation, most fail to scale.

are speculative in nature, seeking short-term valuation bumps rather than long-term business viability. India's dependence on foreign venture capital—without commensurate domestic risk capital—exposes the sector to volatile global interest rate cycles, as seen in the funding winter post-2022.

Let's talk about BYJU'S—the elephant in the startup room that finds a fleeting mention in the article. Once hailed as the poster boy of India's ed-tech boom and valued at over $22 billion at its peak, BYJU'S collapse was neither sudden nor unforeseeable. Its fall was the outcome of systemic rot that plagues many unicorns—growth without governance, expansion without ethics, and valuation without value creation. BYJU'S reportedly delayed financial disclosures, faced allegations of mis-selling, massive layoffs, lawsuits from investors and creditors, and the final insult: regulatory scrutiny for corporate mismanagement. Yet, there has been no independent performance audit of what led to such a rapid descent. Nor has there been a structured policy introspection into the perverse incentives created by valuation-chasing VCs, or the lack of institutional mechanisms to hold startups accountable once they scale.

> Your school says its cricket team is world-class because it has 11 players, new jerseys, and sponsors. But no one checks how many matches it has won.
>
> That's how India's startup data is presented. We count how many startups exist—but rarely ask how many survived, created jobs, or solved real problems. Glitzy stats hide a hollow scorecard.

Kant praises the role of PE (Private Equity) and VC in India's innovation ecosystem, but glosses over the fact that many of these funds are now tightening their purse strings or demanding board control due to repeated instances of founder-led mismanagement and opaque finances. The failed IPOs, shrinking cash reserves, and the pivot-to-profit narrative that now dominates boardrooms are a stark departure from the 'growth-at-all-costs' playbook that helped create these unicorns in the first place.

The op-ed also highlights the government's interventions—ranging from Startup India to the Semiconductor Mission—but fails to offer any independent third-party evaluation of these schemes. There is no mention of audit reports, outcome assessments, or performance metrics verified by institutions like the CAG, NITI Aayog's DMEO (Development Monitoring and Evaluation Office), or reputed think tanks. In fact, several Parliamentary Standing Committee reports and Lok Sabha questions have flagged that data on employment creation by startups is either not maintained or is based on self-declared metrics. The Centre for Monitoring Indian Economy (CMIE) has, on multiple occasions, pointed out that the employment elasticity of the startup sector remains negligible, especially outside a few metros.

Contrary to the optimistic assertion that the startup boom is spreading to Tier II and III cities, hard data tells another story. As per DPIIT data and analysis by the India Development Foundation, over 80% of startup funding and formal registrations are still concentrated in six cities: Bengaluru, Mumbai, Delhi-NCR, Hyderabad, Pune, and Chennai. The so-called rise of Jaipur, Indore, or Visakhapatnam in the startup ecosystem is often anecdotal or based on local incubators whose success rates remain poorly measured. Even schemes like the AIM or the FFS have failed to create a lasting impact beyond metro enclaves due to infrastructural deficits, the absence of angel networks, and the lack of early-stage mentoring in non-metro areas.

Perhaps most troubling is the absence of any discussion in the op-ed about the grim survival rate of startups in India. A study by IBM and Oxford Economics had earlier revealed that 90% of Indian startups fail within the first five years, primarily due to a lack of innovation, poor business models, and funding gaps at the scale-up stage. The problem is not that India lacks ideas—it is that it lacks institutional depth and regulatory foresight to nurture ideas into enterprises of enduring value. There is also a growing mismatch between the skillsets of the Indian workforce and the employment needs of these tech startups, many of which remain capital-intensive but low on job creation.

The op-ed calls for a 'pro-innovation policy regime' and greater investment in IP and R&D. But India's R&D spending remains stagnant at around 0.7% of GDP—a figure unchanged for over a decade and far below China (2.4%) or the US (3.5%). Private sector participation in R&D is equally dismal, and startups, barring a few exceptions in pharma or deep-tech, spend minuscule amounts on true innovation. The 'me-too' replication of Western business models—ride-hailing, grocery delivery, ed-tech, or BNPL (Buy Now Pay Later)—has dominated India's unicorn story far more than original problem-solving rooted in Indian realities.

Finally, the op-ed romanticises the idea that India is well-positioned to become the global hub for innovation by 2047. But that vision will remain a mirage unless we reorient our startup policy architecture towards grounded, measurable outcomes. We need an independent Startup Accountability Commission, regularised audit and disclosure norms, and outcome-based evaluation of schemes like FFS, Stand-Up India, and Startup India. We also need to break the myth that more startups automatically mean more innovation. It is time to ask the uncomfortable but necessary question: are our startups building lasting value, or just flipping ventures for the next valuation bump?

India's startup story has undoubtedly captured global attention, but it risks becoming a hollow narrative unless backed by rigorous third-party evaluations, structural reforms in governance, and a wider base of geographically and demographically inclusive entrepreneurship. BYJU'S is not an exception—it is a symptom. And unless the ecosystem corrects its course, many more such symptoms will continue to disfigure the dream.

References:

1. Department for Promotion of Industry and Internal Trade (DPIIT), Government of India, Startup India Progress Reports (2023–24).

2. Bain & Company, India Venture Capital Report 2024.

3. Tracxn Technologies, 'India Startup Funding Trends', Q4 2023.

4. Bloomberg, 'Byju's Valuation Peaks at $22 Billion', July 2021.

5. Reuters, 'Byju's Faces Legal and Financial Storm as Valuation Plunges', February 2024; Ministry of Corporate Affairs Compliance Tracker.

6. Economic Times, 'VCs Recalibrate India Strategy Amid Governance Woes', November 2023.

7. Lok Sabha Unstarred Question No. 1406, Answered on 5 February 2024; Parliamentary Standing Committee on Industry (2023), Report on Startup India.

8. Centre for Monitoring Indian Economy (CMIE), Employment and Unemployment Survey Reports, 2022–24.

9. India Development Foundation and DPIIT, 'Geographic Spread of Indian Startups: Myth vs Reality', Policy Brief, August 2023.

10. NITI Aayog DMEO Evaluation Report, 'Startup India and FFS Performance Review', 2022.

11. IBM Institute for Business Value and Oxford Economics, 'Entrepreneurial India', 2016.

12. Azim Premji University, 'State of Working India Report', 2023.

13. UNESCO Institute for Statistics, Global R&D Database, 2022; India's Economic Survey 2023–24, Ministry of Finance.

14. https://indianexpress.com/article/opinion/columns/how-india-can-become-the-worlds-leading-startup-ecosystem-9781088/

SECTION III

◆◆◆

BUDGETS, CRISES, AND POLICY PROMISES

From demonetisation to COVID, from Budget speeches to dashboard schemes, this section traces how shocks and slogans have shaped—and scarred—India's small enterprises. It finds that India's defence MSME saga is a paradox of bold reforms and broken execution. Despite DAP 2020, Make-I/II, iDEX and SRIJAN, bureaucratic inertia, delays, and PSU gatekeeping persist. It discusses why 'Make in India' risks becoming 'Missed in India', urging CAG-style audits, faster procurement, and true MSME empowerment.

CHAPTER 8

◆◆◆

Budget 2025–26: Lip Service or Lifeline?

Abstract:

The Union Budget 2025–26 introduced a suite of measures aimed at revitalising India's MSME sector. These interventions focus on enhancing credit access, supporting first-time entrepreneurs, and promoting labour-intensive industries. While the initiatives signal a strong commitment to bolstering the MSME landscape, a critical examination of the underlying data on employment, production, and exports reveals areas that necessitate further scrutiny to ensure objectivity and accuracy.

The MSME sector, understood to be with 5.93 crore registered enterprises employing over 25 crore individuals, stands as a pivotal component of India's industrial framework. In 2023–24, MSME-related products accounted for 45.73% of India's total exports, underscoring their significant role in the nation's economic fabric.

The Budget 2025–26 proposed several key interventions:

i. **Revised Classification Criteria:** Investment and turnover limits for MSME classification have been increased by 2.5 times and 2 times, respectively, facilitating greater scalability and resource access.

Definition of MSMEs Before and After Budget 2025–26

Before Budget 2025–26:

Prior to the 2025–26 Union Budget, the classification of MSMEs in India was based on investment in plant and machinery or equipment, and annual turnover, as per the MSME Development Act, 2006. The criteria were:

- Micro Enterprises: Investment up to ₹1 crore and turnover up to ₹5 crore.
- Small Enterprises: Investment up to ₹10 crore and turnover up to ₹50 crore.
- Medium Enterprises: Investment up to ₹50 crore and turnover up to ₹250 crore.

After Budget 2025–26:

The Union Budget 2025–26 revised the MSME classification criteria to accommodate inflation and changing economic conditions. The updated thresholds are:

- Micro Enterprises: Investment up to ₹2.5 crore and turnover up to ₹10 crore.
- Small Enterprises: Investment up to ₹25 crore and turnover up to ₹100 crore.

Medium Enterprises: Investment up to ₹125 crore and turnover up to ₹500 crore.

This reclassification aims to enable more businesses to qualify for MSME benefits, fostering growth and formalisation.

Meena runs a home-based papad-making business in Indore. She registered herself on the Udyam portal in early 2025. Till then, she borrowed from informal lenders at steep interest rates. In April 2025, she received a pink-coloured micro enterprise credit card loaded with a ₹5 lakh limit—announced under the new scheme in Budget 2025–26. This allowed her to buy a small dough mixer, hire two women from her neighbourhood, and expand her monthly production threefold. Now she's supplying to a local supermarket chain. 'Before this, I was invisible. Now I swipe and scale,' she says, laughing. For her, the credit card was not plastic—it was power.

Definitions of MSMEs or SBCs in Other Countries

United States:

The US SBA defines small businesses based on industry-specific standards, primarily considering the number of employees and annual receipts. Generally, a small business is one with fewer than 500 employees. However, this can vary; for instance, manufacturing and mining industries may have thresholds up to 1,500 employees, while wholesale trade businesses may be classified as small with up to 100 employees. Annual revenue limits also differ by industry, ranging from $1 million to over $40 million.

Saira, a 23-year-old graduate from Aligarh, had always dreamt of opening a café that served local millet-based snacks. But banks kept rejecting her loan requests—she had no collateral and no business history. In June 2025, she applied under the new ₹10,000 crore Fund of Funds and term loan scheme meant for first-time entrepreneurs like her.

United Kingdom:

In the UK, an SME is defined as a business with fewer than 250 employees and either an annual turnover not exceeding €50 million or a balance sheet total not exceeding €43 million.

China:

China's definition of SMEs varies by industry and considers the number of employees, annual revenue, and total assets. For example, in the manufacturing sector, a medium-sized enterprise may have up to 2,000 employees, while in the wholesale sector, the threshold might be lower.

Singapore:

In Singapore, an SME is defined as a company with an annual turnover of less than S$100 million or employing fewer than 200 employees.

South Africa:

South Africa classifies small enterprises based on the number of employees and annual turnover, which vary across sectors. For instance, in the manufacturing sector, a small enterprise might have up to 50 employees and a turnover of up to R13 million.

Bangladesh:

In Bangladesh, SMEs are defined by the number of employees and fixed assets, excluding land and buildings. For example, in the manufacturing sector, a small enterprise may have 10–49 employees and fixed assets between BDT 0.5 million and BDT 15 million.

The redefinition of MSMEs in India's Budget 2025–26 reflects an effort to align with global standards and address the

In Agra, Irfan manufactures leather belts. His unit has been exporting to the UAE since 2022. He recently joined a government-supported cluster for toy, leather, and footwear exporters. With guidance from an MSME export cell, he secured a small buyer in Germany, tripling his export income in six months.

Irfan was happy to hear that MSMEs now account for over 45% of India's total exports. But when asked about how the number was calculated, he smiled. 'Maybe they counted me. But they didn't ask me. I still send invoices in Excel and WhatsApp. Who's aggregating these?' he asked. 'Yes, I export. But do I feel supported? A little. Do I feel counted? Not always.'

evolving economic landscape. By increasing the investment and turnover thresholds, the government aims to accommodate inflationary trends and enable more enterprises to benefit from MSME-related schemes. Comparatively, definitions of SMEs or SBCs vary across countries, tailored to their unique economic structures and policy objectives.

ii. **Enhanced Credit Availability:** The credit guarantee cover for micro and small enterprises has been raised from ₹5 crore to ₹10 crore, aiming to enable additional credit of ₹1.5 lakh crore over five years. Startups and exporter MSMEs are also set to benefit from increased guarantee covers and reduced fees.

iii. **Credit Cards for Micro Enterprises:** A new scheme will provide ₹5 lakh in credit to micro enterprises registered on the Udyam portal, with a target of issuing 10 lakh cards in the first year.

iv. **Support for Startups and First-Time Entrepreneurs:** A ₹10,000 crore Fund of Funds will be established to support startups, alongside a scheme offering term loans up to ₹2 crore for 5 lakh first-time women, SC, and ST entrepreneurs over five years.

v. **Focus on Labour-Intensive Sectors:** Initiatives targeting the footwear, leather, and toy sectors aim to create substantial employment opportunities and position India as a global manufacturing hub in these domains.

> In a remote village near Ranchi, Munshi runs a small brick kiln. He employs 12 labourers seasonally and sells bricks to nearby towns. He doesn't have a GST number, doesn't maintain digital books, and has never registered on the Udyam portal. But when government data says 25 crore people work in MSMEs, his labourers are probably counted—without any formal entry.

While these measures are commendable, the data underpinning the sector's current status warrants a critical assessment. The reported employment figure of over 25 crore individuals within the MSME sector appears substantial, especially considering India's total workforce. This discrepancy raises questions about data collection methodologies and the potential for overestimation.

Similarly, the assertion that MSME-related products constituted 45.73% of India's total exports in 2023–24, while indicative of the sector's export potential, lacks granularity. A more detailed breakdown of the types of products, their value addition, and the specific markets they cater to would provide a clearer picture of the sector's export dynamics.

The Union Budget 2025–26's initiatives for the MSME sector reflect a strategic approach to fostering growth, inclusivity, and global competitiveness. However, for these interventions to yield the desired outcomes, it is imperative to ensure the accuracy and objectivity of the data informing policy

In Mumbai, Preeti, an economics student, interned at a textile firm that claimed to be a leading MSME exporter. She helped prepare an export report for government submission. 'They showed ₹10 crore in exports but most was invoiced through a partner company. Actual production was much less,' she recalled.

This sparked her curiosity about how MSME export data is compiled. 'I realised that the same export can be shown under multiple MSMEs in a supply chain—if you don't filter carefully, it looks like three companies are exporting ₹10 crore each when only one actually is,' she said. For her, the lesson was clear: data integrity in MSME exports is not just a technical issue—it's about painting a true picture.

decisions. Robust data collection and validation mechanisms will be crucial in monitoring the effectiveness of these measures and in making informed adjustments as necessary.

Having discussed some of the significant initiatives of the government in promoting the startup and MSME ecosystem in the country, we now come to a sensitive and delicate area of performance evaluation—the absence of robust, objectively verified data on the outcomes of the various interventions of the government.

CHAPTER 9

When Numbers Lie: The Mirage of MSME Statistics [32]

The Ministry of MSME in India reports significant contributions of the sector to employment, manufacturing output, and exports. However, the reliability and objectivity of these statistics warrant a critical assessment, considering the methodologies employed and the challenges inherent in data collection, especially within the informal sector.

Employment Data

The ministry reports that as of 16 July 2024, MSMEs registered on the Udyam portal employed approximately 20.39 crore individuals, including those from informal micro enterprises registered via the UAP. However, this figure is based on self-reported data at the time of registration and may not reflect current employment levels. The absence of regular updates and verification mechanisms raises concerns about the accuracy of these employment statistics.

32. Chapters 2 and 10 also mention data unreliability (NSSO 2015 outdated; Udyam over-reporting).

Ramesh runs a modest tailoring unit in a small town in Madhya Pradesh. When a local NGO encouraged him to register on the Udyam portal to avail credit benefits, he filled out the form with the help of a cybercafé operator. Under the 'number of workers employed', he optimistically wrote '10'—including part-time help, his cousin who occasionally stitched during festival seasons, and a neighbour's son who visited on weekends. He never updated the registration later, even though half of those people stopped helping him. On paper, Ramesh's unit continues to be counted as a business providing employment to ten people, contributing to the 20 crore-plus employment figures cited by the ministry. But in reality, only Ramesh and his wife work there full-time. This gap between self-declared and actual employment data is one of the biggest flaws in the current MSME statistics.

Manufacturing Output

The MSME sector is reported to contribute around 30% to India's GDP. This estimate is derived from extrapolations of data collected during the 73rd round of the National Sample Survey (NSS) conducted in 2015–16. Given the dynamic nature of the MSME sector and the elapsed time since the last comprehensive survey, these figures may not accurately represent the current state of manufacturing output. The lack of recent, large-scale surveys limits the reliability of these estimates.

Export Contributions

The ministry indicates that MSME-related products accounted for 45.73% of India's total exports in 2023–24. This statistic is based on data from the Directorate General of Commercial Intelligence and Statistics (DGCIS), which classifies exports by product categories associated with MSMEs. However, this method does not account for the scale of the exporting

> Sarla Devi runs a small agarbatti (incense stick) business in a rural corner of Odisha. She started it in 2018 after taking a loan from a self-help group. In her village, many women like her engage in small-scale manufacturing—whether it's papad-making, weaving, or handmade soaps. But when the government calculates how much MSMEs contribute to India's manufacturing output, it relies on data from the NSS conducted way back in 2015–16. Sarla's business—and millions like hers that started after that—aren't even part of the dataset. So while newspapers quote that MSMEs contribute about 30% to India's GDP, they're missing stories like Sarla's. She often wonders why no one has come to count her enterprise. The numbers may look good, but the ground reality has changed, and no one has updated the books.

enterprises, potentially attributing exports from larger firms to the MSME sector. Consequently, the actual contribution of MSMEs to exports may be overestimated.

Data Collection Challenges

A significant portion of MSMEs operate within the informal sector, which poses challenges for data collection and verification. The reliance on self-reported data during registration, without subsequent audits or integration with tax filings and GST returns, undermines the objectivity of the statistics. Moreover, the absence of independent third-party assessments or beneficiary surveys further limits the credibility of the reported figures.

While the MSME sector undoubtedly plays a crucial role in India's economy, the current methodologies for data collection and reporting raise questions about the reliability and objectivity of the statistics presented by the ministry. To enhance the accuracy of MSME data, there is a need for regular, comprehensive surveys,

Ahmed owns a leather goods company in Kanpur that supplies wallets and belts to a large export house. His products eventually reach overseas markets, but he himself doesn't export anything directly. Yet, when the government publishes data on MSME exports, it includes the type of products Ahmed makes—leather goods—assuming they were exported by MSMEs. In truth, the export house that ships these items is a large enterprise. So, while the statistics claim that MSMEs contribute over 45% to India's exports, entrepreneurs like Ahmed—whose goods are exported under another company's banner—are counted in the tally, even though they're not the ones earning foreign currency. This method may inflate the numbers, unintentionally giving MSMEs more credit than they actually deserve.

Shalini runs a beauty parlour in Hyderabad and was thrilled to receive a ₹2 lakh loan under the Credit Guarantee Scheme. The paperwork was done, and she proudly told her friends she was now part of the formal MSME network. But six months later, the business slowed down. She had to divert the loan amount towards household expenses and couldn't repay the EMIs (Equated Monthly Instalments). Her bank has now marked the account as a non-performing asset. But the official statistics still reflect Shalini's loan as part of the ₹2.44 lakh crore sanctioned under the scheme in 2024. There is no mention of whether the loan was used productively or whether it helped Shalini scale her business. To a casual reader, the figures sound like a roaring success, even though her story ended on a note of quiet distress.

integration of administrative data sources such as tax and GST filings, and the implementation of independent verification mechanisms. Such measures would provide a more accurate and objective understanding of the MSME sector's contributions to employment, manufacturing output, and exports.

Evaluating the Reliability of MSME Statistics in the 2024 Year-End Review

The Ministry of MSME released its 2024 year-end review, highlighting significant achievements in formalisation, credit facilitation, and employment generation. This analysis critically examines the objectivity, acceptability, and reliability of the reported statistics, focusing on the methodologies employed and the extent of independent verification.

The ministry's report indicates that as of 26 December 2024, 5.70 crore MSMEs employing 24.14 crore individuals were registered on the Udyam Registration Portal and UAP. While this suggests substantial progress in formalising the sector, the reliability of these figures warrants scrutiny.

The registration process on the Udyam Portal is primarily self-declaratory, relying on information provided by the enterprises without mandatory third-party verification. Consequently, the accuracy of employment data and the operational status of these enterprises remains uncertain. There is a lack of evidence indicating that these figures have been corroborated through independent assessments or beneficiary surveys.

Similarly, the report states that 19.90 lakh credit guarantees amounting to ₹2.44 lakh crore were approved under the Credit Guarantee Scheme in 2024. However, the data does not provide insights into the actual disbursement of these loans, their utilisation, or repayment performance. Without such information, it is challenging to assess the effectiveness of the credit support in enhancing MSME operations.

The report also mentions the registration of 24.77 lakh applications under the Prime Minister Vishwakarma scheme, with 15.05 lakh beneficiaries completing basic skill training. While these numbers indicate outreach efforts, the absence of follow-up data on the beneficiaries' post-training employment or income improvements limits the ability to evaluate the programme's impact.

Furthermore, the reported increase in Khadi and Village Industries (KVI) sales to ₹1.55 lakh crore in fiscal year 2023–24 lacks context regarding the data collection methods and verification processes. Without clarity on these aspects, the reliability of the sales figures remains questionable.

While the Ministry of MSME's 2024 year-end review presents impressive statistics on sectoral achievements, the reliance on self-reported data without independent verification raises concerns about the objectivity and reliability of these figures. To ensure accurate assessment and effective policy-making, it is imperative to implement robust data validation mechanisms, including third-party assessments and integration with tax and financial records. Such measures would enhance the credibility of reported achievements and facilitate targeted support for the MSME sector.

The UK Sinha Committee, established by the RBI in January 2019, conducted a comprehensive review of the MSME sector to identify challenges and propose long-term solutions for its economic and financial sustainability. While the committee did not explicitly state that the data on MSMEs was inflated, it highlighted significant concerns regarding the reliability and comprehensiveness of existing data.

Key Observations:

1. **Inadequate Data Infrastructure:** The committee noted the absence of a robust, centralised database for MSMEs, leading to challenges in policy formulation and implementation.

2. **Credit Gap Estimation:** It estimated a substantial credit gap in the MSME sector, ranging between ₹20 to ₹25 lakh crore, indicating that many MSMEs lacked access to formal credit channels.

3. **Delayed Payments:** The committee observed that MSMEs

often faced delayed payments from buyers, affecting their liquidity and operational efficiency.

Key Recommendations:

1. **Creation of a Comprehensive MSME Database:** To address data deficiencies, the committee recommended establishing a centralised database that integrates information from various sources, including GSTN (Goods and Services Tax Network), Udyam registration, and banks.

2. **Use of PAN as a Unique Enterprise Identifier (UEI):** It suggested adopting the PAN as a UEI for MSMEs to streamline registration and access to services.

3. **Establishment of a Distressed Asset Fund:** The committee proposed a ₹5,000 crore fund to support MSMEs facing financial stress due to external factors.

4. **Fund of Funds for MSMEs:** It recommended creating a ₹10,000 crore government-sponsored fund to encourage venture capital and private equity investments in MSMEs.

5. **Amendments to the MSMED Act:** To ensure timely payments, the committee suggested mandating the uploading of all invoices above a specified amount to an information utility, enhancing transparency and accountability.

6. **Digital Public Infrastructure:** The committee emphasised leveraging digital platforms like the Udyam Registration Portal and TReDS to improve access to credit and reduce transaction costs.

In summary, while the UK Sinha Committee did not directly label MSME data as inflated, it underscored the need for improved data collection and management systems to enhance the reliability of information, which is crucial for effective policy-making and support mechanisms for the MSME sector.

Let us now take a look at what the latest statistics, sourced primarily from NASSCOM, PIB (Press Information Bureau), and Statista, paint a picture of relentless growth, equity inclusion, and financial backing in the Start up sector.

Beneath the Boom – Scrutinising the Startup Euphoria in India

India's startup sector is frequently feted as a symbol of the country's entrepreneurial renaissance, with explosive numbers on DPIIT-recognised startups, jobs created, and unicorns celebrated across reports. However, beneath this glitter lies a fog of unanswered questions around data validation, sustainability, third-party evaluations, and long-term economic impact. This narrative critically examines each major parameter and assesses the credibility and objectivity of the presented data.

As the clock ticked into 2025, India found itself proudly wearing the badge of being the world's third-largest startup ecosystem, boasting a mammoth 1,59,157 DPIIT-recognised startups. These startups are credited with generating over 16.6 lakh direct jobs—figures that would make any policymaker beam with pride. But when one steps beyond this data deluge, critical questions begin to surface: How many of these startups are sustainable? How many still operate today? And most importantly, how trustworthy are these statistics in the absence of any credible, third-party verification?

The most striking figure—over 38,000% growth in recognised startups from 2016 to 2025—feels more like a viral social media post than a grounded economic trend. Recognition by DPIIT is merely registration; it doesn't equate to viability, innovation, or revenue generation. Of the 1.59 lakh startups, only 17,678 are classified as 'established'—a term whose operational definition is never clarified. That's barely 11% of the total. So are the rest simply names on a registry, hanging by the thread of aspiration rather than a working business model?

Further, the oft-repeated claim that Indian startups created 16.6 lakh jobs since 2016 should ideally come with a caveat: Are these full-time, quality jobs with social security and benefits, or informal, short-term gig engagements? The report glibly lists IT services, healthcare, and professional services as employment engines, but does not distinguish between salaried tech developers and part-time delivery boys. Nor is there any clarity on attrition, net employment retained, or regional disparities in job distribution. Without third-party audits or even sample surveys by independent labour economists, these tallies remain suspect.

When it comes to startup failures, the global data paints a sobering reality—90% of startups fail within ten years, and over two-thirds collapse within five. But this figure, drawn from the US Bureau of Labour Statistics, is curiously divorced from Indian ground realities. India lacks a nationwide startup mortality tracking system. There is no standard definition for 'failure'—whether it is formal closure, dormancy, or pivoting into a completely unrelated line. Nor does the NASSCOM-PIB data venture into the murky terrain of zombie startups—ventures that survive on life support from grants and subsidies, without meaningful operations or returns.

The investment story is equally bipolar. The headline ₹10,000 crore boost to AIFs in Union Budget 2025–26 sounds impressive. Yet, the same report acknowledges that 51% of founders found the funding experience 'favourable'—a fall from the previous year. That means nearly half of the ecosystem did not. Also, 25% of founders did not even attempt fundraising. This indicates not confidence, but perhaps fatigue with the opaque funding ecosystem dominated by elite networks. What about startups in Tier II and Tier III cities that lack access to these VCs and angels? Their silence in the dataset is deafening.

The gender representation section reads like a celebratory LinkedIn post—48% of DPIIT-recognised startups reportedly have at least one woman director. But what does this number imply? Is the presence of a woman director nominal, symbolic, or does it reflect actual control and leadership? Without qualitative analysis, this figure becomes a checkbox metric, incapable of capturing the nuanced struggles of women entrepreneurs in patriarchal boardrooms and investor pitches.

The unicorn parade,[33] too, deserves a reality check. India boasts 117 unicorns as of 2025, but not one new unicorn has emerged in the past year. Is this stagnation cyclical or systemic? If Bengaluru leads with 44 unicorns, is the startup scene becoming too clustered in a few metro bubbles? And more critically, what is the post-unicorn survival rate? A unicorn is not a finish line—it's an expensive milestone. Some, like BYJU'S, have even turned into cautionary tales of valuation inflation and governance lapses.

The data source credibility is another elephant in the room. Most of the numbers stem from NASSCOM, DPIIT, Statista, and internal surveys, like those by AngelList India. None are peer-reviewed, none independently audited. There is a complete absence of evaluative studies by reputed public or academic institutions like the Indian Statistical Institute, Centre for Policy Research, or even the CAG. Are we confusing visibility with verifiability?

Moreover, the entire dataset is curated by GrabOn, an e-commerce startup itself. When startups report on the startup ecosystem, there is an inherent conflict of interest. It is like letting coaching centres draft the NEET[34] syllabus or

---

33. A unicorn is a privately held startup company valued at $1 billion or more, typically based on fundraising rounds rather than audited revenues or profits. The term symbolises rarity and high-growth potential, though such valuations often reflect investor optimism rather than proven financial sustainability.

34. NEET stands for National Eligibility cum Entrance Test. It is a standardised entrance examination conducted in India for students seeking admission to undergraduate (MBBS (Bachelor of Medicine and Bachelor of Surgery)/BDS (Bachelor of Dental Surgery)) and postgraduate (MD (Doctor of Medicine)/MS (Master of Surgery)) medical and dental courses in government and private institutions across the country.

stockbrokers write SEBI[35] regulations. Without checks, the possibility of data cherry-picking or framing bias is very real.

Way Forward

If India truly seeks to harness its startup energy for transformative economic growth, it must first embrace brutal honesty. The government must mandate the publication of periodic third-party evaluations of the startup ecosystem—preferably by bodies with statutory independence or academic repute. DPIIT must classify startups not merely by registration, but also by functional status—operational, dormant, defunct—and update this classification annually.

A nationwide startup survivability tracker must be instituted, with standardised definitions of 'failure' and 'scale-up'. The government should also ensure that funding outcomes and investor behaviours—especially in AIFs, SIDBI schemes, and tax exemptions—are made transparently available. Data on women-led startups should shift from presence to participation, tracking real leadership roles and investment traction.

Above all, there is a pressing case for the CAG of India to step in—not because it needs fresh empowerment, but because it already holds the constitutional and statutory mandate to audit public spending and evaluate outcomes. With thousands of crores being funnelled into AIFs, startup incubators, tax breaks, credit guarantees, and policy incentives, the startup ecosystem qualifies—by any standard—as a high-risk, high-visibility expenditure arena. The puzzling question, then, is not whether the CAG can audit this domain, but why it hasn't. Is it inertia? A lack of domain-specific expertise? A deliberate choice to stay away from politically high-pitched zones? Or are there simply too many burning fires elsewhere—

35. SEBI is the equivalent of the SEC (Securities and Exchange Commission) of the US or the FCA (Financial Conduct Authority) of the UK.

health, education, defence procurement, environment—that are crowding out this audit priority? Whatever the reason, the omission is conspicuous. In an era where the rhetoric of innovation is generously subsidised by the exchequer, the absence of a rigorous, all-India performance audit examining the actual outcomes, failures, fund flows, deadweight losses, and success stories in India's startup ecosystem leaves a gaping hole in public accountability. It is high time the CAG treated this not as an optional audit, but as an essential national reckoning.

Let us now briefly discuss what the associations or organised groups of MSMEs have been expecting and demanding from governments in terms of support and assistance.

References:

1. Press Information Bureau, Government of India. Number of DPIIT-Recognized Startups and Employment Generated. Published January 2025. https://pib.gov.in

2. NASSCOM. Indian Startup Ecosystem Report 2024–25. National Association of Software and Service Companies; 2025.

3. Statista. India Startup Landscape: Founder Priorities and Funding Trends, 2024–25. https://www.statista.com/statistics/startup-india

4. Tracxn. Unicorn Startups in India – Sector and Geography Distribution. Published September 2024. https://tracxn.com

5. US Bureau of Labor Statistics. Business Employment Dynamics: Establishment Age and Survival Data. Updated 2024. https://www.bls.gov

6. Bain & Company. Women Entrepreneurs and MSMEs in India: Economic Impact and Job Creation. Published 2023. https://www.bain.com/global-reports/women-entrepreneurs-india

7. AngelList India. Angel Investment Trends and Exit Patterns in Indian Startups. Published 2024. https://angel.co/india

CHAPTER 10

◆◆◆

MSME Voices 2024–25: Associations and Aspirations

Abstract:

In the fiscal year 2024–25, associations representing MSMEs in India presented a series of demands to the Ministry of MSME and the Parliamentary Standing Committee. These demands aimed to address persistent challenges faced by the sector and to seek enhanced governmental support. This chapter summarises the key interventions proposed by these associations and critically examines the objectivity and reliability of data concerning employment, production, and exports within the MSME sector.

The MSME sector, often referred to as the backbone of the Indian economy, has consistently faced challenges related to credit access, delayed payments, and infrastructural constraints. In 2024–25, MSME associations articulated specific demands to the government, emphasising the need for:

1. **Enhanced Credit Facilities:** Associations urged the expansion of credit guarantee schemes and the introduction of collateral-free loans to improve liquidity.

2. **Timely Payments:** There was a call for stricter enforcement of payment timelines from large corporations and government entities to MSMEs, ensuring better cash flow management.

3. **Infrastructure Development:** The need for dedicated industrial zones with adequate facilities was highlighted to support MSME operations.

4. **Digital Integration:** Associations recommended the promotion of digital platforms for marketing and sales to expand MSME reach.

5. **Skill Development:** Emphasis was placed on training programmes to enhance the skill set of the workforce, aligning with modern technological advancements.

While these demands underscore the proactive stance of MSME associations in seeking growth and sustainability, concerns persist regarding the reliability of data on employment, production, and exports in the sector.

Data Reliability Concerns:

- **Employment Figures:** The reported employment statistics often rely on self-declared data during MSME registration, lacking periodic verification, which may lead to inflated numbers.
- **Production Output:** Production data is frequently estimated based on outdated surveys, without real-time tracking mechanisms, questioning its current relevance.
- **Export Contributions:** Export data attributed to MSMEs may not accurately distinguish between small enterprises and larger firms, leading to potential overestimations.

These data challenges highlight the necessity for more robust, third-party assessments and integration with verifiable sources, such as tax filings and GST returns, to ensure accuracy and objectivity.

The demands presented by MSME associations in 2024–25 reflect a concerted effort to address longstanding issues and to seek governmental interventions for sectoral growth. However, for policy decisions to be effective and targeted, it is imperative to base them on accurate and objective data. Implementing comprehensive data verification processes and integrating multiple data sources will enhance the reliability of information, thereby facilitating informed decision-making and fostering a more resilient MSME sector.

MSME Associations' Demands and Government Responses in 2023–24 and 2024–25

In the fiscal years 2023–24 and 2024–25, MSME associations in India actively engaged with the Ministry of MSME and the Parliamentary Standing Committee to address sectoral challenges. This section examines the evolution of their demands, the government's responsiveness, and the associations involved in these advocacy efforts.

In 2023–24, MSME associations primarily focused on implementing immediate relief measures, including enhanced credit access, timely payments, and infrastructural support. The government's response included the introduction of the 'MSME-TEAM' (MSME-Trade Enablement and Marketing) initiative, aiming to promote digitalisation among MSMEs.

By 2024–25, the associations' demands evolved to encompass broader structural reforms, such as increased investment thresholds, streamlined regulatory processes, and targeted support for women and marginalised entrepreneurs. The Union Budget 2025–26 reflected some of these demands by revising the MSME classification criteria and enhancing credit guarantee schemes.

Notable MSME associations that actively represented these demands include:

- **Consortium of Indian Associations (CIA):** Engaged in policy advocacy and provided feedback on government initiatives.
- **Federation of Indian Micro and Small & Medium Enterprises (FISME):** Focused on policy reforms and capacity building.
- **Confederation of All India Traders (CAIT):** Represented the interests of small traders and advocated for simplified tax regimes.
- **Laghu Udyog Bharati:** Emphasised the need for technological upgradation and skill development.

The transition in MSME associations' demands from immediate relief to structural reforms indicates a maturing advocacy landscape. While the government has addressed several concerns, continuous engagement and collaborative efforts are essential to ensure the MSME sector's sustainable growth and resilience.

CHAPTER 11

◆◆◆

Blindsided Twice: Demonetisation and COVID – Survival Stories and Scars

> Imagine you run a roadside tea stall. You deal only in cash. Suddenly, the ₹500 and ₹1,000 notes you've saved are declared useless overnight. Customers can't pay. Suppliers stop delivering. You can't pay your helper.
>
> That's what demonetisation did to millions of micro-businesses. No digital backup, no bank support—just shutdowns and silence

India's MSMEs—its khadi weavers, metal benders, toy makers, garage repairers, food vendors, tech startups, and backyard innovators—have long been romanticised as the real India. They are that silent 63 million-strong (also stated to be 6 crore in some government statistics and reports) economic army that contributes over 30% to the GDP and employs more than 110 million people. But in the span of just four years, this heartbeat of the economy was twice ambushed—first by demonetisation in 2016, then by COVID-19 in 2020. These twin shocks were not just events. They were tsunamis that crashed against the fragile shores of India's informal and small-scale economy, laying bare structural rot and testing resilience like never before.

The Shock That Shattered Cashflow: Demonetisation

It was a televised announcement that would change the fate of millions. On the evening of 8 November 2016, Prime Minister Narendra Modi announced that ₹500 and ₹1,000 notes—86% of the cash in circulation—would cease to be legal tender. While the intent was pitched as an assault on black money, the execution overlooked a brutal truth: India's MSMEs were cash-intensive, unbanked, and unprepared. Overnight, entire businesses were paralysed. Wages couldn't be paid. Inventory lay idle. Transactions halted mid-sentence.

> Picture a small tailoring shop with four workers. In March 2020, you shut shop due to the lockdown. Orders are cancelled, cloth stock lies idle, and workers leave for home. You have no savings, no insurance, no backup.
>
> That's the COVID story for MSMEs. Businesses didn't just pause—they fell off a cliff, especially in the informal and unregistered sector.

The first to crumble were the unregistered micro enterprises. According to a report by the All India Manufacturers' Organisation (AIMO), nearly 35% of micro and small enterprises experienced a sharp decline in revenues within the first few months post-demonetisation. And the worst part? They had no recourse—no insurance, no credit history, and certainly no bailout cushion.

Women-led home businesses, rural service units, and family-owned workshops bore the brunt. They operated outside digital footprints, and the sudden withdrawal of cash choked them out. The death was not dramatic, but silent—enterprises simply stopped showing up.

> Imagine you run a roadside tea stall. You deal only in cash. Suddenly, the ₹500 and ₹1,000 notes you've saved are declared useless overnight. Customers can't pay. Suppliers stop delivering. You can't pay your helper.
>
> That's what demonetisation did to millions of micro-businesses. No digital backup, no bank support—just shutdowns and silence

The Pandemic Punch: Frozen Demand, Broken Chains

Just when some semblance of normalcy was returning, COVID-19 landed like a sledgehammer in 2020. This was no liquidity crisis—it was a full-blown existential halt. Lockdowns froze demand, shuttered operations, and turned supply chains into jigsaw puzzles. Unlike demonetisation, where the rich weathered the storm with digital tools and diversified assets, COVID made survival dependent on agility, tech adaptability, and access to finance—all luxuries for most MSMEs.

According to a 2021 CRISIL (Credit Rating Information Services of India Limited) study, more than 67% of MSMEs reported a significant decline in revenues, and over 30% faced permanent closure risks. A survey by the CIA found that nearly 73% of MSMEs had not received any meaningful support

> Suppose a training centre teaches painting, but sends its students to do plumbing jobs. Employers complain they don't have the right skills.
>
> That's Skill India in many sectors. MSMEs needed specific hands-on skills. But most trainees got generic training not aligned to real-world jobs.

from government relief packages. Gig economy disruptions meant smaller vendors lost both customers and platforms. From Darjeeling's tea sellers to Chennai's auto component workshops, despair was universal.

The most painful stories emerged from the urban-rural fringes—areas where economic opportunity had just begun to sprout. Thousands of migrant workers returned home, rendering MSMEs in urban clusters short of labour. Others simply couldn't restock, rehire, or reopen.

Dried-Up Taps: Liquidity and the Informal Trap

Access to credit has always been the Achilles heel of MSMEs. And during these twin crises, that heel was struck repeatedly. Formal banks, despite elaborate priority sector lending norms, remained risk-averse. Informal credit systems, the lifeblood of tiny businesses, shrivelled post-demonetisation and never recovered to their original strength.

NBFCs too grew cautious. Though the RBI injected liquidity into the system, it never fully trickled down. According to a SIDBI-TransUnion CIBIL {Credit Information Bureau (India) Limited) report (2021}, new MSME credit disbursals declined sharply in the pandemic's first year. The majority of micro units couldn't meet the eligibility norms for new schemes and guarantees.

> Say the government launches an app for farmers to get fertiliser subsidies—but most of them don't have smartphones or network coverage.
>
> That's what digitalisation felt like for many MSMEs. UPI and GST worked for urban sellers, but rural and small-town entrepreneurs struggled with tech, tools, and connectivity. unregistered sector.

The ECLGS launched during COVID was hailed as a lifeline, but the reality was more sobering. Many smaller units, lacking existing bank relationships or collateral, couldn't access the benefits. In effect, relief flowed disproportionately to medium-sized and formal MSMEs, bypassing the informal grassroots segment that needed it most.

> At a grand wedding, you distribute gifts only to wealthy relatives because they are 'easier to track'. The poor cousins get ignored.
>
> That's how government relief flowed during COVID. Medium-sized units got credit support. The smallest players got none—no records, no visibility, no access.

MUDRA Scheme: Promise, Reach, and Real Impact

Launched in 2015, the Pradhan Mantri MUDRA Yojana (PMMY) was billed as a transformative credit channel for micro units. By 2022, over ₹18 lakh crore had been disbursed under the MUDRA scheme. But the scheme's success story is not so straightforward. While the sheer number of beneficiaries is impressive, most loans fall in the 'Shishu' category—under ₹50,000—often used for consumption rather than business creation.

Independent assessments, including one by the Parliamentary Standing Committee on Finance (2021), noted the alarming levels of NPAs in MUDRA loans. The RBI itself warned of the growing systemic risk posed by defaults. What began as an enabling tool has now morphed, in some instances, into a debt trap for economically vulnerable borrowers who were pushed to repay even during lockdowns.

Digital Leap or Digital Divide?

One of the unintended effects of demonetisation was the forced march toward digital payments. Platforms like UPI, Paytm, PhonePe, and BharatPe mushroomed. COVID further accelerated this trend. The government's Digital India pitch found resonance, but mainly in metro and Tier I MSMEs. For many rural or semi-urban entrepreneurs, the promise of digital inclusion remains just that—a promise.

Poor Internet access, limited smartphone penetration, and digital illiteracy created a sharp divide. While some entrepreneurs in Bengaluru or Gurugram used QR (Quick Response) codes and online orders to stay afloat, their counterparts in Moradabad or Imphal struggled to generate even basic invoices. Cyber fraud and a lack of grievance redressal mechanisms added to the woes.

> Suppose you hire a trained driver, but give him only a bicycle. He can't perform, not because he's unskilled, but because the tools don't match.
>
> That's what many MSMEs faced with Skill India hires. They got workers with paper certificates but no practical exposure or relevant trade training.

Moreover, digital success often favoured consumer-facing enterprises. B2B industrial clusters, artisanal craftspeople, and traders in traditional markets still relied heavily on face-to-face transactions and trusted middlemen. For them, the digital revolution felt exclusionary.

Startup India: Celebrated, But Skewed

Startup India was launched with much fanfare in 2016 to turn India into a nation of job creators. And indeed, unicorns sprouted, pitch decks flourished, and investor appetite boomed. But here's the rub—very few of these celebrated startups were rooted in the MSME spirit. Most were tech-driven, urban-centric, and funded through venture capital, not bank credit.

The programme's benefits—tax exemptions, IPR (Intellectual Property Rights) support, regulatory handholding—largely bypassed non-tech, small-scale manufacturing or rural entrepreneurs. A 2022 DPIIT report acknowledged that less than 10% of recognised startups were from Tier II and Tier III towns.

The spectacular rise and fall of BYJU'S (discussed in chapter 7) tells a cautionary tale. Once a darling of ed-tech and the poster child of Startup India, BYJU'S went from a billion-dollar valuation to being mired in governance lapses, audit concerns, and mass layoffs. Its implosion wasn't just about one company's missteps—it exposed the frothiness of India's startup celebration, where hype often raced ahead of substance.

Skill India: The Missing Link

Skill India was supposed to complement MSME growth by supplying a trained workforce. But the outcome has been underwhelming. Between 2016 and 2022, lakhs were trained—but not necessarily employable. MSMEs often found these 'certified' workers ill-equipped to handle real-life production tasks.

A CAG report in 2022 flagged issues of duplication, poor monitoring, and weak post-placement tracking in Skill India programmes. Moreover, the scheme didn't address sector-specific needs. A textile unit needed loom experts, not generic welders. An electronics startup needed embedded coders, not just ITI diploma holders. The disconnect between supply and actual market demand rendered much of the effort symbolic.

Structural Faultlines and Policy Blind Spots

The twin shocks exposed deeper structural issues. First, registration. Less than 25% of MSMEs were registered on the Udyam portal, even by mid-2023. Without formal registration, access to government schemes, bank loans, and grievance mechanisms remained elusive. Second, labour. Rigid labour laws disincentivised hiring beyond 10–20 workers. Many enterprises stayed deliberately small to stay out of compliance nets.

Third, taxation. GST compliance became a nightmare for micro businesses. While the system was meant to formalise the economy, it ended up penalising smaller players who lacked accounting support or real-time invoice systems. Refund delays, input credit confusion, and arbitrary notices became routine.

Udyam, RAMP, CHAMPIONS: Much Promise, Modest Outcomes

To its credit, the government did attempt a course correction. The Udyam portal simplified registration and linked it with PAN and Aadhaar. The RAMP programme, backed by World Bank funds, aimed to improve competitiveness. The CHAMPIONS portal was launched to provide grievance redressal and handholding.

But execution lagged. Udyam registration remained patchy, especially in backward states. RAMP's success was limited by state capacity constraints. CHAMPIONS became more of an information repository than an active facilitator. The gap between intent and outcome continued to haunt policy efforts.

Conclusion: The Road to Redemption

India's MSME sector is like a banyan tree—resilient, rooted, and often ignored in the shade of larger corporate behemoths. Demonetisation and COVID-19 didn't just expose its fragility—they illuminated its centrality. The millions of enterprises that were blindsided by policy and pandemic deserve more than rhetoric. They deserve a state that listens, adapts, and walks alongside them.

What is needed now is not just credit, but capability-building. Not just portals, but people-friendly processes. Not just grand schemes, but ground-level execution. As India eyes a $5 trillion economy, its MSME sector cannot be an afterthought. It must be at the core of economic planning, not merely in slogans but in design, delivery, and accountability.

References:

1. https://aiaiindia.com/wp-content/uploads/2020/04/IMPACT-OF-DEMONETIZATION-ON-MSMES.pdf

2. https://www.assocham.org/uploads/files/MSME-ASSOCHAM-CRISIL%20Study%20April%202022.pdf

3. https://yourstory.com/smbstory/micro-small-businesses-government-stimulus-package-covid-msmes

4. https://www.cenfa.org/mudra-loans-and-the-dangers-of-micro-finance/

5. https://cag.gov.in/uploads/download_audit_report/2024/CHAPTER-5-067ed54fce08929.11140134.pdf

6. https://eparlib.nic.in/bitstream/123456789/994373/1/17_Finance_46.pdf

7. https://www.researchgate.net/publication/334537301_DEMONETIZATION_AND_ITS_IMPACT_ON_THE_MSME_SECTOR

8. https://icrier.org/pdf/Annual-Survey-MSMEs_India_2025.pdf

9. https://stateofthemsme.org/survey/

10. https://www.transunioncibil.com/content/dam/transunion-cibil/business/collateral/report/report-msme-june-2021.pdf?utm_source

11. https://www.cenfa.org/mudra-loans-and-the-dangers-of-micro-finance/?utm_source

12. https://perspectivia.net/servlets/MCRFileNodeServlet/pnet_derivate_00005528/reddy_demonetization.pdf?utm_source

CHAPTER 12

Credit Apartheid – Why Small Borrowers Bleed While Big Defaulters Thrive

In the bustling corridors of India's financial institutions, a silent narrative unfolds—one where the scales of justice seem tipped in favour of the corporate elite, leaving the MSMEs grappling with stringent recovery mechanisms. This dichotomy raises pressing questions about equity, accountability, and the very ethos of our banking system.

Picture this: One man walks into a bank in a luxury car after defaulting ₹500 crore. He gets coffee, a grace period, and a new repayment plan. Another man arrives on a scooter, having missed two EMIs on a ₹15 lakh loan. He gets a notice and a threat of asset seizure.

That's the story of India's credit culture. The bigger you owe, the softer the system becomes.

The Corporate Conundrum

Over the past decade, Indian banks have written off a staggering ₹16.35 lakh crore in bad loans, with public sector banks (PSBs) accounting for a significant portion. Notably, in fiscal year 2019 alone, write-offs peaked at ₹2.36 lakh crore. While Finance

Minister Nirmala Sitharaman clarified that write-offs don't absolve borrowers of their liabilities, the recovery rates tell a different story. Between fiscal year 2015 and fiscal year 2023, PSBs managed to recover only about 15.45% of the written-off amounts.

This leniency appears even more pronounced when juxtaposed with the treatment of large corporate defaulters. As of December 2024, 29 major companies had NPAs exceeding ₹1,000 crore each, totalling ₹61,027 crore. Despite these colossal defaults, the mechanisms for recovery seem sluggish, often entangled in prolonged legal proceedings or benefiting from restructuring schemes.

Imagine you borrow a bicycle from a friend. You're late in returning it, and he demands it back immediately. Someone else borrows a full-sized bus, crashes it, and still gets offered a spare one.

That's how MSMEs and corporates are treated differently. Small borrowers are squeezed. Big defaulters are indulged.

MSMEs: The Struggling Backbone

Contrastingly, MSMEs, which form the backbone of India's economy, face a more stringent financial environment. While credit disbursement to the MSME sector has seen a commendable increase—from ₹10.99 lakh crore in 2019 to ₹21.73 lakh crore in 2024—the sector continues to grapple with challenges in accessing timely and adequate credit. Only 15% of MSMEs in India have a bank loan, a stark contrast to 45% in some European countries.

Moreover, the recovery mechanisms for MSMEs are notably stringent. Unlike large corporates, MSMEs often lack the resources to navigate complex legal frameworks or negotiate favourable restructuring terms. The result is a higher incidence of asset seizures, business closures, and a general sense of financial precarity.

Suppose a school fines students who arrive five minutes late—but does nothing to those who skip class for weeks.

That's how RBI's NPA classification works. MSMEs are penalised for technical delays. But large firms in deep default stay unflagged through evergreening and lenient restructuring.

How True is the Perception that India's Banking System Favours Big Defaulters Over Struggling MSMEs?

It's a tale of two borrowers—one drives a Mercedes into a bank boardroom with a ₹5,000 crore default and walks out with a restructuring deal and a grace period. The other, a small manufacturer from Coimbatore, stumbles into the same branch with an unpaid ₹30 lakh term loan and is promptly slapped with SARFAESI[36] notices, asset seizures, and blacklisting. The contrast is not just jarring—it is systemic, institutionalised, and now deeply resented.

Imagine two runners preparing for a race. One has brand-new shoes, a personal coach, and a head start. The other has no shoes, no track access, and must fill forms in triplicate before starting.

That's India's MSMEs vs big corporates. MSMEs face a maze of compliance, while big players get banker concierges.

Over the past decade, India's banking system has written off a whopping ₹16.35 lakh crore

36. The SARFAESI Act, enacted in 2002, empowers banks and financial institutions in India to recover NPAs without court intervention by enforcing the security interest created on secured assets. It is especially significant for MSMEs and other borrowers, as it allows lenders to seize and auction collateral—such as land, machinery, or inventory—if loan repayments default, making timely compliance and dispute resolution critical for small businesses.

in bad loans. That figure—gleaned from Parliament replies and RBI circulars—is not merely a spreadsheet entry. It is an indictment of policy bias and a mirror to our financial sector's skewed priorities. Most of these write-offs are linked to large corporate accounts. A list of the top 100 wilful defaulters in India reads like a who's who of Indian boardrooms—big infra players, real estate giants, steel magnates, aviation czars. As of 2023, over 90% of gross NPAs by value were from loans exceeding ₹5 crore.

To be clear, a write-off does not mean a waiver. Banks claim they will pursue recovery. But the facts speak otherwise. As per data tabled in Parliament in March 2024, banks managed to recover barely 15% of these amounts over a nine-year span. Meanwhile, those very borrowers float new firms, bid for government contracts, or acquire sick units under the same IBC[37] they previously used to exit their own debts. If the system sounds rigged, that's because it often is.

The MSME Squeeze: Strangled by Rules, Starved of Relief

Flip the coin and you find a very different India. The MSME sector—spread across Ludhiana, Tiruppur, Rajkot, Morbi, and

> Imagine getting a school report card that lists only your English and Math scores—but skips Science and Social Studies.
>
> That's India's banking disclosure system. We know the total write-offs, but not who got them, and how much was recovered by borrower size. Transparency stops where it matters most.

37. 'IBC: The Insolvency and Bankruptcy Code (IBC) is a law that provides a time-bound process to resolve insolvency of companies and individuals when they cannot repay their debts. It aims to either revive the business quickly or close it efficiently, so lenders recover money faster and economic resources are not wasted

Guwahati—employs over 110 million people and contributes more than 30% to GDP. These are job creators, not job seekers. And yet, they face the most brutal lending terms, the lowest tolerance for failure, and the harshest recovery mechanisms.

In Surat's textile markets, small dyeing units shut shop overnight in the wake of GST rollouts and power tariff hikes. In Hyderabad's pharma clusters, small API producers lost orders to Chinese competitors during COVID, missed two loan EMIs, and were declared NPAs. In Bengaluru, first-generation tech entrepreneurs operating with small lines of credit were told to pledge their personal homes when venture capital fell through. The system does not forgive MSME failure—it punishes it.

Even the much-celebrated CGTMSE, touted as a risk-sharing mechanism, is underutilised. Less than 10% of MSME loans across PSBs in the fiscal year 2022 were routed through CGTMSE. The banks often reject coverage due to procedural headaches or low claim settlements. The RBI's 2023 report on priority sector lending admitted that most MSME loans still require collateral, defeating the entire purpose of risk mitigation.

How the Same Default Is Treated Differently

To understand the systemic bias, consider two parallel cases:

In 2019, IL&FS defaulted on over ₹90,000 crore. What followed was a government-initiated rescue operation, board takeover, and legal shielding of promoters under court supervision.

> Say a village clinic treats only the rich patients with free medicine and personal care. The poor are asked to fill out forms, bring old records, and wait in line for days.
>
> That's how schemes like CGTMSE are treated. Despite being meant for MSMEs, banks often reject or delay claims. The very people who need it most are left untreated.

> Imagine being asked for three documents to get a ₹5,000 loan—PAN, Aadhaar, and a utility bill. But the person taking a ₹5,000 crore loan gets a handshake and a 'let's talk terms' meeting.
>
> That's the compliance paradox. Small businesses are buried in red tape, while large borrowers negotiate their defaults.

Though warranted for systemic stability, the same urgency was never extended to MSMEs hit by the twin shocks of demonetisation and COVID-19. In Moradabad, a group of brass exporters who defaulted on working capital loans post-2020 were neither restructured nor rescued. Instead, their assets were auctioned by regional branches of PSBs without even hearing their viability pitches.

Then there's the case of Bhushan Steel—once declared a wilful defaulter. After defaulting on ₹56,000 crore, it was bought out by Tata Steel under IBC with a 37% recovery rate for banks. Meanwhile, in Tiruppur, over 400 MSMEs went into forced closure between 2020 and 2023 for failing to repay small-ticket loans. Their founders, mostly sole proprietors, were chased personally for repayment. There were no buyers, no revival packages, no IBC haircuts—just bank notices and lost livelihoods.

The Razor's Edge of Compliance

For small businesses, the problem is not just credit denial—it is compliance overkill. RBI's Enhanced Due Diligence (EDD) and PSB loan renewal systems require audited financials, GST filings, IT returns, export-import certifications, and, increasingly, integration with portal-based tracking systems. A vegetable dehydration unit in Bhavnagar recently lost a ₹75 lakh cash credit facility renewal because its GST software failed to update vendor-wise supply data. The bank marked it as high risk and refused renewal.

> You miss a bus once, and the driver bans you from riding again. Another passenger crashes ten trains, and still gets a seat.
>
> That's the double standard in wilful defaulter classification. MSMEs are blacklisted for small delays; big borrowers walk away with restructured loans.

Compare this with large companies that routinely get 'evergreened' loans—fresh disbursements to repay earlier dues—and multiple debt restructurings through consortiums. The Kamath Committee recommendations during the COVID period were supposed to help MSMEs restructure. But out of ₹1.7 lakh crore of restructured loans under the scheme, only 18% went to MSMEs. The rest was lapped up by mid-sized and large borrowers.

A Failed Ecosystem of Support

NABARD (National Bank for Agriculture and Rural Development), SIDBI, NSIC, NIMSME (National Institute for Micro, Small, and Medium Enterprises), NIESBUD (National Institute for Entrepreneurship and Small Business Development)—the alphabet soup of MSME support agencies—remain mostly on paper. Field implementation is limited, budgets are thin, and coordination with banks is poor. There's little evidence that any of these agencies have prevented MSME defaults or ensured post-loan handholding. As per a 2023 CAG audit of DC-MSME (Development Commissioner-Micro, Small, and Medium Enterprises) field offices, 68% of 'handholding beneficiaries' under entrepreneurship programmes had no follow-up loan or business activity after training. No wonder critics will jump to say that this is not capacity building, but rather administrative theatrics.

Budget 2025: A Step Towards Equitable Solutions

Recognising these challenges, the Union Budget 2025 introduced several measures aimed at addressing the disparities faced by MSMEs:

1. **Enhanced Credit Guarantee Cover:** The credit guarantee cover for micro and small enterprises has been increased from ₹5 crore to ₹10 crore, unlocking an additional ₹1.5 lakh crore in credit over the next five years. For startups, the guarantee cover has been doubled from ₹10 crore to ₹20 crore, with a reduced fee of 1% for loans in 27 priority sectors. Exporter MSMEs will benefit from term loans up to ₹20 crore with enhanced guarantee cover.

2. **Revised MSME Classification Criteria:** To help MSMEs scale operations and access better resources, the investment and turnover limits for classification have been increased by 2.5 times and 2 times, respectively. This move is expected to improve efficiency, technological adoption, and employment generation.

3. **Support for Startups and First-Time Entrepreneurs:** A new Fund of Funds with ₹10,000 crore will be established to expand support for startups. Additionally, a scheme for 5 lakh first-time women, SC, and ST entrepreneurs will provide term loans up to ₹2 crore over five years, incorporating lessons from the Stand-Up India scheme.

4. **Customised Credit Cards for Micro Enterprises**: A new customised credit card scheme will provide ₹5 lakh in credit to micro enterprises registered on the Udyam portal, with 10 lakh cards set to be issued in the first year.

5. **Focus on Labour-Intensive Sectors:** A Focus Product Scheme for the footwear and leather sector will support design, component manufacturing, and non-leather footwear

production, expected to create 22 lakh jobs and generate a turnover of ₹4 lakh crore. A new scheme for the toy sector will promote cluster development and skill-building, positioning India as a global hub for toy manufacturing.

Fixing the Tilted Playing Field: Real Solutions, Not Sermons

Let us now examine if there are any global lessons and how other nations support their MSMEs or small businesses in times of distress.

While India's MSMEs navigate a labyrinth of compliance and limited support, many developed and developing countries have instituted robust frameworks to bolster their small enterprises, especially during economic downturns. These international practices offer valuable insights into creating a more equitable environment for MSMEs.

Developed Economies: Proactive and Inclusive Support

In the US, the SBA plays a pivotal role in supporting MSMEs. Through programmes like the Paycheck Protection Program (PPP) and Economic Injury Disaster Loans (EIDL), the SBA provided over $800 billion in aid during the COVID-19 pandemic, ensuring businesses could maintain payroll and cover essential expenses. Additionally, the SBA's 7(a) loan programme offers government-backed loans, reducing the risk for lenders and making credit more accessible to small businesses.

Germany's 'Kurzarbeit' scheme is another exemplar, where the government subsidises wages for employees working reduced hours, allowing businesses to retain staff during economic slowdowns. This approach not only preserves employment but also ensures that companies can quickly ramp up operations post-crisis.

Developing Nations: Tailored Interventions for MSMEs

In Indonesia, the government introduced the People's Business Credit (KUR) programme, offering subsidised loans to MSMEs with minimal collateral requirements. This initiative is understood to have significantly improved credit access for small businesses, fostering entrepreneurship and economic growth.

Brazil's National Bank for Economic and Social Development (BNDES) provides targeted financial products for MSMEs, including credit lines for innovation, export support, and working capital. These programmes are designed to address specific challenges faced by small enterprises, ensuring they receive the necessary support to thrive.

Comparative Insights: India's Position

While India has made strides in supporting MSMEs, especially with recent budgetary provisions that enhance credit guarantees and redefine MSME classifications, there remains a gap in the depth and responsiveness of support compared to international counterparts. For instance, during the pandemic, Indian MSMEs faced challenges in accessing timely financial aid, whereas countries like the US and Germany swiftly deployed substantial support mechanisms.

Moreover, India's focus has often been on credit facilitation, with less emphasis on comprehensive support encompassing wage subsidies, innovation grants, and market access programmes. To bridge this gap, India could consider adopting a more holistic approach, drawing lessons from global best practices to create a resilient and inclusive ecosystem for its MSMEs.

If India is serious about its 'Vocal for Local'[38] and 'Atmanirbhar[39] Bharat' slogans, the banking system needs a structural overhaul that treats MSMEs as economic assets, not statistical liabilities. Here's what needs to happen—and fast.

First, the Insolvency and Bankruptcy Code must include a pre-pack resolution model exclusively for MSMEs. This mechanism should allow small businesses to restructure debts under ₹5 crore through a simplified, time-bound process with a single creditor class vote. The UK and Singapore offer templates that work—India must adapt them.

Second, the RBI should mandate that all MSME loan accounts under ₹2 crore must be evaluated for restructuring before being declared NPAs. This pre-NPA restructuring window should have a statutory form, similar to Form 26AS in taxes, where all communications between borrower and lender are recorded and reviewable by the Banking Ombudsman—no more backdoor blacklisting.

Third, CGTMSE must be made mandatory for 20% of all new MSME loans in PSBs and cooperative banks. The Finance Ministry should create a dashboard, tracking approvals, claim settlements, and rejections—accessible to the public and audited by the CAG annually. This would end the current opacity and ensure that the guarantee coverage actually works as intended.

Fourth, we need a Behavioural Credit Rating system for MSMEs based on cash flow data, digital utility payments,

---

38. Vocal for Local is a campaign launched under the Atmanirbhar Bharat initiative that urges Indian consumers to support and promote locally made products and services. The idea is to boost indigenous industries, crafts, and startups by creating demand within the domestic market and eventually making them globally competitive.

39. Atmanirbhar Bharat (Self-Reliant India) is a vision launched by the Indian government in 2020 to make India economically self-sufficient by promoting domestic manufacturing, reducing import dependence, and enhancing local supply chains. It encourages innovation, entrepreneurship, and resilience across sectors, aiming to transform India into a global manufacturing and export hub.

GST returns, and e-commerce performance. Credit bureaus, like CRIF (Centre for Research in International Finance) or Equifax, should be compelled to issue dynamic MSME credit health cards that are updated quarterly and linked to the Udyam registration. Banks must accept this as a valid metric alongside traditional CIBIL scores.

Fifth, wilful defaulter classification norms for MSMEs must have a 'materiality and intent' test, especially for loans below ₹5 crore. A technical delay should not become financial exile. RBI's master circular must be amended to create a three-member independent panel in each bank to vet such classifications.

Sixth, we need MSME Banking Benches at DRTs (Debt Recovery Tribunals). These should be staffed by retired district judges, ex-entrepreneurs, and financial consultants who understand both default and viability. A Financial Services Lokpal for MSMEs with powers akin to SEBI's adjudicating officer must be instituted to handle complaints against high-handed bank behaviour.

And finally, the RBI and Ministry of Finance must be compelled to release a quarterly Default and Recovery Transparency Report. This should show disaggregated write-off and recovery figures by loan size and sector. The public deserves to know whether the bank manager is chasing a pan masala vendor in Kanpur while ignoring a steel baron's ₹3,000 crore default.

Conclusion: The Lasting Cost of Unfairness

India's banking system today rewards size, not sincerity. A small unit with a missed EMI is declared non-cooperative; a large borrower with a ₹10,000 crore hole is invited to lunch. This duality is eroding not just faith in institutions, but the very spirit of enterprise among India's grassroots wealth creators.

The MSME sector doesn't ask for privilege. It asks for fairness, for rules that don't bend with muscle or money, and for a banking system that values viability over visibility. The sooner we level the playing field, the faster India will move from survival to true economic self-reliance.

Let us now examine the results of the evaluation of the achievement of MSMEs by the RBI and issues arising therefrom in the next chapter.

References:

1. The New Wave Indian MSME – a KPMG study, 2015.

2. Enhancing MSMEs competitiveness in India: a study by Institute for Competitiveness for NITI Aayog (March 2025).

3. A Model Comprehensive MSME policy for Indian states by CSIS – Wadhwani Chair in US-China; report by Richard M Rossow (29 November 2022).

4. An Assessment of the State of Risk Capital Finance to the MSME sectors in India: International Finance Corporation – World Bank Group (in partnership with Government of Japan).

5. https://www.data.gov.in/resource/bank-wise-details-loans-written-scheduled-commercial-banks-2014-15-2023-24

6. https://www.niti.gov.in/sites/default/files/2025-05/Enhancing_Competitiveness_of_MSMEs_in_India.pdf

7. https://www.csis.org/analysis/model-comprehensive-msme-policy-indian-states

8. https://www.mckinsey.com/mgi/our-research/a-microscope-on-small-businesses-spotting-opportunities-to-boost-productivity

9. https://www.ideasforindia.in/topics/macroeconomics/is-small-beautiful-a-critical-evaluation-of-msme-policy-and-performance-in-india.html

10. https://assets.kpmg.com/content/dam/kpmg/pdf/2016/03/The-new-wave-Indian-MSME.pdf

11. https://www.ifc.org/content/dam/ifc/doc/mgrt/assessment-of-state-of-risk-finance-for-msmes-in-india.pdf

12. https://pib.gov.in/PressReleasePage.aspx?PRID=2099687

13. https://pib.gov.in/PressReleaseIframePage.aspx?PRID=2098389

14. 'Banks write off bad loans worth Rs 16.35 lakh crore in last 10 years', The Economic Times, April 2025.

15. 'Ministry of Finance says overall credit disbursement to Priority Sectors jumped 85% from 2019 to 2024', Business Standard, March 2025.

16. Swaminathan J, 'MSMEs – bridging the credit gap through improving access to formal finance', Bank for International Settlements, November 2024.

17. 'MSME Finance Gap', SME Finance Forum, 2019.

18. 'Banks wrote off bad loans worth ₹16.35 lakh crore in last 10 years', Hindustan Times, April 2025.

19. 'Rs 16.35 Lakh Crore Bad Loans Written Off by Banks in Past 10 Years', Moneylife, April 2025.

20. 'MSME Report August 2023', SIDBI, August 2023.

21. 'For loans up to ₹25 lakh for Micro and Small Enterprises (MSE)', Press Information Bureau, April 2025.

22. 'CONTRIBUTION OF MSMEs TO THE GDP', Press Information Bureau, July 2024.

23. 'ACCESS TO CREDIT FOR INDIAN MSMEs', UNICTRAL, 2021.

24. 'Banks wrote off Rs 16.35 lakh crore bad loans over decade: Centre', Zee Business, April 2025.

25. 'Priority sector lending', Wikipedia, December 2024.

26. 'Micro Units Development and Refinance Agency Bank', Wikipedia, March 2025.

27. 'Kerala Financial Corporation', Wikipedia, January 2025.

28. 'Small finance bank', Wikipedia, March 2025.

29. 'GetVantage', Wikipedia, April 2025.

30. 'The Regulations That Govern Banking in India', Investopedia, November 2014.

CHAPTER 13

◆◆◆

The UK Sinha Report: Still Waiting for Action

Imagine your bathroom has a leaking tap. An expert architect draws a fantastic blueprint for a full bathroom renovation, with digital faucets, motion sensors, and mood lighting. But no plumber shows up.

That's the Sinha Committee Report. Great ideas—digital invoices, PAN-based IDs, simplified laws—but without real implementation muscle, nothing changes.

The UK Sinha Committee, constituted by the RBI in December 2018, was tasked with an urgent mission: to rescue India's beleaguered MSME sector from systemic neglect, policy confusion, and structural fragility. Armed with insights from industry veterans, central bankers, multilateral agencies, and entrepreneurs across India, the committee's report stands as one of the most ambitious blueprints ever drawn for the revival and long-term sustainability of India's MSMEs. However, while the recommendations brim with vision and urgency, the document also lays bare the deep fissures that have long hobbled this critical sector.

The backdrop was grim. Despite accounting for 30% of India's GDP, over 40% of exports, and employing 111 million people, the MSME sector remained largely informal, underfinanced, and chronically vulnerable. Successive governments had offered schemes in silos—credit here, training there—but never a holistic push to lift the sector out of its reactive, survivalist mode. The committee's starting point was this recognition: that MSMEs were fighting twenty-first-century battles with twentieth-century tools, stuck in a maze of outdated definitions, fragmented data, weak institutions, and vanishing risk capital.

The report begins with a powerful assertion that the time had come to ditch the archaic MSMED Act, 2006, in favour of a comprehensive MSME Code—something akin to a modern, consolidated law that streamlines definitions, simplifies registration, enables data triangulation, and eliminates inspector raj. The current investment-based classification was dismissed as opaque and distortionary. In its place, the committee championed a turnover-based metric, aligned with GST data, and proposed that Parliament delegate definitional authority to the Executive to ensure agility in a rapidly evolving economic landscape.

> Suppose you ask a village farmer to use a drone for spraying fertiliser. But he doesn't have a smart-phone, reliable electricity, or Internet.
>
> That's what many MSMEs face. The committee's digital dreams clash with on-ground realities—low digital literacy, patchy infrastructure, and poor handholding.

Among the most glaring issues the committee dissected was the plague of delayed payments to MSMEs—arguably the sector's single greatest nemesis. Buyers, especially large corporates and PSUs, treat MSME dues as working capital. Despite legal protections under the MSMED Act, enforcement was toothless. The committee made a bold pitch: make it mandatory for MSMEs to upload all invoices above a threshold to an Information Utility regulated by the Insolvency and Bankruptcy Board of India. These invoices would act as digital grenades, naming and shaming defaulting buyers and forcing transparency into the system.

But delays weren't the only form of systemic strangulation. MSMEs faced an obstacle course of overlapping registrations—from Udyog Aadhaar to NSIC to GSTN. The committee's prescription? One enterprise, one identity—PAN should become the universal business identifier across platforms. Similarly, the report took aim at the proliferation of facilitation councils—barely one per state in many cases—and called for a significant expansion to ensure real-time redressal of payment grievances.

On the question of credit, the committee pulled no punches. Banks were chastised for continuing to rely on collateral and outdated lending practices, while data-rich but credit-starved MSMEs were left out in the cold. It advocated for a decisive shift toward cash-flow-based lending, enabled by GST and soon-to-be-operational Account Aggregators. The PSBLoansIn59Minutes portal, while promising, catered only to existing borrowers. The committee demanded it be widened to accommodate first-time borrowers and urged that in-principle approvals be acted upon within ten days, with the loan limit extended to ₹5 crore.

SIDBI, India's apex development bank for MSMEs, was simultaneously praised and burdened with more responsibilities. The committee called for channelling banks' PSL (Priority Sector Lending) shortfalls to SIDBI for cluster development, infrastructure loans to states, and market-making in SME debt. It even floated the idea of a SIDBI-led Fund of Funds to seed venture capital aimed at MSMEs, mirroring models from Israel and Malaysia.

Perhaps the most radical intervention proposed was the creation of a ₹5,000 crore Distressed Asset Fund to revive

MSMEs in clusters hit by regulatory shocks—such as bans on plastic or anti-dumping actions. This was not charity, the committee argued, but a strategic buffer to unlock stuck assets and reboot economic activity. Similarly, the report recommended revamping MUDRA's operating model and extending its guarantee coverage to Self-Help Group (SHG) enterprises, an acknowledgement of the informal sector's contribution to MSME activity.

One of the stark weaknesses the committee identified was the lack of credible, real-time data. The Udyog Aadhaar portal, though well-intentioned, was plagued by self-declared and unaudited data. The Data Bank lacked validation, and Economic Census definitions often excluded retail trade, transport, and services—the very backbone of urban and peri-urban entrepreneurship. The committee called for administrative data collection by the MSME ministry every three years, decoupled from the CSO's (Central Statistical Organisation) Economic Census, and a revamp of Udyog Aadhaar to capture dynamic, validated inputs.

The committee's reflections on global best practices offered a sobering contrast. Countries like China, Malaysia, Brazil, and Mexico have built robust ecosystems—central coordinating agencies, dedicated venture capital channels, cluster-based innovation networks, and public procurement systems that do more than pay lip service to MSMEs. In India, procurement policies remained riddled with loopholes. Even though

> Think of a small-town hospital where one doctor is expected to be the surgeon, pediatrician, radiologist, and pharmacist—all at once.
>
> That's how SIDBI is treated in the report. It's asked to do everything—fund infrastructure, manage venture capital, guide NBFCs, and monitor loans—but lacks the staff and systems to handle such scale.

25% procurement from MSMEs was mandated for PSUs, it wasn't enforced. The committee proposed routing all such transactions through the GeM (Government e-Marketplace) portal to ensure transparency and traceability.

Despite these powerful insights and ambitious proposals, the report also exposed the systemic inertia within the ecosystem. Many ideas—such as EDCs (Entrepreneurship Development Cells) in every district, the integration of GeM[40] and TreDS,[41] the creation of Loan Service Providers (LSPs), and the introduction of e-liens—were either too dependent on inter-agency coordination or vulnerable to turf wars between ministries. The committee admitted as much, urging the creation of a National MSME Council chaired by the Prime Minister and replicated at the state level to break the bureaucratic logjam.

What emerges from the Sinha Committee report is a sector caught in a double bind: immense potential throttled by policy neglect and institutional sclerosis. The recommendations offer a real opportunity for a reset: a simplified legal framework, digitised credit systems, risk capital for innovation, and cluster-based development models. But unless these are pursued with urgency, cross-departmental coordination, and political will, the document risks becoming just another report that gets read, quoted, and forgotten.

---

40. GeM is an online procurement platform launched by the Government of India to facilitate transparent, efficient, and paperless purchases of goods and services by central and state government departments from registered sellers, including MSMEs. It empowers small businesses by offering them direct access to government buyers without middlemen, thus expanding their market reach and improving payment reliability.

41. TReDS (Trade Receivables Discounting System) is a digital platform regulated by the RBI that enables MSMEs to auction their trade receivables (i.e., unpaid invoices) to financiers for early payment at competitive rates. This helps MSMEs maintain healthy cash flows and working capital by resolving the chronic problem of delayed payments from larger buyers or government departments

Imagine making a new rule that only people with passports can get subsidised ration. Most don't have passports, so they're left out.

That's the risk of using PAN as a compulsory ID for MSMEs. Many small units fear formalisation and don't have PANs. So instead of easing access, it may shut the door.

The MSME sector does not need sympathy. It needs systems. The UK Sinha Committee handed us a blueprint. The real question is: Who will implement it, and when?

The Devil in the Details: Where the Sinha Committee Stumbles

For all its breadth and ambition, the UK Sinha Committee report is not without its blind spots, overestimations, and deeply impractical prescriptions. If the report lays out a grand blueprint for MSME revitalisation, it also reveals a bureaucratic optimism that often underestimates ground-level realities and systemic inertia.

At the heart of its impracticalities lies the sheer scale of coordination it demands between ministries, financial institutions, regulatory bodies, and state governments—each a silo with its own pace, priorities, and turf consciousness. The committee recommends a National MSME Council chaired by the Prime Minister, and similar state-level bodies to synchronise efforts. But history offers a cautionary tale: India's policymaking machinery is notoriously fragmented. Between the Ministry of MSME, the Department of Financial Services, the RBI, SIDBI, GSTN, state DICs, and others, the 'whole-of-government' approach is easier written than operationalised. There is no institutional roadmap provided in the report to cut through this bureaucratic tangle.

Another impracticality is the committee's unqualified faith in digital solutions. From invoice uploading to online registration, e-liens, PSBLoansIn59Minutes, and the integration of land records with loan portals, the report imagines a tech utopia where government databases talk to each other, credit risk is auto-scored, and MSMEs glide through a seamless digital interface. The reality is far messier. Even in urban India, MSMEs often lack digital literacy or access to high-speed Internet. In rural areas, connectivity, language barriers, and data integrity issues make such visions aspirational at best. Worse, the proposed linking of platforms like TReDS, GeM, CGTMSE, and land registries assumes interoperability that does not exist today, and would require years of legislative and infrastructural overhaul to materialise.

The proposal to create a ₹5,000 crore Distressed Asset Fund, although well-intentioned, comes with slippery execution terrain. Identifying deserving clusters affected by regulatory shocks (like the plastic ban) is not an exact science. In practice, it could become a honey pot for interest groups and lead to the same leakages and politicisation that afflict most rehabilitation schemes. The analogy to the Textile Upgradation Fund Scheme (TUFS) is telling—TUFS itself has been repeatedly flagged by the CAG and internal audits for inefficiencies and under-utilisation.

Suppose a company says, 'We've set up grievance boxes for all employees.' But there's only one box for 3,000 staff—and it's located in the CEO's cabin.

That's how MSME Facilitation Councils operate. There's often just one per state, making timely redressal of payment delays impossible.

Perhaps one of the most glaring drawbacks is the committee's overreliance on SIDBI. The report places SIDBI at the centre of nearly every solution: infrastructure funding, cluster development, debt market-making, venture capital support, and handholding of NBFCs and MFIs. But SIDBI, in its current avatar, is ill-equipped to shoulder this burden. It lacks the staffing depth, regional penetration, and capital base to play the multifaceted role envisioned in the report. There is also no discussion on how SIDBI will be recapitalised or restructured to meet these expectations.

The idea of making PAN the UEI also has its limitations. Many MSMEs, especially in the micro and informal segments, operate without PAN, and are wary of formalisation due to fear of tax compliance burdens. For such enterprises, PAN as a compulsory gateway may lead to exclusion rather than inclusion, defeating the very spirit of ease of doing business.

> Imagine that the central government announces a national festival—without asking states to join or planning how it'll be celebrated locally.
>
> That's how Centre-heavy the Sinha Report is. It underplays the vital role of state governments in power, land, and compliance—all critical for MSMEs.

Even some of the progressive recommendations falter in feasibility. Making PSUs route all 25% MSME procurement through GeM sounds clean on paper, but it will require rewriting procurement manuals, retraining staff, and re-engineering vendor systems across dozens of central and state PSUs. There is no evidence in the report that such operational hurdles were studied, nor is a phased roadmap provided.

Finally, the committee's silence on the role of state governments beyond token mention is troubling. Land, electricity, local compliance inspections, and much of MSME handholding fall within state jurisdiction. Yet the report treats Centre-led initiatives as the silver bullet, missing the opportunity to deepen federal cooperation or incentivise state-level reforms through competitive rankings or fiscal grants.

In sum, while the UK Sinha Committee is a remarkable intellectual exercise, it veers toward technocratic idealism in places where hard-nosed realism was needed. Its architectural sketches are brilliant, but its civil engineering is weak. Unless translated into time-bound, accountable, and state-integrated action plans, the report risks joining a long list of well-written documents that gather dust, even as MSMEs continue to drown in paperwork, payment delays, and policy neglect.

We will move to a critical evaluation of the achievements of the Office of the Development Commissioner, MSME, with special focus on 2022–23 and 2023-24 in the next chapter.

References:

Primary Source:

1. UK Sinha Committee Report on MSMEs (June 2019).

   Constituted by the Reserve Bank of India to propose long-term solutions for the financial and economic sustainability of the MSME sector.

   Full Text: https://bit.ly/4a6lLsQ

Secondary Sources and Contextual References:

1. Comptroller and Auditor General (CAG) of India Reports on TUFS (Textile Upgradation Fund Scheme).

   CAG reports have raised concerns over inefficiencies, poor targeting, and under-utilisation in TUFS, which the Sinha Committee proposes as a model for the Distressed Asset Fund.

2. SIDBI Annual Reports and RBI's Financial Stability Reports (2018–2023).

   Provide insights into SIDBI's capital adequacy, structural limitations, and performance constraints that cast doubt on its capacity to take on expanded roles as envisaged in the Committee Report.

SIDBI Annual Report archive: https://sidbi.in/en/financials

3. Government e-Marketplace (GeM) Procurement Policy Guidelines (2020).

Details issues with the enforcement of mandatory 25% procurement from MSMEs by PSUs.

Source: GeM portal and Ministry of Commerce procurement circulars.

4. Ministry of MSME Annual Reports (2017–2023).

Contain registration data, status of Udyog Aadhaar portal, and implementation status of schemes such as MUDRA and Cluster Development Programme.

https://msme.gov.in/annual-report

5. Economic Survey of India (2018–2022 editions).

Contextual references for the digital divide, formalisation through GST, challenges in state-level policy implementation, and credit access.

Ministry of Finance, Government of India: https://www.indiabudget.gov.in/economicsurvey/

6. NITI Aayog Discussion Paper on Reforming MSME Policy (2020).

Critiques centralisation and lack of state government engagement in MSME reform design.

https://niti.gov.in

7. World Bank Group (2018). 'Principles for Public Credit Guarantee Schemes for SMEs'.

Cited in the Sinha Committee report for best practices on regulating credit guarantee schemes like CGTMSE.

https://documents.worldbank.org/en/publication/documents-reports/documentdetail/576061543411490762

8. Standing Committee on Finance (2018–19): 'Credit Flow to the MSME Sector' (Lok Sabha Secretariat).

Discusses issues in delayed payments, weak TReDS uptake, and bottlenecks in schemes like MUDRA.

https://loksabhadocs.nic.in/

9. India Stack and Account Aggregator framework documentation by RBI and NPCI.

Supports analysis of overdependence on digitised data aggregation for MSME lending without sufficient on-ground infrastructure or borrower preparedness.

https://www.rbi.org.in, https://www.npci.org.in

CHAPTER 14

◆◆◆

Self-Certified Glory: DC-MSME's Reports vs CAG's Reality

> Imagine a school that publishes a glossy brochure saying, 'We taught 10,000 students this year!' But it doesn't say how many passed, dropped out, or learned anything.
>
> That's what DC-MSME's skill programmes look like. Thousands may have been 'trained', but no one tracks if they got jobs, started businesses, or even finished the course.

If annual reports were .the sole metric of performance, the Office of the Development Commissioner (MSME) would appear to be in top gear—churning out numbers, launching schemes, showcasing digital dashboards, and proudly recording milestones in entrepreneurship training, employment, and cluster development. But scratch the surface and a less flattering story emerges—of patchy implementation, questionable data verifiability, overstated outputs, underwhelming outcomes, and a growing disconnect between headline claims and grassroots realities.

The Development Commissioner (MSME), as an attached office of the ministry, carries the institutional legacy of promoting MSMEs through a web of 32 Development and Facilitation Offices (DFOs), 30 Technology Centres (Tool Rooms), and other autonomous bodies. On paper, its functions span everything from policy advice and market intelligence to facilitating credit, technology upgradation, skill development, and exports. However, in 2022–23, these sprawling responsibilities yielded a mixed bag of results that merit far more scrutiny than celebration.

Let's start with the headline numbers in skill development. The Entrepreneurship and Skill Development Programme (ESDP), one of DC-MSME's flagship offerings, claims to have trained 66,502 beneficiaries through 1,105 programmes up to January 2023. But here's the catch—there's no audit trail of how many of these trainees transitioned into viable self-employment or sustained jobs. The report proudly lists expenditure of ₹34.21 crore against an allocation of ₹40 crore, but does not bother to publish post-training impact metrics, drop-out rates, or third-party evaluation findings. The achievements, therefore, are volumetric, not qualitative.

> Suppose you throw a wedding, and later claim '2,000 family members attended'—including the flower vendor, the security guard, and the DJ's assistant.
>
> That's how SFURTI (Scheme of Fund for Regeneration of Traditional Industries) defines 'beneficiaries'. People attending a workshop or camp are shown as artisans uplifted, even if they were never part of any income-generation plan.

Tool Rooms and Technical Institutions (TRs and TIs)—another arm under the commissioner—claim to have supported 31,554 units and trained over 1.4 lakh youth in the previous year (2021–22). However, the 2022–23 report is

Think of a restaurant with an impressive digital menu, QR codes, and an app—but no kitchen, no chef, and no food.

That's what the ministry's 97.67% digital claim feels like. The backend is digitised, but actual MSME users—especially in rural areas—still rely on cash and paper. It's digital for the system, not the people.

strikingly silent on the corresponding outcomes or even revised numbers. Have these TRs generated sustained livelihoods? Has the training kept up with Industry 4.0 demands? The silence is revealing.

The situation becomes murkier when one examines employment figures. Under the PMEGP scheme, 46,808 new enterprises were financed, with a reported subsidy outgo of over ₹1,500 crore. But even here, the report glosses over the crucial data point: how many of these enterprises survived beyond the first year, or worse, how many were ghost units submitted to claim margin money subsidies? No verification mechanism, geo-tagged inspections, or cross-referenced bank data are presented to back these numbers.

The numbers under the KVI sector—a favourite of every annual report—claimed 1.66 crore employment as of December 2022 and a projected 1.70 crore by March 2023. This figure increased to 1.87 crore in 2023–24 and 1.94 crore in 2024–25—all estimated and not verifiable independently or objectively. The real questions are left unanswered: Is this cumulative or concurrent employment? What is the nature of this work—full-time, part-time, or seasonal? Are the earnings even above subsistence levels? As the CAG and other studies have shown earlier, employment numbers in khadi are notoriously inflated through conversion formulas based on yarn production and not actual man-hours.

Even the much-touted cluster development efforts under SFURTI, where over 20 lakh artisans were reported as 'beneficiaries' in 2022–23, suffer from similar opacity. The term 'beneficiary' is used elastically, often referring to people merely covered under awareness camps or incidental contacts rather than sustainable livelihood interventions. No income benchmarks or third-party audits are cited to validate these 'regeneration of traditional industries' claims.

> You spend lakhs setting up a gym in your society. But there's no trainer, no regular users, and the machines gather dust. Still, you proudly list it as a 'fitness initiative'.
>
> That's what many Common Facility Centres under SFURTI have become. Nice infrastructure, little usage, and no real impact.

On the infrastructure and digital fronts, too, the achievements sound impressive until examined closely. The ministry reports that a dazzling 97.67% of all financial transactions were done digitally up to December 2022. But this is aggregated across all departments—including NSIC, Coir Board, and others—without differentiating the value or volume per agency. Moreover, no audit or independent digital literacy assessment of actual MSME users is referenced to verify whether the intended target groups (often first-time rural entrepreneurs) are truly transacting digitally or whether the offices themselves are merely pushing backend digital entries to meet KPI (Key Performance Indicator) targets.

> Suppose a student registers for a five-day class but drops out after Day 1. Yet the school marks them 'trained' and adds them to its success tally.
>
> That's how ESDP numbers are often inflated. Attendance, completion, and outcomes are rarely verified.

Even in grievance redressal, a sector that speaks directly to governance sensitivity, only 60 pending cases are reported on CPGRAMS,[42] and a separate 'eSamadhan' portal has been launched. However, there is no commentary on closure quality, average redressal time, or whether complaints related to corruption, fund delays, or discrimination are handled with transparency.

Meanwhile, the ministry also proudly showcased its presence in multiple international expos, signed MoUs with 19 countries, and conducted high-profile summits in association with bodies like FICCI (Federation of Indian Chambers of Commerce & Industry). However, such diplomacy-heavy, event-centric activities, while excellent for optics, have little bearing on the everyday struggles of MSMEs dealing with power cuts, GST refund delays, unpaid dues from PSUs, or bank credit rejections.

> Imagine giving a debit card to someone who's never used an ATM (Automated Teller Machine). You then declare, 'We've enabled 100% digital financial access!'
>
> That's the digital inclusion illusion. Backend staff may record digital entries, but frontline MSMEs often don't know how to transact online.

The most telling indicator of performance, however, lies in the discrepancy between budget allocations and actual fund utilisation. Despite fancy targets, several schemes show underwhelming expenditure. For instance, under the Digital MSME initiative—a scheme intended to mainstream Industry 4.0 tools like ERP (Enterprise Resource Planning) and cloud computing—not a single rupee was spent as of 31 December 2022, despite an allocation of ₹7 crore. Similarly, the Lean Manufacturing scheme spent barely ₹2.25 crore out of the ₹8.34 crore allocated. This is not just bureaucratic inertia—it is a

42. CPGRAMS: 'Centralised Public Grievance Redressal and Monitoring System'.

symptom of chronic incapacity to roll out complex, technology-heavy initiatives with the speed and sophistication the sector desperately needs.

A glaring limitation across the report is the absence of independent, third-party evaluations. Most achievements are self-reported. Beneficiary feedback is cherry-picked or absent. Outcome indicators are replaced by input counts. No red-flag mechanisms, exception reports, or audit validations are shared. This lack of objectivity and critical introspection reduces the annual report to little more than a bureaucratic compliance exercise.

In sum, the 2022–23 performance report of the Office of DC-MSME is a classic case of achievement inflation. It reads more like a promotional brochure than a diagnostic report. The numbers may look big and bold, but when stripped of their context, clarity, and credibility, they reveal a machinery that is struggling to keep pace with India's complex, competitive, and rapidly digitising enterprise landscape. The gap between planning and execution, between headline and impact, remains as wide as ever.

You build a flashy app for students to apply for scholarships. It works only in English, crashes on older phones, and requires high-speed Internet.

That's like launching e-portals for MSMEs without testing real user access, language support, or connectivity. Usage stats often reflect system-side uploads, not real empowerment·

What's urgently needed is not more schemes or social media campaigns, but grounded reforms in monitoring, scheme design, last-mile delivery, and data integrity. Only then will 'achievement' in official reports begin to reflect achievement in real life.

Critical Insights into DC-MSME's 2023–24 Performance

In the 2023–24 annual report, too, the Office of the DC-MSME outlines an ambitious push, flooding the ecosystem with credit, capturing digital momentum, and uniting domestic and international outreach. Yet, without independent scrutiny, the narrative risks veering into one-sided cheerleading. Despite claims of expanded registrations, infrastructure upgrades, and scheme roll-outs, questions about effectiveness and verifiable impact linger. This critique explores what's celebrated, what needs caution, and how DC-MSME might forge credibility by tightening evaluation.

A Surge in Numbers, A Whisper of Substance

The report touts nearly 4.77 crore MSMEs registered via Udyam by mid-2024, with 2.49 crore added in fiscal year 2024. This surge speaks to successful digital outreach, yet mere registration masks the real test—whether these newly formalised units are productive, sustainable, and inclusive. Overstated quantitative gains without qualitative analysis may inflate perceptions, especially in the absence of a third-party audit.

DC-MSME also highlights a full rollout of digital and credit mechanisms. With 49.22% of GeM portal orders going to micro and small enterprises, the digital thrust shines. But engagement depth matters. The ministry reports ₹34,500 crore disbursed under the ECLGS.

MSME—an impressive figure whose actual trickle-down effect on MSME solvency, job retention, or expansion remains opaque.

Programmes Galore – Yet Missing Independent Lens

The extensive description of initiatives—lean manufacturing, global tie-ups, targeted regional pushes—portrays a dynamic agenda.

However, DC-MSME frequently refrains from sharing third-party evaluations or outcome metrics on productivity gains, debt sustainability, or export performance. Without neutral assessment, the narrative feels like marketing copy rather than a reflective organisational learning exercise.

This absence of external validation is more than a formality. Independent reviews act as mechanisms for accountability, granting confidence to stakeholders—from entrepreneurs and financiers to civil society and policy planners. In their absence, DC-MSME's self-reported triumphs hover in a vacuum of unverified claims.

Objectivity in Numbers – But Not in Interpretation

Figures bristle throughout: hundreds of conclaves, millions of registered enterprises, billions in credit guarantees. The sheer volume communicates seriousness. Yet, DC-MSME rarely contrasts cadre-specific before-and-after baselines, or interrogates scheme overlaps and cost-benefit trade-offs. Are all 49% GeM procurements to quality-compliant MSMEs, or is it just small-value orders skewing statistics? We don't know.

Moreover, the report's focus on process—registration counts, training sessions held, and MoUs signed—leaves outcome evaluation weak. There's little insight into whether trained beneficiaries started sustainable ventures, scaled up, or graduated to Tier I vendors.

Reliability and Acceptability – Too Much Trust on Self-Assertions

By channelling the narrative through internal metrics and admin-focused achievements, DC-MSME creates an internally coherent document—yet fails the litmus test of acceptability in policy and public spheres. Without an external audit or academic study, any sector stakeholder—MSMEs, investors, or NGOs—is left wondering how much weight to give these claims. The report's authority is constrained by a lack of triangulation or critical peer review.

From Numbers to Narratives of Impact

To transform future reports into credible mirrors of progress, DC-MSME should institutionalise independent evaluation. Commission peer reviews with NIMSME or even independent think-tanks. Tighten KPIs to include the survival rate of trained enterprises, uplift in profit margins, diversification of product portfolios, and wage growth. Introduce randomised control trials for select interventions—for example, comparing clusters with lean-manufacturing training against control groups to assess productivity gains.

Encourage stakeholder feedback loops—testimonial recording should be systematic, cross-verified, and open to public scrutiny. Release detailed data dashboards online, enabling civil society and media to analyse scheme uptake and verify regional impact. Openness to third-party audits and critiques would boost legitimacy and inform adaptive learning.

Conclusion

DC-MSME's 2023–24 report, much like its report of the preceding year, is bold and brimming with ambition—unprecedented registrations, rapid digitisation, and multi-pronged schemes. But beneath the veneer, the narrative remains self-referential, lacking external validation and deep impact metrics. To shift from self-promotion to genuine progress, a pivot is needed: embed independent evaluation, prioritise outcome analysis over administrative checkboxes, and foster transparency. Only then can the DC-MSME construct a narrative that not only dazzles but also withstands scrutiny and builds the transformative MSME ecosystem India needs.

The CAG Speaks – A Reality Check on DC-MSME's Claims

Amidst the polished tables and glowing summaries of the DC-MSME's 2022–23 annual report, one might be forgiven for believing that India's small enterprise ecosystem is thriving on all fronts. But such confidence is shaken when confronted with the findings of the nation's constitutional auditor. The CAG, in its performance audits over the years—including recent ones feeding into the broader oversight of MSME schemes—has regularly punched holes in the projected efficacy, reach, and impact of the very schemes celebrated by DC-MSME.

> Suppose 1,000 people register for a marathon. Only 300 show up. Of them, 50 complete the race. But the organisers declare, '1,000 successful runners!'
>
> That's how performance is reported in schemes like PMEGP. Units are 'assisted', but there's no clarity on survival, sustainability, or ghost registrations.

The ESDP, with its glossy claim of training over 66,000 beneficiaries in just one fiscal, is another classic case of form trumping substance. The CAG has earlier flagged the absence of performance benchmarking across institutions, resulting in wide quality disparities between Tier I and rural training centres. More worryingly, tracer studies—designed to track post-training employment or entrepreneurial ventures—are rarely undertaken. Thus, 'beneficiary' in the report could very well mean an attendee who dropped out after the second day of a five-day programme, with no intent or capability to pursue enterprise development.

Even in infrastructure and credit access, the story is more illusion than impact. The CAG's audit findings on the Credit Guarantee Scheme and MSE-CDP (Micro and Small Enterprises – Cluster Development Programme) schemes have shown not only low penetration in backward and rural areas, but also alarming delays in fund utilisation and irregularities in beneficiary identification. The 2022–23 annual report claims widespread success but conveniently omits the CAG's caution that cluster infrastructure projects have suffered from delays of up to five years, with common facilities either underutilised or lying defunct due to poor planning and local buy-in.

As for digital adoption, the report sings paeans to a 97.67% digital transaction rate across the ministry's agencies. Yet the CAG's performance assessments caution that these figures often represent backend accounting entries—digitisation by the ministry's own staff—rather than actual MSME users transacting online. There is no survey presented in the report to validate that rural MSMEs have actually embraced UPI, BHIM (Bharat Interface for Money), or digital lending platforms for credit access, despite multiple past CAG directives to assess such ground-level impact through third-party evaluators.

A more structural critique by the CAG relates to the lack of cohesive scheme convergence. Many schemes run in silos—KVIC, NSIC, Coir Board, and the Office of DC-MSME often report overlapping beneficiaries and outcomes without integrating data or impact assessments. The 2022–23 report does little to correct this fragmentation. While it celebrates 'digital dashboards' and portal integrations, there is no mention of whether these systems enable inter-agency de-duplication or real-time monitoring of beneficiary outcomes—long-standing recommendations from both the CAG and Standing Committees of Parliament.

Most worryingly, the CAG has time and again noted the absence of independent third-party evaluations across schemes—a point completely ignored in the self-congratulatory tone of the annual report. From SFURTI to PMEGP to the CHAMPIONS portal, beneficiary satisfaction surveys, dropout analyses, and long-term sustainability metrics are all missing. Instead, the Office of the Development Commissioner continues to rely on internal reporting, which risks masking ground realities and perpetuating a culture of compliance over consequence.

In short, the CAG's findings, though not explicitly reproduced in the 2022–23 or the later annual report, form a damning counter-narrative to the claims of achievement. The report reads like a balance sheet focused on 'number of trainings', 'expenditure incurred', and 'units supported', whereas the CAG demands answers on efficiency, equity, sustainability, and outcomes. And it is in this yawning gap—between what is reported and what is real—that the credibility of the DC-MSME's achievements truly begins to fray.

Unless the ministry integrates audit findings, mandates third-party validations, and shifts from input counting to outcome measurement, annual reports will continue to showcase progress only on paper, while India's vast MSME base continues to grapple with the same old challenges under the veneer of new schemes.

References:

1. Primary Source: Annual Report 2022–23, Ministry of MSME.

- Title: Annual Report 2022–23
- Publisher: Ministry of Micro, Small, and Medium Enterprises, Government of India
- Relevant sections cited:
    - Chapter 2: Growth and Performance of MSMEs
    - Chapter 3.2: Office of the Development Commissioner, MSME – Schemes, Tool Rooms, Technology Centres
    - Annexes: Budget allocations, scheme-wise expenditure, procurement from MSEs

    - Specific citation: https://msme.gov.in/msme-annual-report-2022-23?utm_source

2. CAG Reports and Audit Observations.

- Report of the CAG on Performance Audit of Prime Minister's Employment Generation Programme (PMEGP)
    - Report No. 36 of 2017 (Union Government – Economic Services Ministries)
    - Findings:
        - 23% of units not physically verified.
        - 17% of inspected units were non-functional or fictitious.
        - Weak monitoring of employment generation claims.
    - Available at: https://cag.gov.in

- Report of the CAG on Performance Audit of Cluster Development Programme for Micro and Small Enterprises (MSE-CDP)
    - Report No. 41 of 2015 (Union Government – Economic Services Ministries)
    - Findings:
        - Delay in infrastructure projects up to 60 months.
        - Underutilisation of Common Facility Centres.
        - Inadequate selection criteria for SPVs.
    - Available at: https://cag.gov.in

- CAG Compliance Audit Reports on the Ministry of MSME
    - Highlight persistent issues in:
        - Data inflation in employment numbers (especially in khadi sector)
        - Overlapping beneficiaries under multiple schemes (PMEGP, SFURTI, SRI Fund)
        - Non-evaluation of schemes like Digital MSME and Lean Manufacturing
        - Ineffective grievance redress platforms (CPGRAMS and Champions)

- Related Standing Committee Reports:
    - Parliamentary Standing Committee on Industry
        - 311th Report (2021): Highlighted lack of independent evaluation of MSME schemes
        - 329th Report (2022): Noted irregularities in fund utilisation and duplication of scheme beneficiaries

CHAPTER 15

◆◆◆

From Refugee Camps to Digital Rupee: MSMEs in the Budgetary Journey

Abstract:

India's journey from the trauma of Partition to the threshold of a digital economy has been driven, shaped, and often dramatised by one annual spectacle—the Union Budget. More than just a statement of accounts, the Budget has served as India's moral compass, political manifesto, economic GPS (Global Positioning System), and populist battleground. This expanded narrative captures the defining themes relating to the MSME/startup sector, its turning points, and quirky footnotes from every significant Budget from 1947 to 2025. From levying taxes on crossword puzzle winners to abolishing the angel tax on startups, every Budget attempted to carry the pulse of its time—bold reforms, bureaucratic retreats, welfare experiments, and poetic flourishes. With verified milestones and contemporary cross-references, this chapter chronicles how India's annual 'Book of Numbers' has grown from a colonial ledger to a statement of aspirations and sometimes, audacity.

The Grand Inauguration: Budgets of Survival (1947–1965)

> Imagine a family displaced by a flood, suddenly handed a survival kit—some rice, some medicine, and a roofing tarp. That's what India's first few Budgets felt like. In 1947, freshly torn apart by Partition, the country's Union Budget was more rescue manual than financial roadmap. Half the outlay went to defence, the rest to food, rehabilitation, and building the skeleton of a State. Fast forward 75 years, and that same Budget morphs into a sleek digital download, with QR codes linking to policy documents, tax slabs, and subsidy apps. From feeding 3 crore refugees in 1948 to disbursing e-RUPI vouchers in 2023, the Budget has mirrored India's transformation—from analog chaos to digital ambition. But somewhere in this evolution, MSMEs have often been the silent passengers—occasionally thrown a lifebuoy, rarely given the oars.

The very first Union Budget of independent India, presented on 26 November 1947, by RK Shanmukham Chetty, was a grim ledger of a nation born in trauma. Nearly 46% of the total outlay went to defence, reflecting the deep security anxieties post-Partition. But beyond defence, the Budget hinted at a vision—allocations for refugee rehabilitation, food procurement, and infrastructure stabilisation set the tone. Chetty also introduced the concept of the 'interim budget' in 1948–49, institutionalising a practice now typical of election years.

The 1950–51 Budget announced the formation of the Planning Commission, the architect of India's Five-Year Plans, reflecting Nehru's socialist resolve. In the next few years, budgets became tools of fiscal engineering with heavy reliance on direct taxes. The exemption limit for income tax was raised (1953–54), ICICI (Industrial Credit and Investment Corporation of India) was birthed (1954–55), and capital gains tax was scrapped and later reintroduced. A distinctive 1957–58 Budget brought in Wealth Tax, targeting high-net-worth individuals, and in 1958–59, Prime Minister Nehru, doubling as finance minister, introduced the Gift Tax.

India also began engaging international institutions—the Ford Foundation's assistance in 1952 symbolised, if one may call it, early public-private partnerships. The structural refinement of clubbing Plan and Non-Plan expenditure in 1959–60 improved transparency in public spending. This period laid the institutional and fiscal groundwork for future developmentalism.

The Populist Decade and Budgetary Theatre (1966–1984)

The late 1960s and 1970s witnessed budgets serving as populist pamphlets. Morarji Desai, India's finance czar for much of the 1960s, introduced the Voluntary Disclosure Scheme (1965–66), an early attempt to tackle black money. In 1967–68, Desai served both as Prime Minister and finance minister. Meanwhile, tax structures became increasingly convoluted: super profit tax (1963), expenditure tax (1964), and its removal (1966) highlighted the policy oscillation.

The 1970–71 Budget, presented by Prime Minister Indira Gandhi, made her the first woman to do so. She used budgets as tools for welfarism and political consolidation. Foreign travel tickets were taxed (1971–72), crossword puzzle prize winnings were brought under tax (1972–73), and affluent villagers faced scrutiny (1973–74). In 1975–76, the Incentive Bonus Scheme encouraged public savings amidst high inflation.

The 1976–77 Budget introduced the 20-Point Programme targeting poverty, land reform, and health. In 1978, under the

Janata government, demonetisation struck ₹1,000, ₹5,000, and ₹10,000 notes—foreshadowing the 2016 move. Tobacco farmers got excise relief (1979–80), and taxes on food and drinks in 1980–81 curbed aspirational consumption.

Picture this: you're sipping chai in 1972, poring over your morning newspaper. You solve the crossword, send in your entry, and—voilà—you win ₹500. But wait, here comes the taxman! That year's Union Budget taxed even crossword prize winnings, in a bid to increase revenue and reduce the 'unearned' riches of the middle class. This quirky footnote isn't just a trivia nugget—it tells you how obsessed post-Independence Budgets were with extracting revenue from every possible corner. MSMEs, many of whom operated as informal or cash-based setups, got swept up in the same tide of suspicion. For every reform measure, there was often a penalty lurking nearby, creating an atmosphere of compliance fatigue, especially among small entrepreneurs just trying to stay afloat.

This era blended taxation eccentricities with expanding state control. It was theatrical but transformative, punctuated by political instability and economic idealism.

Economic Liberalisation and Fiscal Awakening (1985–2000)

The late 1980s laid the groundwork for India's economic awakening. In 1985, VP Singh introduced the Board for Industrial and Financial Reconstruction (BIFR) to revive sick industries, including many small-scale enterprises. MODVAT (Modified Value Added Tax), introduced in 1986–87, simplified the excise structure for manufacturing MSMEs (then called SSIs (Small Scale Industries)), reducing cascading tax effects. A year later, Minimum Alternate Tax (MAT) was introduced (1987–88) to ensure that zero-tax-paying companies contributed a minimum amount to the exchequer.

Think of the Indian Budget as a big joint family dinner. The loudest kids—corporate India on one end and farmers on the other—always get served first. MSMEs? They're like the middle child. Not big enough to throw their weight around, and not poor enough to demand urgent rescue. Every year, they're promised attention—some loan waivers, some skilling, a new website—but by dessert, most of the talk has moved elsewhere. Whether it was the Tax Holiday for startups in 2016 or CGTMSE's collateral-free loans since the 2000s, MSMEs have always been the 'also beneficiaries' of big ticket announcements. What they rarely got was sustained, sector-specific nurturing. The result? Most MSMEs continue to feel like Budget afterthoughts, not central characters.

In 1988–89, the launch of Kisan Vikas Patra (KVP) gave small savers a secure investment avenue. The 1989–90 Budget introduced Equity Linked Savings Schemes (ELSS), providing long-term investment options. These were targeted not just at salaried classes but also at small business owners.

But the epochal shift came with the 1991–92 Budget, when Finance Minister Dr Manmohan Singh liberalised the economy. Foreign investment norms were eased, and licensing requirements were drastically pruned. This reform spirit extended to SSIs in the form of simplification of investment caps, removal of industrial licensing for many SSI sectors, and easing of export-import restrictions.

The 1993–94 Budget laid the foundation for capital market reforms with the establishment of the NSE. In 1995–96, Singh pushed insurance sector reforms and proposed the IRDA (Insurance Regulatory and Development Authority) to break the monopoly of LIC (Life Insurance Corporation of India) and GIC (General Insurance Corporation of India), ultimately benefiting SSIs seeking insurance and credit services.

The Foreign Investment Promotion Board (FIPB), introduced in 1996–97, streamlined FDI approvals, encouraging global investors to consider joint ventures with Indian MSMEs. The 1997–98 Voluntary Disclosure of Income Scheme (VDIS) also provided tax amnesty to small businesses holding undisclosed wealth.

Special schemes for NRIs (Non-Resident Indians), such as the Resurgent India Bonds (1998–99), helped banks mobilise long-term funds that were eventually channelled into priority sectors, including SSIs. The late 1990s witnessed consistent efforts to integrate Indian small industries into a liberalised market system, albeit with variable success due to limited institutional handholding.

Welfare Expansion and Inclusive Growth (2001–2014)

The 2000s witnessed a convergence of welfare economics and growth ambitions. Budgets were now instruments of targeted intervention—more populist but increasingly data-driven. In 2004–05, Finance Minister P Chidambaram announced a 'New Deal for Rural India', focusing on employment and agriculture. One of the biggest milestones was the 2005–06 Budget, which launched the National Rural Employment Guarantee Scheme (NREGS)—later renamed MGNREGA (Mahatma Gandhi National Rural Employment Guarantee Act). Though primarily a rural employment scheme, it could be considered to have indirectly supported SSIs by boosting rural purchasing power.

For SSIs, this era saw critical structural steps. The 2006 MSMED Act gave a statutory definition and protection to MSMEs. It mandated payment within 45 days for supplies to large buyers, introduced a facilitation council mechanism, and pushed for procurement reservations. In parallel, the SIDBI-led CGTMSE was strengthened, enabling collateral-free credit to lakhs of units.

Chidambaram's 2007–08 Budget began tracking tax evasion via art and non-financial assets. By 2008–09, the historic ₹60,000 crore farmer loan waiver made headlines, while MSMEs got additional allocation under the Technology Upgradation Fund (TUF).

> Visualise this: a roadside tea vendor in Kanpur dreams of expanding his stall. He doesn't own land, has no credit score, and no collateral to offer. Yet, in 2015, he walks into a bank and walks out with ₹50,000 under the PMMY. For the first time in decades, the Budget had created a backdoor for micro-entrepreneurs to bypass the fortress of traditional banking. MUDRA wasn't perfect—defaults mounted, middlemen flourished—but it was revolutionary in spirit. The chaiwala no longer needed a guarantor; his ambition was enough. That's the kind of democratising push Budgets must keep replicating—where credit is a right, not a reward for pedigree.

The 2009–10 Budget set up UIDAI (Unique Identification Authority of India)—a revolution in welfare delivery. With Aadhaar's eventual linkage to subsidy transfers, leakage in MSME and rural schemes reduced. Subsequent Budgets introduced venture capital support and market development assistance for MSMEs, including participation in international trade fairs.

2012–13's retrospective tax and the 2013–14 'super-rich surcharge' worried foreign investors, but the Budget also introduced a special Women Entrepreneurs Fund under SIDBI. Budgets of this period, in sum, mixed welfare populism with targeted regulatory reforms that helped MSMEs gain legitimacy, finance, and legal clarity.

Recasting Fiscal India: Modi Era Budgets (2014–2025)

When Arun Jaitley took charge in 2014, his maiden Budget was a record-breaker in speech length and scheme announcements. It symbolised a new political economy—pro-reform, market-facing, but populist when needed. Twelve flagship schemes were launched in one go, and key public banks received capital infusions under Project Indradhanush (2016–17).

MSME support became central. The MUDRA Yojana (2015) extended collateral-free loans to micro units under the PMMY, creating a new credit pipeline for informal entrepreneurs. Budgets from 2015 onwards also promoted Startup India and Stand-Up India, pushing institutional and funding support for first-time entrepreneurs, including women and SC/ST groups.

In 2017–18, three major changes transformed budgetary governance: the Railway Budget was merged into the Union Budget, the Plan/Non-Plan distinctions were removed, and Budget Day was advanced to 1 February. This streamlining is supposed to have helped the faster implementation of schemes, including MSME procurement, skill development, and digitisation initiatives.

> Imagine putting up a signboard outside a housing society that says: 'Only residents may park here.' Seems clear, right? Now imagine every security guard reading it differently. That's what happened with the 2006 MSMED Act. It was supposed to be a one-rule-fits-all declaration: define MSMEs clearly, offer them statutory protection, mandate payments within 45 days. But across India, implementation became a maze. Big firms delayed payments, facilitation councils sat on disputes, and registration stayed patchy. Even with Udyam and Aadhaar integration in the 2020s, the spirit of the 2006 Act—of protecting the small guy—remains honoured more in intent than execution. The Budget may have laid the rule, but the enforcement never quite followed through.

The 2018–19 Budget capped cash payments above ₹10,000 and began regulating NGOs and trusts. In 2019, Nirmala Sitharaman became the second woman finance minister to present the Budget. Her first full Budget was notable for abolishing the briefcase and introducing the traditional '*bahi-khata*'.

Amid COVID-19, the 2020–21 Budget increased deposit insurance from ₹1 lakh to ₹5 lakh, boosting confidence in banks where MSMEs often parked their savings. The 2021–22 Budget introduced the Voluntary Vehicle Scrappage Policy to stimulate the auto sector, with downstream benefits to auto parts MSMEs.

The 2022–23 Budget focused on digital currency and payments. CBDC (Central Bank Digital Currency) and e-RUPI were introduced to enhance digital finance. 2023–24's Agri Accelerator Fund encouraged rural agri-tech startups—many of which operate at micro or small scale. The 2024–25 interim Budget's allocation of ₹1,11,11,11 crore for capex was symbolic, while the final Budget abolished the angel tax for all categories of investors, removing a major funding bottleneck for MSME startups and early-stage ventures.

Conclusion

From a wartime survival document in 1947 to a vision statement for a trillion-dollar digital economy in 2025, the Indian Union Budget has reflected the country's evolving ethos. It has walked a tightrope between socialism and liberalisation, welfare and fiscal prudence, symbolism and substance. Every Budget—whether introducing MODVAT or e-RUPI, funding wars or startups—has tried to steer India closer to a complex but essential goal: inclusive growth with financial discipline.

MSMEs are supposed to have emerged as consistent beneficiaries across eras. Whether through statutory protections under the 2006 Act, financial plumbing like MUDRA and CGTMSE, or digital tools such as Aadhaar, Udyam, and digital payments, successive Budgets have tried—sometimes timidly, sometimes boldly—to support the most entrepreneurial layer of India's economy. The way forward lies in backing these efforts with real-time audits, focused and objective outcome monitoring (instead of relying on estimations), and decentralised empowerment.

The Budget is no longer a mere book of numbers. It is now a national moment—a reflection of intent, a commitment to course-correct, and a crucible of bold ideas. As India approaches its centenary of independence, its Budgets must continue to lead the way—not just by measuring what we spend, but by revealing who we want to become.

References:

1. 'History of Budget', The Organiser, 2024.

2. Government of India, Ministry of Finance Budget Speeches Archive: https://www.indiabudget.gov.in

3. Reserve Bank of India – Handbook of Statistics on Indian Economy.

4. 'From License Raj to Liberalisation: Manmohan Singh's 1991 Budget', Economic & Political Weekly, 1991.

5. 'Union Budget Highlights (Various Years)', PRS Legislative Research.

6. 'Budget Documents', Press Information Bureau, GoI.

7. D Subbarao, *Who Moved My Interest Rate?* Penguin India, 2016.

CHAPTER 16

◆◆◆

Make in India or Missed in India – The MSME Saga Inside Defence Manufacturing

Abstract:

India's defence MSME story brims with bold policy moves yet struggles with sluggish execution. Since 2016, a slew of reforms—from new procurement procedures to innovation schemes—promised to catapult small enterprises into the heart of 'Make in India' defence production. In reality, those ambitions often stalled on the ground. This chapter, through a performance-audit lens, cuts through official narratives to examine actual outcomes. While policies like DAP 2020, Make-I/II, iDEX, SRIJAN, and revamped offset guidelines aimed to empower MSMEs, their impact could have been blunted by bureaucratic bottlenecks, delayed deliverables, and half-fulfilled promises. The result is a saga of intent versus implementation—one crying out for a thorough audit and course correction to truly unleash India's defence MSME potential.

The Post-2016 Reform Tsunami – Hopes for the Small Fish

In the second half of the 2010s, India's defence establishment unleashed a wave of reforms explicitly targeting indigenisation and the inclusion of MSMEs. The Defence Procurement Procedure 2016, overhauled as the DAP 2020, exemplified this shift. DAP 2020's preamble even spotlighted MSMEs, noting that 'the Make in India initiative aims to increase the involvement of Indian vendors, notably MSMEs', and that the 'Make' system was being improved to be more objective and deadline-driven for industry, 'particularly MSMEs'. Lofty words, indeed, as policymakers promised a more level playing field for the little guys in a sector long dominated by hulking public-sector units and foreign Original Equipment Manufacturers (OEMs).

Several new categories and schemes were rolled out under DAP 2020 to walk the talk. The 'Make' Procedure was split into sub-categories: Make-I (government-funded prototypes) and Make-II (industry-funded prototypes). In Make-I, the Ministry of Defence (MoD) would fund up to 70% of development costs for ambitious indigenous projects, an unprecedented hand-up for the domestic industry. Make-II, on the other hand, invited companies—often expected to be MSMEs or startups—to propose defence solutions using their own funds, with the promise that if their prototype succeeded, the military could directly place an order. This was touted as a 'game-changer' to harness private innovation without the red tape of tenders. By mid-2021, MoD had already given preliminary approval (Acceptance of Necessity) to 58 Make-II projects pitched by the army, navy and air force. The message was clear: there's a new welcome mat for small innovators at the defence ministry's door.

Next came a flashy new initiative, iDEX. Launched in 2018, iDEX set up a platform for innovators—often startups and MSMEs—to work on problem statements given by the Armed Forces. It offered grants (capped at around ₹1.5 crore per project) and a fast-track route for promising prototypes to be tested and procured. The aim was to 'democratise defence innovation' and connect youthful talent to military needs.

Politicians talked it up with zeal; the defence minister even exhorted young entrepreneurs to create India's first defence tech unicorn, vowing the government would support them 'at every step from ideation to implementation'. By 2025, the government claimed that more than 650 iDEX winners had emerged, with prototype orders worth over ₹3,000 crore facilitated—a 'revolution in India's defence innovation landscape', in the minister's words. It all sounded like an MSME founder's dream come true.

Other policy moves also targeted the indigenisation ecosystem. The SRIJAN portal, launched in August 2020, started listing thousands of imported components used by the Armed Forces and Defence PSUs, essentially a matchmaking board for items that could be indigenised by local industry. By mid-2023, over 30,000 such defence items were put up on SRIJAN for grabs by domestic firms (including MSMEs) to 'become partners in the indigenisation process', according to the MoD. Notably, by early 2025, the government reported that of 38,000+ items offered, about 14,000 had been successfully indigenised—progress, but indicating a long road ahead.

To address a perennial pain-point—the lack of test facilities—the government launched the Defence Testing Infrastructure Scheme (DTIS) in 2020, aiming to set up six to eight new testing labs where private players could validate their products. This was meant to especially help MSMEs, who often couldn't afford expensive trials or lacked access to military firing ranges and labs.

Even the decades-old Defence Offset Policy got a makeover. Offsets—which require foreign vendors to invest a portion of contract value back into India—were originally conceived as a golden ticket for Indian industry (including small suppliers) to benefit from big international deals. However, a damning 2019 CAG audit revealed that from 2007 to 2018, offsets had largely flopped: only 59% of due offset credits were discharged, and a mere 8% of the total offset value was actually validated as fulfilled. In other words, tens of thousands of crores meant to boost the Indian industry never materialised. Stung by these failures, the DAP 2020 actually reduced the scope of offsets—it scrapped offset requirements for government-to-government or single-vendor deals (which cover many of the biggest purchases). The logic was that offsets weren't delivering and were deterring vendors; the unintended signal, however, was that a key avenue that might have channelled work to Indian MSMEs was now being shut off. Critics noted that this policy change effectively conceded the offset game, potentially depriving local firms of future business that could have come from, say, a Rafale or S-400 type import on the horizon.

On paper, then, the policy ambition was sky-high: simplified procurement, funds for development, innovation challenges, indigenisation lists, testing support—a comprehensive toolkit to propel MSMEs into the defence production mainstream. The stage seemed set for the 'small' to do something big. But as the next act would show, grand policies don't automatically translate to grand outcomes. For many MSMEs, the saga has felt less like Make in India and more like Missed in India.

Ground Reality Check – The MSME Experience in the Trenches

If we walked into a defence industry event or an expo in the late 2010s, we could sense the buzz of new entrants—spunky startups and small manufacturing firms hoping to land that big opportunity. Yet, if we talked to their founders for a few minutes, a different picture would emerge: one of exasperation with systemic hurdles. The hard truth is that while reforms opened the door, the journey beyond that door often remained/remains an obstacle course for MSMEs.

Take the essential hurdle of quality control and certification. An MSME can design a world-beating gadget, but if it cannot clear the gauntlet of defence testing and quality assurance, it's game over. Consider a fictional composite: Aarav Electronics, a Pune-based MSME that developed a rugged radio for the army. Enthused by Make in India, Aarav's team toiled on the design and even got an opportunity to field-test under a Make-II proposal. That's when they hit the wall called DGQA—the Directorate General of Quality Assurance.

Every component of their radio had to pass rigorous inspections and trials supervised by DGQA. Nothing wrong with that—soldiers' lives depend on a quality kit. But the process turned Kafkaesque: tests were scheduled, delayed, repeated, documentation was sent back for tiny errors, and as soon as one round of trials passed, another round of 'confirmatory trials' was mandated. Months stretched into years. 'It felt like a never-ending loop—test, tweak, re-test—while our order hung in the balance,' the (composite) founder recounts.

Such stories are common folklore among defence suppliers. In fact, the MoD itself eventually recognised this bottleneck. In 2024, it announced a major reorganisation of DGQA to speed up quality assurance and 'reduce layers of decision-making', conceding that the old ways were too slow. The restructure aims to provide single-point QA (Quality Assurance) support and even set up a dedicated testing facilitation unit. These are welcome steps—but ask MSMEs and many will say, 'We'll believe it when we see it.' Years of navigating DGQA's maze have left them sceptical that the culture will change overnight.

Delayed payments pose another deadly threat to MSME survival. Defence procurement is notorious for its long payment cycles—a small firm might supply parts to a giant PSU or directly to a military workshop, only to wait months beyond the contractual 30- or 45-day period for their money. For big companies, delayed payments are an annoyance; for a tiny supplier, they can be a life-and-death cash flow crunch.

India's MSME ministry set up an online portal, Samadhaan, for small businesses to report and resolve delayed payments, and the data is eye-opening. As of January 2025, over 2.18

lakh delayed payment complaints had been filed by micro and small enterprises, amounting to nearly ₹48,000 crore in dues.

Tellingly, central public sector units (which would include defence PSUs) accounted for over ₹5,500 crore of these unpaid bills. The defence sector's share isn't broken out, but anecdotal evidence abounds.

Picture a Coimbatore-based precision machining MSME that supplies components to a big Defence PSU—let's call them Coimbatore Engineering Co. They deliver a batch of parts for a missile programme, worth say ₹50 lakh, in January. The payment is supposed to come by March. March becomes July, then Diwali, and still no sign of cash. The proprietor nervously juggles bank loans to pay his workers and electricity bills. It takes a stern letter—and a veiled hint at legal action—before the PSU finally clears the dues after a year. By then, the MSME has aged a decade under stress. Sadly, this isn't a rare horror story; it's close to the norm. Government rules ostensibly mandate interest on late payments to MSMEs, and even threaten tax disallowances for late-paying buyers, but enforcement is weak. Until the culture shifts to 'pay up on time, every time', MSMEs will remain financially fragile when selling to MoD or its primes.

Then there is the matter of testing infrastructure (or lack thereof). Vikram Aerotech, another composite MSME from Bengaluru, developed a new drone as part of an air force innovation challenge. When it came time to test the drone's endurance and sensor range, Vikram's team found there was no readily available facility to simulate the required conditions. Private labs were not certified for defence standards; DRDO and service labs were booked solid for months with their own projects. This delay in testing meant a delay in certification, which meant a delay in any potential order—a chain reaction all too familiar to small defence tech firms.

The DTIS aimed to plug this gap by co-funding new test ranges and labs accessible to industry. Yet progress has been slow—by mid-2023, a few projects were in the pipeline (e.g. an advanced materials test facility in Tamil Nadu, an unmanned systems test site in Uttar Pradesh's defence corridor), but most MSMEs haven't felt relief yet. The testing bottleneck continues to bite. In recognition of this, the DGQA reorganisation in 2024 also talked of a new Directorate of Defence Testing and Evaluation Promotion to better allocate test facilities. That sounds promising on paper; in practice, Vikram Aerotech and its peers could still be waiting for those promised world-class test centres to actually open their doors.

Another source of frustration is procurement fragmentation—the convoluted routes an MSME must navigate to win defence business. Consider the bewildering array of channels: direct contracts under DAP (which often favour larger players unless it's a small-value tender), Make-II programmes run separately by each Service HQ, innovation challenges under iDEX, R&D grants under DRDO's Technology Development Fund, vendor registration portals for each DPSU (Defence Public Sector Undertaking) and the Ordnance Factory Board (now corporatised into seven companies), plus the SRIJAN indigenisation portal and GeM for off-the-shelf items. For a small company with limited manpower, just figuring out 'Where is the opportunity?' is a full-time job.

One week, the MSME is preparing a proposal for an army Make-II project (issued via an EOI (Expression of Interest) on some army website), the next week it could be pitching to an iDEX jury for a grant, and simultaneously trying to get its CNC part registered on a DPSU's vendor list. It's easy to miss an announcement or misread the fine print and lose out.

There is no single, streamlined window for MSMEs to engage—instead, it's a hydra-headed labyrinth of acronyms and portals. 'You need a map and a few mentors just to navigate the system,' quips a defence startup founder only half-jokingly. The fragmentation often means the left hand of the system doesn't know what the right is doing. In one instance, an MSME was developing a component under an iDEX contract, while a DPSU simultaneously floated a tender to import a similar component—unaware (or unconvinced) that a local solution was in the works. Such a lack of coordination undermines the very purpose of these MSME-focused schemes. If the defence establishment truly wants to harness small innovators, it must make the process more coherent and user-friendly—a consistent feedback from industry roundtables.

Perhaps the most structural challenge is what many MSMEs perceive as PSU gatekeeping and the absence of mandated opportunity. Despite all the talk of MSMEs being the 'unsung heroes' of Atmanirbhar Bharat, the reality is that the MoD and its PSUs are not bound by the same procurement rules favouring MSMEs that other ministries must follow. Under the general Public Procurement Policy of 2012 (amended in 2018), most government buyers must source at least 20–25% of their purchases from MSMEs, and certain items are reserved exclusively for small units. But remarkably, the defence ministry was exempted from this rule—a carve-out that industry experts flag as a glaring obstacle for defence MSMEs. Even though DPSUs have adopted a few measures (like a price preference for MSME bidders in some cases), there is no binding quota or reservation ensuring that, say, a fifth of HAL's (Hindustan Aeronautics Limited) or BEL's (Bharat Electronics Limited) subcontracting goes to small enterprises. The list of 358 reserved items under the 2012 policy contains 'no significant defence items' at all.

In effect, whether an MSME gets a chance or not often depends on the goodwill of individual officers or the enlightened self-interest of a DPSU, rather than any enforceable obligation. For many MSMEs, it feels like hitting an invisible wall: the big players talk about indigenisation but still keep critical work in-house or within a tight circle of established vendors.

One composite anecdote: Rajesh, owner of a small firm making high-grade fasteners, has been trying for three years to become a supplier to aircraft-maker HAL. Each time he applies, there's either a bureaucratic delay or an incumbent supplier undercutting by a tiny margin. 'They always find a way to prefer the devil they know,' he says wryly. The Strategic Partnership (SP) model in DAP 2020 was supposed to change this dynamic by mandating that big private integrators foster a vendor ecosystem of MSMEs. And indeed, new mega-contracts (like building naval helicopters or submarines under SP) will require the chosen Indian conglomerate to source many parts locally, presumably from smaller firms. But those projects are still on the horizon. For now, MSMEs largely remain junior partners by grace, not by right.

Finally, we come to offsets—the missed opportunity. Offsets could have been a windfall for capable Indian MSMEs by forcing foreign arms suppliers to engage local partners for components or services. However, as noted earlier, the execution was dismal: out of over ₹19,000 crore worth of offset obligations due by 2018, only 59% were actually claimed as discharged, and merely 48% of those claims passed audit—just 8% of total offset credits properly realised. The failures ranged from vendors simply not delivering on promises to shoddy verification by the MoD to a lack of penalties for defaulters. For example, one contract for maritime patrol aircraft had 90% of its offset credits claimed by the supplier, but only 6% verified as legitimate—the rest were in limbo. What does that mean on the ground? It means Indian sub-contractors who were supposed to get work (or technology transfers) via those offset deals never did, because the foreign OEM either found loopholes or the agreements were poorly enforced. In some cases, the foreign vendor didn't even bother to secure a bank guarantee for the offset, so there was no financial consequence when they failed to fulfil it. It's not hard to see why MSMEs feel cheated—the much-trumpeted offset policy turned out to be, as one commentator put it, a 'rotten state of affairs' that neither transferred cutting-edge tech nor generated steady business for India's small suppliers. And with

DAP 2020's change, many future deals won't have offsets at all, effectively closing that door. Unless India radically rethinks how to leverage foreign deals for local gain (perhaps through stricter enforcement or new forms of industrial partnership), offsets will remain a story of promises not kept—and MSMEs will have to pin their hopes elsewhere.

The Innovation Mirage – iDEX, Make-II, and the Reality of Conversion

No discussion of the MSME saga in defence is complete without examining the flagship innovation schemes—iDEX and Make-II—which were supposed to be the springboards for small players. Both have shown flashes of success, but both face a common criticism: great prototypes, few production contracts.

Let us start with iDEX. By design, iDEX picks multiple winners (startups/MSMEs) for each problem statement, gives them modest funding to develop prototypes, and then the services may choose to procure the successful solutions in limited quantities (often under a special provision for innovative procurement). Since 2018, there have been hackathons, grand challenges, and hundreds of startups entering the fray.

The government, as noted, loves touting the numbers—350+ contracts signed with startups by mid-2024, leading to 35 new items being procured worth at least ₹2,000 crore; by early 2025, 430 contracts and 43 items worth ₹2,400+ crore were on the books. On paper, that's impressive: it means dozens of new technologies, like drone swarm systems, AI surveillance software, lightweight body armour, etc., developed by Indian startups, are being bought by the Armed Forces. But if we do the math, 35 items out of 350 agreements is only a 10% conversion rate to a 'material contract'. In other words, nine out of ten iDEX deals did not culminate in the military actually inducting the product in any significant way.

A few went into extended trials, some prototypes failed to meet requirements, and many simply languished after the initial grant money was used up. Winning an iDEX challenge is only part of a long story, as one defence startup mentor remarked. The startup must then deal with certification, user trials, staff evaluation, and price negotiations—a process just as complex as any regular defence procurement, only this time the company is burning its own cash while waiting. 'The chances of winning are 50/50 because field trials are subjective…,' admits Abhishek Tomar, CTO of startup AjnaLens, which won an iDEX contract in 2019 and whose product is still stuck in trials as of 2024. This illustrates the 'valley of death' problem: the gap between prototype and production. Many startups, after proving a concept, find no budget line or bureaucratic will for a bulk order. If the Armed Forces don't quickly embrace the new tech, the small company will be left holding an expensive demo with no customer.

Unsurprisingly, some have pivoted away. Staqu Technologies, for instance, tried to offer an AI video analytics solution through iDEX but found the process 'complicated and non-transparent' and eventually shifted focus to civilian markets. Another, Skylark Labs, secured an iDEX contract for a drone solution but struggled with 'slow decision-making' in the procurement system and couldn't sustain their defence line of business. These cases reflect a sobering statistic: roughly only 10% of iDEX agreements led to real contracts, while many startups saw their defence prospects fizzle out. The government recognises this issue—by late 2023, there was talk of a dedicated 'iDEX procurement window' to fast-track successful prototypes into purchases. Until such measures take effect, however, iDEX will continue to generate more headlines than lifelines for most startups.

Make-II, similarly, has been a mixed bag. It was hyped as the flexible, industry-driven path for MSMEs to propose solutions the military didn't even know it needed. The good news: it cut out a lot of paperwork (no necessity for the government to issue a tender first; industry could *suo motu* propose projects). By 2022, dozens of Make-II project ideas had been greenlit—autonomous combat vehicles, wearable robotic exoskeletons for aircraft maintenance, mountain tanks, you name it.

The bad news: converting these into actual inducted products has proven arduous. Many Make-II projects are still 'in development hell', with prototypes not yet ready or stuck in testing. As of the end of 2023, officials said 26 projects were being progressed under Make-II (and ten under the funded Make-I). One notable success story came from the navy: an upper-air sound monitoring system (UASS) for meteorological use was developed under Make-II with ten MSMEs collaborating, and the navy was impressed enough to place an order for 60 units right after successful trials. This was hailed as proof that Make-II can work—a ₹40 crore prototype effort leading to a production contract, all driven by Indian SMEs.

Yet for every UASS, there are other projects, like the army's advanced surveillance systems or autonomous vehicles that, after two or three years, have yet to see a single order. Part of the problem is the inherent uncertainty of R&D: not every attempt will yield a deployable product. But part is also bureaucratic lethargy—the 'Atmanirbhar' rhetoric sometimes collides with a risk-averse procurement culture. If a foreign off-the-shelf option exists, there's often a faction that prefers to buy proven gear rather than bet on an untested indigenous prototype. That mindset defeats the purpose of Make-II. One army officer candidly admitted (off record) that some within the system view Make projects as 'science fair experiments'—nice to show off, but not to actually rely on. Overcoming this bias will require accountability: the brass must ask why, if an indigenous solution meets 80% of the requirement, are we not adopting and improving it, rather than importing 100% solutions. Without a push from the top to convert prototypes to production, Make-II will remain largely a story of unrealised potential.

In short, iDEX and Make-II have generated enthusiasm but not enough outcomes. They were designed as bridges for MSMEs into big defence contracts, yet too many MSMEs find themselves stuck midway on those bridges, looking at a chasm between them and the promised land of orders. Bridging that chasm is the next big challenge if the MSME ecosystem is to truly flourish inside defence manufacturing.

Way Forward – Auditing the Gaps, Bridging the Divide

The saga so far has been one of high hopes tempered by harsh realities. So what's the prescription to cure what ails the Indian defence MSME ecosystem? We need a multipronged fix—equal parts accountability, policy fine-tuning, and cultural change. Here's a roadmap to consider:

Shine a Light with a Performance Audit: It's time for a no-nonsense CAG-led performance audit focused exclusively on MSMEs in defence manufacturing. Such an audit should examine whether the lofty promises translated into results. Are the Armed Forces and DPSUs meeting even informal targets for engaging MSMEs? How have schemes like iDEX, TDF (Technology Development Fund), Make-I/II actually fared in terms of tangible outcomes versus funds spent? Are there systemic patterns in certification delays, re-testing loops, and procedural rejections faced by small vendors? An audit would provide an objective scorecard—cutting through the self-congratulatory press releases to show what worked and what didn't. For instance, it could reveal how many of those '650 iDEX winners' actually saw service orders, or how many Make-II projects got shelved. It could call out specific choke points, like the average time for DGQA clearance for MSME-supplied items or the quantum of pending payments by DPSUs to MSMEs. Much like a diagnostic MRI (Magnetic Resonance Imaging), a well-scoped audit would identify the fractures and soft-tissue injuries in the ecosystem.

Enforce Complexity-Weighted Procurement Metrics: One reason MSMEs struggle is that procurement decisions often default to L1 (lowest cost) and large volume norms, which favour bigger players. The MoD should implement complexity-weighted metrics for certain categories, meaning procurements are segmented by complexity level and size. For example, simple, low-value items (nuts, bolts, cables, basic tech) could be mandatorily sourced from MSMEs, while mega-integrations (fighter jets, tanks) understandably go to big players. However, in many cases, subsystems and components of complex platforms can be broken out and procured from smaller firms if they meet specs. A complexity-weighted approach would intentionally give MSMEs a fighting chance in their weight class, rather than pitting them head-to-head against conglomerates for the same pie. It echoes the idea of the 20% MSME procurement policy but tailored to defence by focusing on appropriate categories. The MoD could, for instance, declare that for any contract under ₹100 crore that doesn't involve cutting-edge weaponry, an MSME-only tender will be preferred (if at least two MSMEs are qualified, as DAP 2020 actually hints at). Likewise, maintenance, repair, and overhaul (MRO) services—a huge spend area—could be opened up more to MSMEs with domain expertise, rather than renewed single-source contracts to large PSUs.

Tie Payments to PFMS (Public Finance Management System) Triggers: To kill the menace of late payments, the answer may lie in technology and transparency. The government's PFMS can be configured to enforce automatic payment triggers. For defence contracts with MSMEs, the moment a delivery is marked as accepted in the system (or a milestone is approved by the project manager), the payment should be released directly via PFMS to the MSME's bank account within a fixed window (say seven days), failing which it flags at the highest level. In essence, make delayed payment a technical impossibility by removing manual hold-ups. This might require policy tweaks—perhaps an amendment that defence capital budget funds can be placed in escrow for MSME contracts, or simply a strong order from MoD that no invoice shall sit beyond X days. It also requires cultural change: officials must treat MSME dues as sacrosanct as salaries or strategic payments. The MSME ministry's move to disallow tax deductions for late payers is a good disincentive; however, in defence, accountability to timely pay should be part of performance appraisals. Basically, pay on time or face the music—that message needs to be sent loud and clear through the ranks.

Accelerate and Expand DTIS – Testing Labs in Every Corridor: The DTIS must move from plan to reality post-haste. The government should treat the setting up of testing facilities as critically as building highways or power plants. Fast-track the partnerships with private industry or academia to establish these labs. And think beyond the initial six to eight labs—India's two defence industrial corridors (in Uttar Pradesh and Tamil Nadu) should each have a cluster of specialised test centres (for electronics, ballistics, aerospace, etc.) within the next couple of years. Also, make existing government test ranges more accessible: the new DGQA testing directorate should create a single-window scheduling portal where any certified Indian company can book time at a firing range, EMI/EMC (Electromagnetic Interface/Electromagnetic Compatibility) lab, or environmental chamber, for a reasonable fee, without month-long approval notes. If a Pune-based MSME needs to test a new armour plate, they should be able to get a slot at an army proving ground within weeks, not be told to wait indefinitely. These measures will shorten the development cycle for indigenous tech, giving MSMEs a fair chance to prove their product and iterate quickly.

Impose Vendor Development Obligations on DPSUs: It's time to crack the whip on Defence PSUs to proactively nurture MSME suppliers. DPSUs could have yearly targets: e.g., add X new MSMEs to the vendor list, handhold Y number of MSMEs to achieve quality certifications, subcontract Z% of component spending to MSMEs. And these targets shouldn't just be lip service—link them to the performance bonuses of PSU leadership. If, say, Mazagon Docks or Hindustan Aeronautics knows that its chairman's appraisal or the company's Navratna status depends in part on MSME outreach, one can bet they'll pay more attention. This could also include mandatory publishing of MSME procurement share: transparency can shame poor performers. The MoD can publish an annual scorecard: How much did each DPSU procure from MSMEs (directly or via tiered vendors) as a percentage of total procurement? Today, one has to pry those numbers via parliamentary questions; making them public would spur competition (for example, 'BEL sources 22% from MSMEs, why is BEML at only 5%?'). Furthermore, DPSUs and large private integrators should be required to hold open vendor meets and innovation days where MSMEs can pitch solutions for the primes' supply chain needs. Some DPSUs do this sporadically; it needs to be institutionalised and frequent.

Bridge the Prototype-to-Production Gap: Perhaps the toughest nut to crack is ensuring that promising indigenous developments don't die on the vine. Here, a few approaches can help. First, for iDEX and Make-II winners, institute a 'Champion's Bonus'—a guaranteed minimum procurement order if they meet the Qualitative Requirements. For instance, if a startup develops a new sniper rifle sight that meets 80% of specs, the army could be mandated to procure, say, 100 units for further troop trials. It's like a Phase 2 validation—not full induction, but enough order to keep the company afloat and iterating. Second, create a special budget head (or use the existing innovation budget) solely for taking proven prototypes into limited series production. Often, the services might like a product but haven't planned money for it in that year's budget. A central fund can bridge that timing issue—essentially 'buy it now, adjust in next procurement plan'. Third, encourage dual-use commercialisation. Many defence startups survive by finding civilian markets (drone startups offer services to agriculture, surveillance startups pivot to industrial security systems, etc.). The MoD, in conjunction with other ministries, could launch programmes to use defence-developed tech in civil sectors—e.g., an iDEX-developed autonomous vehicle could get a pilot in disaster management or the mining sector via government support. This keeps the MSME solvent while defence orders ramp up. Finally, bring the user (Armed Forces) into the loop early and often. Programmes like iDEX have done this by letting service officers give problem statements. Extend that to Make-II: have service representatives co-create the prototypes with MSMEs, so that by the end, the user has skin in the game and is eager to induct them. In essence, the mindset must shift to 'fail fast, fix fast, and field fast'. The military should tolerate a Version 1.0 of a local product if it's upgradeable and better than waiting five years for an import. Only then will we see the conversion rates improve from that paltry 10%.

In conclusion, a bit of irreverence: India's defence MSME saga so far might well be titled 'Much Ado About Small Things'. The government rolled out red carpets in policy, but forgot to remove the tripwires of procedure. We have no shortage of entrepreneurial talent—over 8,000 MSMEs are already supplying India's defence needs in some capacity, and that number could easily double with the right ecosystem. These firms have shown that they can produce everything from missile components to advanced software. Yet, systemic issues have made them observers rather than drivers of the grand 'Atmanirbharta' parade. It's not too late to set things right. The way forward demands a frank appraisal (hence the CAG audit), structural adjustments (hence the policy tweaks), and a change in attitudes within the defence establishment. If done well, the next chapter of this saga could see India's MSMEs truly rise as the backbone of defence manufacturing—innovating, competing, and thriving. The end goal? An India that doesn't just chant 'Make in India' as a slogan, but lives it as a day-to-day reality on the shop floors of Pune, Coimbatore, Lucknow, and Cochin alike—with our MSMEs proving that the only thing small about them is their size, not their impact on national security and growth. That's the real 'Atmanirbhar' win waiting to happen. Can we make sure we don't miss it this time? A trillion rupee question indeed!

References:

1. DAP 2020 emphasis on MSMEs in defence procurement.

2. Make-I & Make-II procedures under DAP 2020, with 70% govt funding in Make-I and industry-funded Make-II projects approved.

3. iDEX launch and government's claims of over 650 winners and ₹3,000 crore in prototype orders by 2025.

4. SRIJAN indigenisation portal – over 30,000 imported items listed for MSMEs (2023); ~14,000 items indigenised by 2025.

5. CAG report on Defence Offsets (2007–2018) – only 59% of due offsets discharged, and just 8% of total offset value accepted as fulfilled.

6. DAP 2020 removal of offsets for G2G or single-vendor deals (policy change).

7. DGQA reorganisation in 2024 aimed at speeding up quality assurance and reducing decision layers.

8. Data on delayed payments to MSMEs: ₹48,000 crore across 2.18 lakh cases (2017–2025); ₹5,595 crore pending against central PSUs.

9. Public Procurement Policy 2012 (amended 2018) – 20% procurement from MSMEs mandated for ministries/PSUs except MoD, hindering defence MSMEs.

10. DAP 2020 provisions giving preference to MSMEs for bids up to ₹100 cr if 2+ MSMEs participate.

11. iDEX results as of 2024: 350+ agreements signed, but ₹2,000 crore orders.

12. Defence startup challenges in converting prototypes: AjnaLens example – product still in trials 4+ years after winning contract.

13. Only ~10% of iDEX agreements resulted in contracts; many startups exiting defence space due to slow procurement.

14. Examples of startups facing hurdles: Staqu (complicated process) and Skylark (slow decisions) struggled despite iDEX.

15. Make-II success example: Navy's UASS weather system – 10 MSMEs developed it, Navy ordered 60 units after trials.

16. MoD Year-End 2023: 26 projects under Make-II and 10 under Make-I being pursued.

SECTION IV

◆◆◆

INSTITUTIONS UNDER THE SCANNER

Institutions meant to nurture MSMEs have too often smothered them. This section lays bare the decay, tokenism, and lost revolutions inside India's support structures.

CHAPTER 17

◆◆◆

Khadi and the Lost Revolution – KVIC and the KRDP[43] Saga

Introduction

Khadi is no ordinary fabric—it is the handspun, handwoven cloth that became a symbol of India's independence and rural self-reliance under Mahatma Gandhi's charkha movement. In 1956, the government set up the KVIC with a mandate to promote khadi and similar village industries as a means of empowering rural artisans. Today, KVIC boasts an extensive network: over 2,863 registered KIs employing nearly 5 lakh (500,000) artisans. On paper, this sounds impressive, yet beneath the homespun ideal lies a sobering reality. Over the decades, KVIC's mission has drifted off course, mired in bureaucratic inertia, dubious data, and perpetual dependence on subsidies. Even a 2006 legislative overhaul (which expanded KVIC's scope and autonomy) failed to cure its ills. The following narrative dissects how the proud khadi ecosystem spun out of control, examining fake 'khadi' products, phantom workers, failed reforms, internal turf wars, fudged job claims,

43. While Chapter 17 is a broader history, Chapter 18 is audit-focused on this subject.

supply chain woes, and other dysfunctions that plague the commission. The tone is frank and critical, much like the facts demand.

Khadi's Identity Crisis and Fake Khadi

At the heart of KVIC's troubles is an identity crisis over what 'khadi' truly means. Legally, khadi is strictly defined as any cloth hand-spun and hand-woven in India from natural fibre (cotton, silk, wool) on a handloom, and certified by KVIC as genuine. In practice, however, khadi has morphed into a brand that KVIC aggressively polices—often in court—while the market is flooded with imitations.

A simple and fairly reliable way to tell genuine khadi from fake 'khadi' is to look closely at the yarn twists in the cloth—something one can do even without special equipment.

Here's how it works in plain terms:

Genuine khadi is made from yarn that has been hand-spun on a charkha. Because it's spun by hand, the yarn has tiny, natural variations in thickness and twist. When you hold real khadi up to the light, you'll notice that:

- The threads aren't perfectly uniform—some are slightly thicker or thinner along their length.
- In the warp and weft (the vertical and horizontal threads in the weave), the twist of the yarn is usually in opposite directions.
- This is because spinners twist one set of threads (say, the warp) in an 'S' direction and the other set (the weft) in a 'Z' direction. This opposite twist helps the cloth stay strong and gives khadi its distinct texture and drape.
- If you gently rub the fabric between your fingers, you'll often feel a subtle irregularity—a soft 'live' texture—rather than the perfectly smooth, even feel of mill-spun cloth.

By contrast, fake khadi is usually made from mill-spun yarn, which is machine-twisted. Here:

- The thickness of the thread is uniform and mechanical-looking.
- Both warp and weft yarns generally have the same twist direction (either both 'S' or both 'Z'), which you can spot if you untwist a small end of yarn from the edge and compare.
- The surface feels more slick and consistent, lacking the slight unevenness that hand-spinning creates.

In short:

Real khadi = irregular thread thickness + opposite twists in warp and weft.
Fake khadi = uniform threads + same twist in both directions.

The KVIC has trademarked the term 'khadi' and insists that it is not a generic word; it has even sued foreign firms and website domain squatters for misusing the name. Yet, this legal defensiveness has not stemmed the tide of fake khadi. Outright fakery is rampant: many shops slap 'khadi' labels on mill-made cloth or even imported fabric, wrapping a power-loom product in a homespun halo. In 2020, KVIC had to publicly warn vendors to stop selling 'fake khadi' personal protective equipment (like masks and gowns) bearing its logo without authorisation. Even some official Khadi Bhandar outlets (Gramodyog Bhavans) have been caught quietly selling non-handmade textiles procured from private mills operating under defunct khadi units. Insiders estimate that perhaps 90% of 'khadi' on the market is imposter cloth, with only a thin sliver genuinely handspun and handwoven. This 'brand contamination' not only deceives consumers but also undermines honest artisans. KVIC has responded with lawsuits and raids, signalling that it takes brand protection seriously; yet, the proliferation of fakes continues unabated—a symptom of how far khadi's image has strayed from its Gandhian roots.

Smoke-and-Mirrors Numbers: Ghost Jobs and Phantom Sales

KVIC routinely trumpets rosy figures about its achievements—soaring sales, booming production, and lakhs of jobs created. But scratch the surface, and the numbers often turn out to be smoke and mirrors. Official statistics swing wildly from year to year, undermining their credibility. For example, one year's parliamentary report boasted an all-time high khadi sales turnover (in the thousands of crores), only for the next year to show a sharp dip. Likewise, KVIC's flagship credit scheme, the PMEGP, reported job creation jumping from 3.2 lakh to 4.1 lakh, then plunging to 2.57 lakh within a few years. Such volatility raises eyebrows, and independent audits have found little transparency or verification behind these figures. The CAG noted that KVIC's data collection was historically ad hoc and unreliable, often compiled from perfunctory institutional reports or outdated surveys and estimates rather than any rigorous headcount. Even recent attempts at digitisation have not fully solved the credibility problem—by 2023, the CAG still found that comprehensive, accurate data compilation 'remains a work in progress' despite the new IT systems.

Digging deeper reveals why KVIC's statistics deserve scepticism. Ghost outlets and phantom artisans have inflated the ledgers for years. A live audit discovered that out of 92 government-run khadi sales outlets on record, only 18 were actually open and operational—yet KVIC had been counting all 92 as active 'sales units' in its reports. In another case, two venerable khadi sales centres had quietly been taken over by private parties selling unauthorised merchandise and pocketing the revenue, even as those sales went unrecorded (or perhaps were siphoned off) in KVIC's books. The CAG dryly observed that such irregularities suggest that KVIC's official sales figures may be overstated or unreliable, since private players were generating income off the record.

On the employment side, KVIC's claims have been even more fanciful. For decades, the commission counted tens of thousands of nominal 'artisan' positions that did not actually exist—a phenomenon akin to a school register where half the students are long absent but never taken off the rolls. When the government finally forced a cleanup by linking artisan payrolls to Aadhaar unique IDs, the result was dramatic: 'hundreds of thousands' of phantom artisans suddenly vanished from KVIC's statistics. These weren't layoffs—just a long-overdue correction of fiction. KVIC had been disbursing subsidies for spinners or weavers who had long since quit, retired, or even died. In short, the glossy numbers cited in annual reports and press releases were often 'spinning yarns' of their own. Without independent verification, KVIC's output and job figures were basically taken on trust—a trust that audits have found to be misplaced.

One stark example is the PMEGP (Prime Minister's Employment Generation Programme) scheme, for which KVIC is a nodal agency. PMEGP provides loans and subsidies to entrepreneurs, and each funded micro-enterprise is assumed by policy to create five to seven jobs. KVIC has dutifully added up these assumptions to claim lakhs of jobs 'created' each year. But reality doesn't follow bureaucratic assumptions. No one really checks if a PMEGP-funded workshop or shop actually hired the five to seven employees projected on paper. In many cases, a beneficiary might take the government grant, start a tiny unit, and employ perhaps one or two family members—far short of the notional target. When sample audits and surveys were finally conducted, the average actual employment per PMEGP project turned out to be under the assumed figure, meaning a significant shortfall in job creation despite the funds spent. In parliamentary discussions, even government officials conceded that the oft-repeated PMEGP job numbers (for example, 17.6 lakh jobs claimed over 2014–2018) were likely 'highly inflated', based on extrapolations rather than hard data. Tellingly, once Aadhaar-based verifications and stricter tracking were introduced for PMEGP, the reported new jobs plummeted by more than half in one year (from 5.87 lakh in 2018–19 down to 2.57 lakh in 2019–20). The steep drop wasn't due to an economic crash—it was the result of weeding out duplicate or fake entries and forcing some grounding in reality. The 'miracle' of KVIC's employment stats often dissolves upon closer scrutiny: much of it has been a mirage of paperwork and optimistic assumptions, rather than verifiable livelihoods on the ground.

Stuck in the Subsidy Trap

Exaggerated sales and job numbers might be laughable if the underlying economics were sound, but KIs are largely unsustainable without government aid. The sector exists in a state of perpetual subsidy, undermining the claim that it empowers artisans through a self-sufficient industry. In truth, khadi units survive on grants, rebates, and soft loans rather than on profits from the market. The evidence for this dependence is stark. Between the mid-1990s and mid-2010s, KVIC's annual expenditure on the khadi sector skyrocketed from a few hundred crore rupees to over ₹1,450 crore, even as actual khadi production, sales, and employment went into decline. In other words, more and more public money was thrown in, but less and less output was coming out. The CAG summed it up bluntly: KVIC was 'ineffective in utilising plan funds for khadi sector promotion,' resulting in wastage of public monies. Government-run khadi shops (the Gramodyog Bhavans) routinely operate at a loss and require constant bailouts. Many khadi-producing institutions can barely break even without the 40% rebate that the government provides to make khadi cloth affordable to buyers. It's a classic subsidy trap: the moment you withdraw support, the entire edifice collapses, yet pouring in more support often doesn't increase genuine self-sufficiency.

Paradoxically, any improvements in efficiency tend to undermine employment—the very thing KVIC is supposed to sustain. Since khadi, by definition, must be handmade, boosting productivity usually means finding ways to produce the same cloth with fewer human hours, which directly conflicts with maximising jobs. A telling case is KVIC's attempt to modernise the spinning wheel. A few years ago, the commission introduced a new multi-spindle charkha (spinning wheel) to replace the traditional one-spindle wheel, hoping to increase yarn output per spinner. Technically, it worked: one person could spin much more yarn in a day with the improved device. However, as a senior KVIC official dryly admitted, the faster charkha 'could be the cause of some job loss'—fewer spinners were needed to produce the yarn. What might be a productivity win in any other industry was seen as a threat in the khadi world. Faster spinning defeated KVIC's raison d'être of providing maximum employment. Consequently, progress has stalled: much of rural khadi production still relies on antiquated, low-output charkhas and handlooms. Any suggestion of further mechanisation (even modest steps like semi-automatic looms) draws political backlash, since nobody wants to be accused of 'spinning away' village jobs. The result is a cruel bind: khadi's productivity remains punishingly low—an economic disadvantage in a competitive textiles market—yet efforts to boost efficiency run into the wall of job protection. KVIC finds itself subsidising an output that is too costly at market rates, yet unable to modernise in ways that might reduce the subsidy burden, for fear of undercutting employment. It is a vicious cycle of stagnation.

The KRDP Debacle: Reform Wears Khadi and Runs for Cover

By the late 2000s, it was glaringly obvious that KVIC's traditional ways were not delivering results. In 2009, a grand experiment was launched to drag khadi into the modern era: the KRDP, backed by a $150 million soft loan from the Asian Development Bank (ADB). This infusion of global capital and expertise came with strings attached—exactly the medicine many felt KVIC needed. The KRDP laid out a series of reform benchmarks and conditional funding tranches, aiming to transform KIs from sleepy charities into competitive, accountable enterprises. The premise was straightforward: fund and support KIs to become financially viable, but require them to implement modern accounting, transparent governance, and measurable performance improvements in return. Key goals included empowering individual spinners and weavers with direct bank payments (cutting out middlemen), phasing out 'ghost' workers and idle capacity, upgrading technology, and instilling a corporate work ethic in an organisation long run like a bureaucratic relic. At the core of the plan was a technological leap: a comprehensive Khadi Institution Management and Information System (KIMIS) to digitise everything from artisan attendance and wage payments to inventory, production, and sales data across hundreds of institutions. If successful, KRDP promised a leaner, self-sustaining khadi sector no longer addicted to government grants.

It didn't go as planned. In fact, KRDP turned into a textbook case of reform defeated by inertia and resistance. Over nearly a decade, India could utilise only about one-third of the $150 million that ADB had made available, before the frustrated donor effectively pulled the plug. The first problem was sheer absorption capacity: many KIs simply couldn't meet the eligibility criteria to receive funds because they failed to modify to fulfil basic reform conditions. Most KIs were utterly unprepared for ADB's demands. Auditors found that many KIs did not maintain proper accounts or balance sheets, had no credible business plans, and lacked qualified managers. These institutions were used to a lax environment and were unable (or unwilling) to adopt the new discipline. With audit trails missing, records fudged, and internal controls nonexistent, a

2015 CAG audit reported that KRDP was 'plagued by non-compliance', as the intended beneficiaries couldn't qualify for assistance due to not implementing even rudimentary reforms. In other words, the sector flunked its own makeover.

Second, the artisan-focused measures that were supposed to be the soul of KRDP got lost in transit. Funds were meant to bypass the old institutional bottlenecks and flow straight to artisans' bank accounts—but that threatened the power of the middlemen running the KIs. These local managers had long controlled the purse strings and disbursement of wages, often opaquely. Under KRDP, they were asked to relinquish that control and become facilitators rather than gatekeepers. Not surprisingly, many KIs dragged their feet or actively obstructed efforts to link artisans directly with bank payments and individual incentives. Training programmes and awareness campaigns for spinners and weavers were half-hearted. Many artisans remained in the dark about the new benefits they were supposed to receive, while KI managers continued business as usual. The direct benefit transfer model largely fizzled because the last-mile institutions wouldn't cooperate in empowering the very people they purported to serve.

Third, a chunk of the KRDP money was spent in arguably superficial ways. ADB's funding was used to renovate and rebrand khadi showrooms across the country. Admittedly, some Khadi Bhavans desperately needed a facelift—dank, dusty outlets with decades-old decor were unlikely to attract modern shoppers. The makeovers brought in bright lighting, new displays, and fresh paint. But this was akin to repainting a house infested with termites. The core issues—outdated looms, unskilled marketing, unreliable supply chains—were left largely untouched. Nicer stores selling the same old stock did little to boost sales in any meaningful way. In fact, the revamped showrooms sometimes faced higher operating costs (air-conditioning, maintenance) without commensurate revenue, worsening their sustainability. Critics quipped that

KRDP ended up 'painting the façade while termites ate the beams', as cosmetic changes took precedence over substantive fixes.

The biggest piece of KRDP was the new digital Management Information System (MIS), KIMIS, which ADB and KVIC hyped as a game-changer. In theory, KIMIS would track every ounce of cotton, every metre of fabric, and every rupee of subsidy through a centralised online platform. Thousands of khadi spinners and weavers would be registered with photo IDs; their daily output would be logged; inventory at each unit would be monitored in real time; sales from even the smallest village outlet would be uploaded to the cloud. This panopticon of data was supposed to bring unprecedented transparency and enable performance-based funding (e.g. releasing grants only when actual production targets are met, as evidenced in KIMIS). On paper, it sounded visionary. In practice, it was a disaster in slow motion.

KVIC rolled out KIMIS in stages, first as standalone software in 100 pilot institutions, then supposedly upgrading to a web-based system in over 1,800 KIs by 2017. Reams of reports, user manuals, and screenshots were produced to show compliance; by late 2017, KVIC even claimed the MIS was fully implemented in the requisite 400 institutions needed to satisfy ADB's conditions. But ADB's verification visits told a different story. Many KIs either could not or would not use KIMIS in any meaningful way. The software itself was complex and unintuitive for the typical KI employee. Training sessions fell flat—field officers often struggled to understand the system, let alone ageing khadi gramodyog secretaries who were more comfortable with handwritten ledgers. Reliable electricity and Internet connectivity, prerequisites for a cloud-based MIS, were absent in numerous rural centres. Data entry was patchy and riddled with errors; many units simply stopped updating the system once the initial hand-holding ended. In effect, KIMIS became a fancy digital diary that few bothered to write in. Some institutions uploaded partial or false data just to tick the box, while continuing their usual manual record-keeping on the side. As a result, the centralised database never had reliable information. In fact, instead of revealing truths, the MIS often institutionalised new forms of fiction: gross under-reporting (or over-reporting) of production that then stalled fund releases tied to those reports. ADB reviewers flagged serious 'data integrity issues' and the lack of any third-party validation of what KIMIS was spitting out. By 2017, ADB had grown deeply sceptical. When KVIC claimed to have met the milestone of an 'operational MIS in 400 KIs', ADB auditors asked pointed questions: How many institutions are actually submitting real-time data? Is anyone using this system to make decisions or disburse funds? Can KVIC show a live dashboard of production and sales? The answers did not convince. In standard donor fashion, ADB suspended further disbursements, effectively freezing the loan after only a couple of tranches had been utilised. The remainder of the $150 million never came because the promised reforms never materialised on paper, let alone on the ground.

By the early 2020s, KRDP had fizzled out, and ADB quietly exited the partnership. The grand rescue plan for khadi ended not with a bang but a whimper. An insider assessment noted that KVIC managed KRDP 'like another government scheme, not a strategic transformation programme', meaning it showed none of the urgency or ownership needed for true reform. The fancy software was there, the funds had partially flowed, but the mindset and accountability remained unchanged. In the final analysis, ADB's initiative failed because it tried to transplant a high-accountability, high-tech solution into a deeply traditional, change-averse ecosystem without first ensuring the soil was fertile for reform. Money was spent, reports were filed, but change remained elusive. As one observer wryly put it, you can spin a yarn in India, but you can't always spin reform. KRDP became a cautionary tale in development circles: pouring in global funds and technology is futile if local institutions are unwilling to rise to the occasion. The 'ruptured dream' of a revived khadi sector demonstrated the limits of external catalysts when met with internal resistance. Ultimately, KRDP left behind some renovated stores, a half-baked MIS, and reams of lesson-learning documents, but little meaningful improvement for khadi artisans.

Dysfunctional Governance: Budgeting Without Accountability

Even as KVIC struggled with external reforms, its internal governance has continued to hobble progress. A prime example is the dysfunctional budgeting process for KIs. Every year, KVIC doles out funds to hundreds of khadi-producing institutions under various subsidy heads—wages, raw materials, marketing, infrastructure, etc. In theory, these allocations should be based on performance and need. In practice, budgeting has been done with a blindfold on, rewarding asks rather than outcomes. KIs have grown adept at proposing bloated budget estimates, knowing that KVIC often approves them with minimal scrutiny. It's akin to giving a teenager more pocket money without ever checking how last month's allowance was spent. A recent standard operating procedure (SOP) for annual budget preparation tried to tighten the screws by demanding online submission of figures through the KIMIS portal and linking proposals to past performance. But compliance remains spotty at best. Many institutions either file their budgets late, enter only partial data into KIMIS, or simply upload inflated numbers that look good on paper. KVIC's central office, for its part, often lacks the will or capacity to rigorously verify these claims. As a result, grants get approved largely on the basis of historical entitlements ('we got ₹X last year, so give us ₹X or more this year') and political lobbying, rather than any real performance metrics. In short, the budget sanction process has long rewarded compliance in form, not in substance.

The consequences are pernicious. Inefficient or even defunct institutions can survive for years on government largesse, while more dynamic or deserving units might be starved of funds if they lack the right connections. A 2019 evaluation found glaring mismatches between reported outputs and the funding given—yet there was no penalty for underperformance, no matter how wide the gap. Indeed, KIs that achieved barely half of their targeted production or employment still often got the same or higher budget sanctioned the next year. There is virtually no outcome-linked accountability. KVIC does not typically cut off an institution for non-performance; the worst that happens is a mild rebuke or a delayed fund release. In contrast, it is not unheard of for politically well-connected khadi organisations to get special increases or relaxed conditions, even if their track record is mediocre. The whole system creates moral hazard: why strive to truly grow sales or improve efficiency if your funding isn't actually contingent on it? As long as an institution files the right forms and plays the bureaucratic game, the money keeps flowing. This has bred a culture of complacency and 'grantsmanship', where running a KI is sometimes more about navigating paperwork and patronage than about weaving cloth or selling products.

KVIC's attempts at instituting tighter financial monitoring often collapse under their own contradictions. For instance, the latest budgeting guidelines urge 'timely scrutiny' and digital record-keeping, yet still require physical file movements through a multi-layered hierarchy of officials for approvals. The mixture of old-school bureaucracy (dozens of dossiers shuttling between state offices and headquarters) with half-hearted digital tools results in delays, duplication of effort, and an accountability vacuum. By the time budgets are finalised and funds are finally disbursed, the financial year might be half over, leading to rushed spending or funds lying idle.

Furthermore, KVIC's role often seems to be that of a passive treasurer rather than an active steward of the khadi sector. It collects proposals, rubber-stamps many of them, and releases money, without investing in capacity-building or enforcing reforms at the institutional level. The commission's field officers are too few (and arguably too politicised) to provide meaningful oversight on how each KI uses its grants. Consequently, the annual budget cycle becomes a revolving door: funds are given out, partially utilised, poorly accounted for, and then new funds are requested to repeat the cycle. As one internal report lamented, this is 'budgeting for survival, not for outcomes'. Without a drastic change in how KVIC links money to results, the commission will continue throwing good money after bad, propping up underperformers and missing opportunities to truly revitalise promising units.

Power Struggles and Turf Wars at the Top

Structural issues within KVIC's governance further complicate any reform effort. The commission has an unusual power dynamic built into its design: the KVIC chairman, a political appointee, functions as a full-time executive head with sweeping authority, while the organisation is simultaneously under the oversight of the Ministry of MSME, which controls the budget and policy direction. This dual control structure has led to periodic turf wars between the chairman's office and the bureaucrats in the MSME ministry. In theory, both should work in tandem—the chairman providing leadership on the ground and the ministry providing support and supervision. In practice, it often devolves into a struggle over 'who runs the class'. Observers describe an implicit tug-of-war: a proactive chairman may push new initiatives or assert their authority, only to meet resistance or delays from career officials at the ministry who prefer to tighten purse strings and micromanage from Delhi. Conversely, if a chairman is inactive or politically weak, the ministry might dominate, reducing KVIC to a mere subordinate office. Either way, accountability becomes diffused. As one assessment noted, it's often unclear 'who's really in charge—the chairman or the ministry mandarins?', and this lack of clear command has made decisive leadership a casualty.

A historical example illustrates the oddity: The high-level Sukthankar Committee (2005), which reviewed KVIC, pointed out that the chairman had become the de facto chief executive of KVIC, wielding control over all departments—a concentration of power atypical for a public institution. Normally, in government bodies, a CEO or member-secretary would handle day-to-day operations while the chair oversees policy. In KVIC's case, the law itself creates a powerful executive chairman. This was intended to allow swift decision-making, but in reality, it sometimes spawns personality clashes and politicised decision chains. For instance, if the chairman is aligned with the ruling party's agenda and the MSME ministry has a different view (or vice versa), KVIC can be pulled in different directions (Chapter 18 discusses this in detail) or left in paralysis awaiting 'clearances'. There have been episodes where major initiatives (like aspects of the KRDP reforms or restructuring proposals) stalled because of differences between KVIC's leadership and the ministry. The losers in these ego battles are ultimately the khadi artisans, who see needed decisions delayed or diluted. Strong, consistent leadership is hard to achieve when the very structure encourages a 'two masters' problem, and KVIC's top management often ends up spending energy on internal turf guarding instead of focusing solely on sector outcomes. Critics point to this governance quirk as one reason many well-intentioned plans have faltered: with power so tangled, no one is squarely held accountable when targets are missed. Unless KVIC's governance is streamlined and depoliticised, attempts to reform its workings risk being undermined by the next tug-of-war between its overseers.

Raw Material Crunch and the Paradox of Productivity

While KVIC grapples with structural and administrative challenges, the ground reality for khadi production is no less troubling. The supply chain from cotton to cloth has become another stress point, highlighting KVIC's reactive and stopgap approach. Consider the recent cotton price shock that hit the sector. In late 2021, cotton prices in India skyrocketed within a matter of months—from roughly ₹36,000 per candy (a standard unit) to as high as ₹78,000. This kind of spike can be ruinous for khadi spinners and weavers, who operate on thin margins. As raw cotton became unaffordable for village artisans, KVIC was forced into emergency action: it dipped into a special Price Adjustment Fund to cover an extra ₹4.06 crore worth of raw cotton costs out of its own pocket, rather than passing the price increase onto the spinners. This stopgap measure protected artisans in the short term, but it underscores how vulnerable the sector is to commodity swings. The wider textile industry responded to the cotton inflation by cutting production by an estimated 30–35%. KVIC, meanwhile, had to scramble to procure enough cotton bales for its KIs at vastly higher prices, planning to spend ₹13.25 crore on cotton in fiscal year 2022 compared to ₹9.2 crore the previous year. Such volatility can wipe out the modest profits of khadi units and make planning impossible. Yet, KVIC has limited tools at its disposal beyond using contingency funds or lobbying for subsidies from the central government to subsidise raw materials.

Next comes the stage of processing cotton into sliver (the carded fibre ready for spinning). KVIC operates six Central Sliver Plants (CSPs) that convert bales of cotton into sliver for distribution to khadi spinners. These CSPs have become a chronic bottleneck. Instead of ensuring a consistent supply of quality fibre to artisans, they have been the target of frequent complaints. Artisans and KIs allege that the sliver provided by

KVIC's plants is often of uneven or low quality, and sold at high prices—hardly a service to the community. The CAG has noted (Chapter 18 discusses this at length) repeated reports from the field about overpriced, substandard sliver being forced on khadi units, which not only raises their costs but also affects the quality of the final fabric. This puts genuine khadi producers in a double bind: cotton is expensive if they try to buy it independently, but the 'official' sliver is also costly and sometimes inferior, hampering their productivity and output quality. Here again, KVIC's management seems reactive—addressing complaints after damage is done—rather than instituting a robust quality control and fair pricing mechanism for its sliver supply.

Finally, we circle back to the paradox of technology in the khadi sector, partly touched on earlier. Nowhere is this more evident than in weaving and processing. Khadi's charm is its hand-made quality, but that also means it is labour-intensive and slow. While powerloom and automated mill fabrics churn out yards by the minute, a khadi weaver may spend hours to weave a single metre of cloth. KVIC has experimented with marginal technological improvements (like decentralised solar-powered spinning wheels or slightly better looms), but any significant leap confronts the dilemma of potentially reducing the labour force. The organisation's own reports acknowledge this tension. When multi-spindle charkhas were tried, they increased output per spinner by as much as two to three times, but immediately triggered fears of job cuts, leading some within KVIC to question such upgrades. Similarly, attempts to introduce pedal-driven or motor-assisted carding machines (to replace manual cotton fluffing) have met resistance on the grounds that they take away work from labourers. This aversion to productivity-enhancing tools means khadi remains trapped in a time capsule. An anecdote often cited: a single modern textile mill in one day produces more fabric than an entire state's khadi units do in a year. That is an exaggeration, but it contains truth about the scale mismatch. Consequently, khadi struggles to compete on cost, consistency, or volume in wider markets. It survives in a niche of patriotism, government patronage (e.g. mandatory khadi purchases by ministries), and eco-conscious consumer curiosity. But to transition from an old-style subsidy-driven cottage industry to a self-sustaining rural enterprise network, KVIC would need to resolve this paradox—finding innovations that increase artisans' earnings and product marketability without simply rendering many artisans redundant. So far, it has not squared that circle.

In summary, the KVIC finds itself fighting fires on all fronts: spurious 'khadi' products eroding its brand, unreliable data and ghost beneficiaries eroding trust, subsidy dependence eroding financial viability, failed reforms eroding donor confidence, bureaucratic turf wars eroding effective governance, and supply chain and technology snafus eroding productivity. The cumulative effect is a flagship rural institution that, despite noble intentions and considerable funding, has not delivered to its full potential in recent years.

Conclusion: Reclaiming the Spirit of Khadi

Khadi was born as more than a fabric—it was the material embodiment of self-reliance, dignity of labour, and an economic vision for empowering the poorest of the poor. Today, that spirit is tattered but not beyond repair. The story of KVIC's woes is not just one of incompetence or inertia; it is also a story of missed opportunities and the need for courageous change. To reclaim the soul of khadi, cosmetic fixes won't suffice. A meaningful turnaround would require a cultural overhaul within KVIC and its network.

Accountability must be the new mantra. This means instituting third-party monitoring and independent audits at every level—no more trusting self-reported figures blindly. Whether it's production tallies, sales, or job creation, an external eye should verify outcomes before public money is spent. Funding should be tied to results: if a KI chronically fails to meet even a reasonable fraction of its targets and cannot justify the funds it received, it must see consequences (budget cuts, leadership change, or even de-listing from KVIC). Conversely, those that perform well and innovate should be rewarded with greater support. As radical as it sounds, KVIC may need to cull the deadwood—shutting down or merging units that have become phantom entities—so that resources can be focused on real, functioning enterprises. The goal should be a leaner, transparent, and efficient khadi ecosystem rather than a bloated one riddled with ghosts.

Digitisation, done right, still holds promise. KIMIS, in its current avatar, might be a flop, but a robust MIS is indispensable for a geographically dispersed operation of this scale. The lesson from the KRDP failure is that technology must be introduced with proper training, appropriate simplification, and phased adoption. A revamped KIMIS (or a successor platform) should incorporate user-friendly mobile interfaces, vernacular language support, and offline functionality for areas with poor connectivity. It also needs to be integrated with other government databases (GST, banking, Aadhaar) to automatically flag discrepancies like duplicate beneficiaries or impossible production claims. In parallel, KVIC must invest in digital literacy and change management among its staff and artisans so that the technology is embraced rather than feared.

Governance reforms are equally critical. KVIC has to shed its image as a patronage-driven bureaucracy and reinvent itself as a professional development agency. This could mean bringing in outside experts (as the 2006 amendment attempted, at least on paper) and empowering them to make decisions. The KVIC Board should include independent voices who can push for innovation and hold the organisation to benchmarks. At the same time, the overlapping controls of the commission and the ministry need rationalisation. Clear lines of authority—and responsibility—should be drawn. If the chairman is the CEO, then let him/her truly run it (and be answerable for outcomes) without constant ministerial interference; alternatively, appoint a strong CEO and let the chairman be a non-executive guide. But the present neither-here-nor-there structure must be fixed to enable accountable leadership.

The ministry's role also needs to be clear—it cannot 'boss' over KVIC or meddle in its day-to-day management. At the same time, appointments to top management of KVIC should be streamlined so that the ministry and KVIC are on the same page—this is perhaps the most challenging aspect of all. Both are two wheels of the same cart and should stop pulling in different directions. Often, 'ego' issues or one-upmanship dominate the scene and spoil the working relationship, so essential to the sector's progress. Quite a few secretaries and ministers withdraw themselves from actively and positively intervening for the betterment of the sector (apart from participation in ceremonial events) precisely due to these entirely man-made issues. No amount of instructions and amendments to the statute would work unless the top echelons of the two engines (the chairman, KVIC, and the ministry) drop their pretences and work together for the real betterment of the sector and the artisans. The chairman, KVIC, and the minister of MSME rarely meet. The secretary of MSME does not take any interest other than what is unavoidable. Unfortunately, the sad state of affairs continues, with no end to the almost 'cold war'-like situation between the mandarins of the two engines, despite the 2006 amendments to the KVIC Act, proving that it is implementation that really matters rather than the textual intent of the amendments. The contribution of technical and marketing members in the KVIC to the improvement of the sector has almost become perfunctory, if not zilch. Nobody appears interested in admitting the well-known problems, let alone attempting to solve them, though almost all officials in the institution, as well as the ministry, are aware.

On the operational side, KVIC should address the supply chain and marketing gaps that hobble khadi's competitiveness. This could involve bulk purchase agreements for raw cotton to hedge against price shocks, modernisation of sliver plants with quality audits (or outsourcing to better performers if KVIC's own units can't deliver), and upgraded common facility centres where artisans can access improved tools without losing jobs (for instance, a model where productivity gains translate into artisans being able to produce more and earn more in less time, rather than being laid off). The khadi brand, meanwhile, needs rejuvenation in the marketplace. There is a growing global demand for sustainable, ethically-made textiles. Khadi—authentically handmade, organic, and with a nationalistic legacy—could tap into this niche with the right branding and design innovation. KVIC has started to talk about 'Fashion Khadi' and tie-ups with designers; such efforts should be scaled up so that khadi is not sold only as a nationalist duty, but as an appealing product in its own right.

Above all, KVIC and policymakers must remember that khadi's true USP (Unique Selling Point) is the empowerment it offers to rural artisans. Every reform or scheme must ultimately be measured by that yardstick: Does it improve the livelihoods and dignity of those who spin and weave? That was Gandhi's original intent. It can still be the guiding light. To translate that into reality today, KVIC will need to be honest about its failures and bold about changes. It must move from being a clearinghouse of subsidies to a catalyst of sustainable rural industry. The road ahead calls for tough love—pulling the plug on chronic inefficiencies, demanding real performance, and fostering genuine entrepreneurship among khadi clusters. The government, too, must back KVIC's overhaul not just with money (which it always has) but also with a political will to resist pressures that perpetuate the status quo.

The khadi sector's slow decline can be halted and reversed, but only if all stakeholders stop treating it as a nostalgia-driven welfare relic and start treating it as a viable enterprise sector that needs discipline and innovation. In a country proud of its 'startup culture' and 'Make in India' mantra, there is no reason khadi cannot find a meaningful place—combining tradition with technology—in the contemporary economy. The spinning wheel may be a metaphor of the past, but the ethos of self-sufficiency and dignity it represents is timeless. The KVIC, if it cleans up its act, can still spin a new yarn of revival—one in which every inch of handspun thread carries real weight in the fabric of India's future.

References:

1. Asian Development Bank. Khadi Reform and Development Programme (KRDP). Loan No. 2225-IND, ADB India Country Program; 2009.

2. Ministry of MSME (India), Asian Development Bank. Mid-Term Review and Restructuring of KRDP. Joint Review Report; 2013.

3. Comptroller and Auditor General of India. Performance Audit on Implementation of Promotional Schemes in KVIC. Report 12 of 2016, Chapter 4:35–42.

4. Internal Evaluation Report on KIMIS (Khadi Institution Management Information System). Ministry of MSME (India); 2022. Unpublished internal document.

5. Comptroller and Auditor General of India. Performance Audit on Khadi and Village Industries Commission. Report 18 of 2020:47–52.

6. National Institute of Labour Economics Research and Development (NILERD). Evaluation of Budgeting and Financial Monitoring Practices in KVIC. Report commissioned by NITI Aayog; 2019.

7. KVIC (Khadi and Village Industries Commission, India). Annual Administrative Report 2023–24. Ministry of MSME, Government of India; 2024.

8. Parliamentary Standing Committee on Industry (Rajya Sabha, India). Impact of KVIC Schemes on Artisan Employment. 313th Report; 2022.

9. KVIC. Progress Report: IT-MIS Implementation in 400 Khadi Institutions. Internal report; October 2017. (Details the MIS rollout, hardware provision, training, and challenges.)

10. KVIC Letter No. RIDA (RDP/3rd Tranche conditions)/2017–18 dated 30 October 2017 to Ministry of MSME. (Asserting that the MIS was implemented in 400 KIs and requesting the Ministry to report compliance to ADB.)

11. Asian Development Bank. Loan Agreement for Khadi Reform and Development Programme. Loan No. 2366-IND (KVIC KRDP); 2008. (Includes disbursement conditions and tranche-linked reforms.)

12. Asian Development Bank. Periodic Financing Request Reports – Tranche 2 and 3, KRDP. Internal ADB evaluation documents; 2014–2017.

13. Ministry of MSME (India). Annual Reports 2009–2018 (especially 2016–17 and 2017–18) – References to KRDP implementation, ADB loan tranches, and digitisation challenges.

14. KVIC. KIMIS User Manual. Khadi and VI Commission; 2018. (Step-by-step guide for stock entry, artisan registration, billing, etc., illustrating system complexity.)

15. Asian Development Bank. Project Documents for KRDP (Project No. 38424-013). ADB Project Portfolio; 2008–2017. (Includes project evaluations, progress summaries, and tranche release updates.)

16. Comptroller and Auditor General of India. Performance Audit Reports on KVIC and Artisan Schemes. New Delhi; 2010–2020. (Periodic audits noting KVIC data reliability issues and fund utilisation problems.)

17. Ministry of MSME (India). Parliamentary Q&A and Standing Committee Proceedings on KVIC (2015–2021). (Includes discussions on KRDP target shortfalls and ghost workers identification.)

18. Field Reports from Maharashtra, Uttar Pradesh, Gujarat Khadi Institutions. (Collected feedback on KRDP and KIMIS from grassroots artisans, 2012–2015.)

19. Planning Commission of India/NITI Aayog. Working Group Papers on KVIC and MSME Reforms. 2012 & 2017. (Context on institutional constraints in KVIC and rationale for seeking international assistance.)

20. Sukthankar Committee Report. High Powered Committee on KVIC Reforms; 2005. (Examined KVIC's organisational structure; noted Chairman's excessive executive role.)

21. Press Information Bureau (India). 'KVIC Achieves Record Turnover and Jobs in 2023–24'. Release ID 194511; 9 July 2024. (Claims 1.55 lakh crore turnover, 400% sales growth, 10 lakh new jobs vs 2013–14.)

22. Khadi and Village Industries Commission (KVIC). Data Compilation and Verification Methods. KVIC Policy Circular 17; 2023. (Discusses improvements via KIMIS and remaining data gaps.)

23. Media Reports on KVIC Reforms:

24. The Hindu Business Line. 'ADB holds back funds over Khadi reform compliance shortfall.' 5 June 2017.

25. LiveMint. 'Khadi digitisation hits snag as KVIC struggles with IT adoption.' 18 December 2016.

26. Down To Earth. 'Khadi reforms unravel as KVIC misses transformation targets.' 10 February 2018.

27. Khandekar N. Reforming Khadi: Between Gandhian Ideals and Global Finance. Economic & Political Weekly. 2019; 54(30). (Discusses the ideological and operational conflicts in the KRDP era.)

CHAPTER 18

◆◆◆

The CAG vs KVIC – Audit Trails and Uncomfortable Truths

It began, like many things wrapped in the national tricolour, with the dream of Mahatma Gandhi. A dream spun on the humble charkha—a dream of self-reliance, dignity in labour, and rural resurgence. When the KVIC was established in 1956 by an Act of Parliament, it carried with it the moral weight of the freedom movement and the economic aspirations of independent India. KVIC was not just another bureaucracy—it was supposed to be a movement, a mission, a bridge between the dusty village looms and the gleaming urban markets, between the artisan and the customer, between Bharat and India.

But dreams, when not nurtured with integrity and urgency, can unravel.

The CAG's 2023 compliance audit of KVIC is not merely a technical assessment. It is a dissection of a broken promise—a mirror held up to an institution that once carried the hopes of rural India but is now trapped in inertia, outdated methods, and indifferent management. Spread over four years, the audit turned the spotlight on the Departmental Trading Units (DTUs) of KVIC—units that were supposed to be the physical arms of production, procurement, and marketing. What the audit found was devastating.

Of the 92 DTUs created over decades, only 18 were functional as of March 2021. That's a survival rate of less than 20%. The remaining 74 had become defunct. Some simply withered away without notice, others were formally shut down, but the common thread across most closures was this: KVIC had no clue why they failed. No internal reports. No stakeholder impact assessments. No lessons learned. In 11 out of 25 defunct units that CAG examined, even the basic paperwork explaining the reasons for closure was missing.

And the few cases where reasons existed were often more frustrating than illuminating. Take the CSP at Etah, Uttar Pradesh. It was established to supply cotton roving to KIs in the northern belt. However, for two decades, it functioned entirely on diesel generators, thanks to an unresolved power supply issue. KVIC's proposals for restoring electricity or installing solar alternatives remained stuck in bureaucratic limbo. Even when four registered KIs expressed willingness to revive the plant, KVIC declined the offer. Instead, it let ₹79 lakh worth of equipment lie idle and continued spending ₹69 lakh more on guarding the defunct unit.

The CSP at Etah didn't fail because of market forces. It failed because KVIC failed it.

The farce deepens when you realise what was happening outside KVIC's purview. During the same period that KVIC's units lay defunct, 87 private players in West Bengal and 11 in Rajasthan were merrily selling products branded 'khadi'—without authorisation. Their combined turnover? A staggering ₹1,025 crore between 2017 and 2021. These were not certified institutions. They were counterfeiters, riding on the goodwill of the khadi brand while the real artisans and certified suppliers languished without access to KVIC showrooms.

Inside the surviving DTUs, things weren't exactly humming either. The Khadi Gramodyog Bhavans (KGBs)—KVIC's flagship retail outlets—were meant to be showcases of rural enterprise. From khadi garments to honey, herbal cosmetics to wooden toys, they were envisioned as urban windows to India's villages. But in reality, they had become dusty, understocked, poorly managed relics of a bygone era.

The rules governing procurement were clear—annual procurement plans based on market demand, fair selection of suppliers, and transparent pricing. But the Bhavans operated more like old boys' clubs. The same set of vendors received repeated orders year after year. Just eight suppliers accounted for more than 20% of sales across multiple Bhavans, while 80% of registered suppliers were barely represented. In Kolkata, only 10% of empanelled institutions got any shelf space. Procurement plans, if they existed at all, were unrealistic. Market trend analysis? Non-existent. Product catalogues? Outdated or missing. And the mandated Procurement Committees either didn't meet or simply went through the motions.

This opacity had predictable consequences. In four Bhavans alone, unsold stock worth ₹8.19 crore was found rotting—some of it over a decade old. Worse, these Bhavans were still procuring on a consignment basis, even though the GST regime prohibited it after July 2017. Suppliers were supposed to be paid within 180 days, failing which KVIC would lose its input tax credit. But payments were being delayed until after sales, pushing smaller artisans and institutions to the brink and exposing KVIC to financial risk.

And then came the scandal of fake khadi. The khadi brand, protected under trademark law and subject to quality certifications, is not just a label—it's a promise of handspun, handwoven fabric made from Indian fibre. Yet, CAG found rampant non-compliance in testing protocols. At Bhopal's Bhavan, eight of 14 samples in one year turned out to be fake, machine-made fabric falsely sold as khadi. In Mumbai, a consumer complaint led to the discovery of a similar scam. KVIC's reaction? Ban the supplier, but take no systemic steps to strengthen checks.

Despite all this, KVIC claimed that things were under control. It said that new systems like the KIMIS were now in place. But the CAG found that while KIMIS existed, it was rarely used effectively. It contained modules for item-wise and supplier-wise sales analysis, but nobody extracted the data. Nobody used it to shape procurement or marketing. It was a digital monument to missed opportunity.

KVIC's marketing reforms were equally hollow. Funds were allocated for refurbishing Bhavans, hiring consultants, launching e-commerce platforms, opening franchise outlets, and setting up Khadi Plazas. But most of these initiatives remained on paper. Consultants were hired without clearly defined deliverables. Franchisees were opened without feasibility studies. Not a single Khadi Plaza was built despite multiple schemes and budget allocations. The entire marketing strategy resembled a cloth stitched with invisible thread—elusive and insubstantial.

Even the much-hyped Khadi Trademark enforcement was toothless. While KVIC had secured legal rights over several marks, including 'Khadi India', 'Sarvodaya', and the 'Khadi Mark', it took little to no action against hundreds of violators. No civil suits. No FIRs (First Information Reports). No injunctions. This passive approach allowed counterfeiters to dominate markets while certified institutions floundered.

Financial governance was another disaster zone. KVIC couldn't recover ₹6.81 crore worth of receivables from closed units. Fixed assets worth lakhs were neither transferred nor auctioned. In some cases, employees of defunct units remained on payroll for up to ten years after closure. Bank reconciliations were not done. Internal audits were perfunctory, and even when they flagged serious issues, top management took no corrective action.

At its heart, the KVIC story is not just a story of administrative failure. It's a story of betrayal. For every defunct DTU, there are artisans who lost their livelihoods. For every monopolised Bhavan, there are producers who never got a fair chance. For every fake khadi product sold, a genuine artisan was robbed of income and dignity.

The CAG has made 26 recommendations. From revamping procurement practices and enforcing quality control to strengthening internal audits and launching viable marketing schemes, the path to reform is well mapped. But these recommendations are not checkboxes—they are lifelines.

KVIC must act. Not tomorrow. Not when another audit looms. Now.

The revival of khadi is not a romantic project. It is an economic necessity. In a country where millions are migrating from rural to urban areas in search of dignity and livelihood, institutions like KVIC are vital. They can anchor artisans in their communities, promote sustainable production, and project India's soft power globally. But only if they reform.

If KVIC fails to heed the warnings of this audit, it risks becoming a museum piece—a forgotten corner in the Ministry of MSME's archives. But if it reforms, modernises, and recommits to its founding ideals, it can still reclaim its legacy. It can once again become the backbone of rural enterprise, the torchbearer of Gandhi's vision, and the symbol of an India that remembers not just how to grow, but how to grow with dignity.

The CAG has handed KVIC a mirror. What it does next will decide whether the khadi story spins back into relevance—or fades into the folds of history.

References:

1. Comptroller and Auditor General of India, 'Report No. 9 of 2023: Compliance Audit on KVIC', submitted under Article 151 of the Constitution, pp. iii–x.

2. Ibid., Executive Summary, p. v–vi: 18 functional units out of 92; 74 units defunct with no clear documentation.

3. Ibid., Chapter III, pp. 7–12: Case study of CSP Etah and offers from four Khadi institutions for revival.

4. Ibid., Chapter III, p. 9: ₹716.7 crore turnover of unauthorised firms in West Bengal; ₹309.07 crore in Rajasthan.

5. Ibid., Chapter IV, pp. 13–20: Skewed procurement, consignment model post-GST, and fake khadi testing results.

6. Ibid., Chapter V, pp. 45–80: Non-implementation of marketing schemes, failure of consultants, and absence of Khadi Plaza success.

7. Ibid., Chapter VI, pp. 81–92: Internal audit deficiencies, unrecovered dues, and delayed re-deployment of staff.

CHAPTER 19

The State of India's MSME Incubators (2018–24): A Reality Check

In theory, India's MSME institutions (NIESBUD, NIMSME, .NSIC, and the DC–MSME's field offices) are the launchpads for new entrepreneurs. On paper, they've trained millions: for example, NIESBUD alone claims to have taught 14.65 lakh people by March 2024 (around 44,000 in 2018–19 and roughly 12 lakh since its inception). But independent reviews raise red flags. A 2021 CAG report blasted these programmes for poor monitoring, padded records, and unreturned grants. In other words, the buzzwords (millions trained, high placement rates) outshine actual outcomes. Let's unpack each institution:

Imagine joining a coaching centre that promises to prepare you for government exams. But there's no attendance record, no teacher evaluations, and no test results. When asked, the centre claims 'thousands trained'—but can't name a single student who passed.

That's how NIESBUD and NIMSME functioned. They claimed lakhs trained, but audits found missing course records, no outcome tracking, and even fake placement data.

NIESBUD

This NOIDA-based institute is perhaps the best-known 'incubator'. It indeed runs thousands of courses—its website boasts training about 44,000 students in 2018–19 (part of ~1.2 million since start), reaching 14.65 lakh trainees by 2024. But quantity has not guaranteed quality. The 2021 CAG audit found serious lapses in NIESBUD's tracking and finance:

> Say your dad gives you ₹1,000 to buy school books. You spend ₹700 and keep the rest. But when he asks what happened to the balance, you say, 'I saved it for future opportunity cost.'
>
> That's what NIESBUD did with ₹2.78 crore. Instead of returning unspent government funds, it claimed to be 'retaining it for opportunity value'. The CAG rightly called this out as unjustified hoarding

- Dodgy accounting: Auditors discovered NIESBUD (and partner NIMSME) held back large unspent balances—₹2.78 crore in NIESBUD's case (₹1.27 cr in NIMSME)—without reporting it to the ministry. NIESBUD even defended itself by saying it was keeping ₹0.96 cr principal + ₹1.83 cr interest as 'opportunity cost'—a claim the audit flatly rejected.

- Outsourced delivery: It turns out NIESBUD's Noida centre subcontracted 99% of its own courses to private agencies. The audit noted that those files often lacked completion reports or trainee certificates, meaning NIESBUD itself had no proof that thousands of students were actually taught.

No outcome proof: NIESBUD liked to tout 'Rozgar Melas' (job fairs) and course completions, but the audit warned that even its claim that '36% of trainees found jobs' is unverified fluff. In fact, the audit bluntly concluded the training scheme 'largely failed to achieve envisaged outcomes owing to inadequate monitoring and poor implementation'.

In short, NIESBUD pumped out headcounts of trained people, but a government audit found that it had flouted rules,

> Think of a school where every single class is taught not by its own teachers, but by temporary outsiders—often without credentials. The school doesn't even collect the final marksheets.
>
> That's what NIESBUD did. It subcontracted 99% of its training programs to third parties, often without completion reports or certificates. So how can we be sure training even happened?

fudged data and hid funds. Its own success stories thus, must be taken with a grain of salt—independent checks show little real follow-up on whether the graduates became viable entrepreneurs.

NIMSME

NIMSME (formerly CIETI (Central Industrial Extension Training Institute)) is MSME's principal entrepreneurship training arm. It runs advanced management programmes and thematic courses. Like NIESBUD, it boasts large numbers of 'trained entrepreneurs' (exact tallies are sketchy online). However, the same CAG audit exposed NIMSME's blind spots:

- **Undeclared money:** The audit found NIMSME kept ~₹1.27 crore unspent (plus interest) from government grants during 2012–18 without telling the ministry—effectively concealing funds. (This, combined with NIESBUD's ₹2.78 crore, meant ₹4.05 crore of training money was not accounted for in reports.)
- **Weak tracking:** NIMSME was supposed to monitor partner institutes and verify placements. The auditors noted no evidence

that NIMSME staff ever effectively oversaw those programmes. In fact, NIMSME couldn't even produce documents to show they'd trained the trainers or visited field centres.

- **If it worked, nobody knows:** Official data claim tens of thousands of NIMSME trainees got wage or self-employment, but the audit highlighted big discrepancies (see tables). Crucially, auditors said without independent verification, 'the claim of 36% employment generation cannot be relied upon'—applying to all apex institutes, including NIMSME.

So NIMSME, too, has been flagged for bookkeeping gaps and a lack of evidence that its long courses actually produce new businesses. In practice, the institute has struggled to prove its impact. The government has even admitted that it must tighten schemes to 'convert training into livelihood'—tacitly conceding that until now, little follow-up has happened.

NSIC

NSIC is a central PSU (now Mini-Ratna–I) focusing on credit, marketing, and technology support for small enterprises. It runs

> Imagine a school that hands out certificates to everyone who walks through the gate—no classes attended, no exams passed, no feedback taken. When asked about student success, it just shrugs.
>
> This is how MSME field offices operate. They conduct short-term courses, distribute participation certificates, and then leave trainees to figure things out—with no post-training support or tracking.

technical centres, a well-known Performance and Credit Rating scheme (to ease bank loans for SMEs), and the national SC/ST Hub (promoting SC/ST-owned MSMEs). According to official slides, NSIC also delivers training: e.g., it reported about 45,000 entrepreneurship/skill trainings by 2017–18, and served ~9,000 units via common facilities that year. However, independent analyses of NSIC's effectiveness are thin. NSIC, unlike NIESBUD/NIMSME, didn't show up in the 2021 skill audit's findings on placement rates. Its main measures—number of MSMEs rated or SC/ST beneficiaries reached—are mixed proxies at best. (For instance, by 2024, PMEGP has helped ~9.87 lakh enterprises with bank loans, but that's a different scheme outside NSIC's direct purview.)

> Say your friend borrows your book but never returns it. Worse, he lies about it. And you keep giving him more books.
>
> That's what happened with MSME training funds. Institutes like NIESBUD and NIMSME withheld ₹4.05 crore from the government and didn't disclose it. Yet, they kept getting new funds without consequences.

In short, NSIC talks the talk on MSME growth (and does run large programmes), but data on real business outcomes is lacking. Even a parliamentary report notes that NSIC has run without budgetary aid since 2007—implying it must earn/recover costs from its services. There's no clear independent tracking showing how many NSIC-trained entrepreneurs got credit or scaled up. Anecdotally, NSIC's credit rating scheme has helped some units get bank loans, but there is no public audit of the 'graduates' success rate'.

DC-MSME Field Offices (MSME-DIs (MSME Development Institutes), DFIs (Development Finance Institutions), etc.)

At the grassroots, the Office of DC-MSME's regional centres and district institutes run the bulk of ESDPs, awareness camps, and industrial facilitation. In theory, these should feed 'trained' candidates into startups or employment. In reality, however, the same problems recur. Government audits and committees have warned that placement claims are unreliable. For example, the blanket figure, '36% of ESDP trainees placed', is drawn from conflicting data sets (ministry vs institute reports), so it has no audit backing. The CAG report bluntly said that in the absence of hard evidence, such employment statistics 'cannot be relied upon'.

> Picture a driving school that teaches only road signs and traffic rules—but never lets you drive a real car. Then it says you're 'road ready'.
>
> That's what MSME incubators are doing. They teach entrepreneurship in classrooms but offer no real business mentoring, handholding, credit access, or field support. So the 'entrepreneurs' remain stranded.

No wonder the field units have no easy mechanism to track entrants after training. A Parliamentary Standing Committee has repeatedly urged follow-ups (e.g., encouraging internships, handholding); yet, in practice, these offices mostly deliver courses and then leave trainees to fend for themselves. In other words, the field network expands the funnel of trained people, but doesn't guarantee the launch of businesses. As the CAG concluded, the ministry 'largely failed to achieve envisaged outcomes'. In plain terms, we can count certificates handed out, but we have little proof of actual jobs or viable firms created at scale.

Key takeaways: Across the board, the MSME institutional push is output-heavy and outcome-light. Milestones like 'train 14 lakh people' are cited, but no one's tracking whether they spawn 1.4 lakh enterprises. Audits repeatedly point to weak oversight: institutes often ran courses without proper monitoring or evidence (even falsified records). They also mismanaged funds: for instance, NIESBUD/NIMSME hid ~₹4.05 cr of grants. The government's own reviews admit these gaps, urging better KYC checks and post-training support. Until such fixes happen, the grand numbers on 'MSME training success' will remain suspect.

References:

1. Official MSME scheme documents, institutional reports and news releases, and government audit/committee findings (CAG audit Report No.16 of 2021, Ministry of MSME annual report data, press statements, etc.).

2. https://niesbudtraining.in/Pages/Home.aspx

3. https://cag.gov.in/uploads/download_audit_report/2021/9_Chapter%205-061c1b9cd5bd077.38754359.pdf#:~:text=during%20 2012,XXXV

4. https://msme.gov.in/sites/default/files/Performance-of-under-various-scheme-of-MSME.pdf#:~:text=served%20%28Nos,2007

5. https://pib.gov.in/PressReleseDetailmaspx?PRID=2089308®=3 &lang=1

6. https://timesofindia.indiatimes.com/business/india-business/ skill-development-minister-reviews-reviews-niesbud-performance/ articleshow/70487804.cms

CHAPTER 20

◆◆◆

Inside the Ministry: Bureaucratic Apathy, Political Atonement

Abstract:

India's MSMEs are the spine of its economy, reportedly employing over 110 million people and contributing over 30% to the GDP. Yet, they remain orphans in the governance ecosystem—paraded in slogans, neglected in strategy, and stifled by bureaucratic inertia. This chapter critically explores how decades of institutional apathy, politicised leadership, and flawed administrative practices have derailed MSME policy formulation and implementation. Drawing from an insider's anguished note and additional insights, it lays bare the revolving door of disinterested secretaries, ornamental ministers, token budgets, and chronic mismanagement in institutions like KVIC. It also highlights the few exceptions—bold bureaucrats who tried to change course—and how their initiatives were diluted or derailed. It calls for a radical overhaul of MSME governance if India truly wants to walk the talk on 'Make in India'.

The Farce of Policy and the Fraud of Commitment

If India's MSMEs had a face, it would be bruised from decades of being patted with slogans while being pummelled by systemic neglect. The sector—diverse, dynamic, and indispensable—is the darling of government speeches but the stepson in actual governance. Why? The answer begins with the top.

Imagine a hospital ward where the doctor treating critical patients is changed every two weeks. The new doctor doesn't read the file, doesn't know the patient's history, and leaves before seeing results.

That's what happens in the MSME ministry. No secretary completes a full tenure. Reform plans come and go. Continuity is lost. Progress resets every time the nameplate changes.

Look at the tenure of secretaries (Appendix 2) posted to the Ministry of MSME in the last 20 years. Only one had completed a full two-year term. Instead, the ministry has been reduced to a loop line—where civil servants are shunted just before retirement, often as consolation postings for careers that didn't culminate in the glamour of finance, defence, or commerce. Most Secretaries arrive with neither domain knowledge nor any real desire to leave a legacy. One CMD (Chairman-cum-Managing Director) of the NSIC, functioning under the Ministry of MSME, reportedly told a secretary, 'Sir, I'll be around for the next MoU. But you won't.' The telling cynicism reflects a larger truth: institutional memory is zero, ownership of initiatives is absent, and incentives for reform are rare if not perverse.

Suppose a trained railway engineer is asked to run a toy train—and told it's a 'ministerial role'.

That's how MSME ministers are often chosen. Political lightweights or retirees with no sector knowledge are placed in charge of a sector that fuels one-third of India's economy.

Worse, many of these secretaries are risk-averse to a fault. Little or knowing that they have nothing to gain post-retirement and everything to lose from stirring the pot, they sit quietly, sign files passively, and ensure no waves are created. They rest content with trying to get the budget allocation spent without surrenders in the financial year. Those who try something radical are either outvoted or outlasted. As an insider aptly puts it, '*Isliye woh na karta hai na karne deta hai.* (That's why he neither does anything nor lets others do anything.)'

But not all were duds. Two exceptions stand out—Anupam Dasgupta (IAS-70, Maharashtra) and Dinesh Rai (IAS-74, UP). Their tenures between 2005 and 2009 brought tectonic changes. Under Dasgupta, the MSMED Act was conceptualised and steered, creating for the first time a statutory definition of MSMEs, inclusion of services in the definition of MSMEs, mandatory procurement quotas, and prioritisation of MSME dues, to name a few. Good old legacy institution, KVIC's structure was attempted to be revamped to include a supposedly professional board with experienced representatives from banking, marketing experts, and engineering professionals. Under Rai, the reforms were carried forward, such as rationalising the biennial surveys of MSMEs, refining and expanding the scope of the Credit Guarantee Trust Fund for MSMEs, and getting $150 million in financial assistance for Khadi Reforms and Development.

> Picture a school where one student, who already has resources, gets all the new books and supplies, while the rest share torn pages.
>
> That's how MSME schemes work. Most of the budget benefits small and medium units. The vast majority—micro enterprises—are left behind.

Madhav Lal (20 February 2013 to 30 June 2015) took several initiatives to strengthen the Public Procurement Policy. Orders were issued to mandate 4% annual procurement by Central Ministries/ Departments and Public Sector Undertakings from

SC/ST enterprises with effect from 1 April 2015. Under Anup K Pujari (30 June 2015 to 31 January 2016), the Ministry of MSME took initiatives to improve the ease of doing business. He advocated the need for handholding of budding entrepreneurs, which later laid the foundation of Startup India, one of the flagship programmes of the Government of India. In September 2015, under the MSME Development Act, 2006, it was notified that every MSME unit shall file online a simple one-page Udyog Aadhaar Memorandum (UAM) on http://udyogaadhaar.gov.in, replacing the need to file Entrepreneurs' Memorandum (EM part-I & II) with the respective states/UTs (union territories). Over 95,000 UAMs were filed within a short period of three Months. Krishan Kumar Jalan (1 February 2016 to 30 June 2017) initiated the first-of-its-kind online MSME Internet Grievance Monitoring System (MSME-IGMS), which was aimed at not only addressing the grievances of entrepreneurs but also providing necessary guidance to new entrepreneurs. This online system was later developed into a full-fledged CHAMPION portal. Since the Government of India introduced the GST during his tenure, MSME-IGMS was made to provide a dedicated link for GST-related grievances, making it easier for MSMEs to resolve tax concerns. In December 2016, the Union Cabinet approved the cadre review and formation of a new service in the name of 'Indian Enterprise Development Service (IEDS)' to strengthen the organisation and achieve the vision of 'Startup India', 'Stand-Up India' and 'Make in India' to achieve growth in MSME sector through a focused and dedicated cadre of technical officers. Much credit goes to Amarendra Sinha, IAS-81 (UK), who was the DC-MSME.

In October 2016, the National SC/ST Hub was launched with an initial allocation of ₹490 crore for 2016–2020. Although procurement from SC/ST enterprises was mandated in 2015 to be a minimum of 4%, it was actually less than 1%. Hence, the hub, which was made to operate from the NSIC HQ in Delhi, supported by a special cell created for this purpose, was meant to primarily aid in strengthening market access/linkage, monitoring, capacity building, leveraging financial support schemes and sharing industry best practices, etc. with the entrepreneurs belonging to SC and ST.

But reform doesn't survive in a vacuum—it needs follow-through. KVIC, instead of becoming a lean and professional body, slid into internecine feuds. Ministers and chairmen, often political appointees from rival factions, stopped speaking to each other. CEOs and joint secretaries were reduced to fire-fighters, spending more time managing egos than managing programmes. Secretaries, true to form, distanced themselves. The result? A ministry-within-a-ministry where KVIC consumed the lion's share of the MSME budget but remained 'independent' only on paper. This is despite the efforts of a well-meaning and experienced CEO at the helm, who had to walk a tightrope between three ministers and the chairperson, who was once a governor of a state and considered the ministers her juniors, despite being of cabinet rank.

Let me now narrate some peculiar features of appointments, inter-personal relationships, and wasted opportunities in the management of the Ministry of MSME, largely in the last 18 years.

Power Games in the MSME Ministry – How Egos Trump Efficiency

The Ministry of MSME was designed to be the lifeline of India's small entrepreneurs. Instead, it often turns into a theatre of intrigue, power struggles, and ego clashes that sap its very capacity to deliver. The script is as old as LBSNAA's (Lal Bahadur Shastri National Academy of Administration) lessons: the minister and the secretary are supposed to be the twin bullocks pulling the governance cart forward. But in practice, one often pulls sideways, the other digs in, and the cart is left stranded in the dust.

At the heart of the dysfunction lies the peculiar cocktail of statutory boards, political appointees, and fragile bureaucratic egos. KVIC and the Coir Board, unlike other agencies, are helmed not by seasoned civil servants but by political heavyweights—retired governors, ex-MPs (Members of Parliament), or men (and occasionally women) with direct blessings from the top political offices. The minister, ironically, has little say in these crown appointments; they arrive with a chit from the PMO (Prime Minister's Office), bypassing the niceties of recruitment rules or meaningful qualifications. The appointment orders are silent on something as basic as their reporting line or appraisal authority. Does the chairperson report to the minister? To the secretary? To no one? The answer, in practice, has often been the last.

That vacuum breeds friction. A secretary who has spent decades in service is expected to defer to a parachuted chairperson, who may have once ruled a Raj Bhavan or Parliament. A minister, even if only a minister of state, assumes primacy by virtue of political authority. Add to this mix a chairperson who enjoys perks but faces no appraisal or disciplinary control, and you have a recipe for daily turf wars. KVIC has seen this drama repeatedly. Chairpersons chosen at the very top treat ministers as ceremonial inconveniences and secretaries as meddlesome clerks. Ministers and their staff retaliate by bypassing the chairperson and leaning on the CEO of KVIC or the Coir Board for pliant action—be it transfers, consultancies, or contracts.

The CEO, a career officer, is left in the most unenviable position—walking a tightrope between political masters, bureaucratic bosses, and a domineering chairperson. Who writes the CEO's Annual Confidential Report becomes a tug-of-war. If the CEO is installed by the chairperson, then the secretary's pen is often reduced to a rubber stamp. If the CEO owes allegiance to the minister, the chairperson fumes and sulks, making life miserable for the officer. Governance recedes into the background; survival becomes the only policy.

Petty one-upmanship even seeps into trivial matters. Foreign travel proposals of chairpersons, often essential for business promotion or international cooperation, are held hostage to delays, approvals withheld until the eleventh hour or denied altogether unless the chairperson enjoys special clout. Export promotion suffers, reputational damage accrues, but the satisfaction of 'teaching a lesson' prevails.

Even the ministry's own senior mandarins are not spared. At various times, the DC-MSME and the secretary have refused to speak to each other for months. Technically, the secretary writes the DC's appraisal, but in practice, the minister overrules or sanitises adverse remarks. This open defiance of hierarchy corrodes morale, leaving officers demotivated and programmes adrift.

The KRDP, a $150 million ADB-backed reform initiative (discussed earlier), is a cautionary tale. Because it was stamped as the brainchild of the DEA (Department of Economic Affairs) and pushed by the KVIC chairperson, the secretary of MSME kept it at arm's length, barely showing up even at milestone events. Ministers basked in optics but shied from steering. Joint secretaries were left firefighting bureaucratic egos instead of implementing reforms. The project limped, not because of a lack of funds, but because the institutional triangle of minister-secretary-chairperson collapsed into a Bermuda triangle of mistrust.

This is not governance. Instead of being the engine of MSME growth, the ministry becomes a circus ring where bullocks gore each other while the cart lies unmoved.

The Way Forward

The malaise is structural, not episodic. First, appointment rules for statutory boards must be codified—clear qualifications, defined status, and an explicit reporting and appraisal system. If a chairperson is to be treated as equivalent to a secretary, say so in law, and prescribe who writes their performance review. Without accountability, authority degenerates into arrogance.

Second, the CEO should be unambiguously a career appointment under the secretary, not a pawn in political-bureaucratic games. Ministers and chairpersons should not meddle in day-to-day administration. Their job is to give direction, not dictate transfers.

Third, Parliament's committees should strengthen their oversight of statutory boards. If boards bypass ministries or clash endlessly with them, Parliament must demand answers. Today, accountability is deflected in the fog of overlapping egos.

Finally, the culture must change. Political bosses must stop seeing statutory bodies as parking lots for loyalists, and bureaucrats must shed their turf-guarding rigidity. MSMEs are too critical to the Indian economy to be sacrificed at the altar of petty ego battles. Without a systemic reset, the Ministry of MSME will remain less a ministry of small businesses and more a museum of small-mindedness.

A Ministry in Name, A Sideshow in Practice

The choice of ministers heading MSME betrays the intent. They are often those who need to be 'accommodated'—political lightweights or sidelined veterans. They come without a sectoral background and, worse, without curiosity and almost into their 80s. One senior official observed: 'The minister is least interested, with zero background and experience of MSMEs.'

> Think of a car where the ignition works, the horn blares, but the wheels don't turn. Everyone claps at the startup, but the destination is never reached.
>
> That's the MSMED Act. It promised legal backing and structural support for MSMEs—but without proper enforcement or follow-through, it's motion without movement.

What follows is a complete disconnect between policy and purpose. Even when problems are raised, they remain unsolved because neither the minister can influence the Prime Minister, nor does the secretary have any skin in the game.

> Suppose you send out 100 wedding invites without checking if the addresses are correct or if the people still live there. You assume everyone got the message.
>
> That's how DC-MSME measures success. It counts beneficiaries trained or supported—but never checks if they stayed, survived, or succeeded.

The ministry itself has surrendered vital policy space to others. SIDBI, technically supposed to be a catalytic financier, operates under the Ministry of Finance, not MSME. The NSIC remains underutilised. CGTMSE—an ambitious credit guarantee mechanism—remains the go-to name in reports, but a ghost in terms of ground-level implementation. Instead of expanding their capacities or asserting control, the ministry appears content passing the buck.

Meanwhile, MSME schemes get token allocations. Most of the budget is cornered by KVIC, which oversees the khadi sector and implements the prestigious Prime Minister's Employment Generation Scheme or PMEGP, a back-ended subsidy scheme for self-employment through micro and small enterprises. What's left is barely enough to run legacy schemes. New programmes often appear, not based on need or evidence, but on the whims of a departing secretary trying to leave a mark. Others are buried for the same reason.

The Curse of Categorisation and the Mirage of Definitions

The very nomenclature—Micro, Small, Medium—has turned policy into a pretzel. Despite revisions in 2006 and later in

2020, 2025 the categorisation[44] continues to create distortions. 'Micro' units, which constitute over 95% of the total MSME population, are invisible in policymaking. Their representation is symbolic; their share in benefits is minuscule. Budget after budget talks of empowering MSMEs, but most schemes are directed at the upper end—small and medium units. That, too, often in urban clusters.

> Imagine a factory where the power, water, raw materials, and security are all managed by different departments—but they never coordinate.
>
> That's India's MSME governance. SIDBI, NSIC, KVIC, DC-MSME, and the Coir Board often work in silos, duplicating efforts and failing to deliver results.

> Think of a cricketer who gets out on zero and is banned from the next ten matches. No coaching, no second chance.
>
> That's how failed MSMEs are treated. There's no exit policy, no rehabilitation plan, no support to restart—only blame and blacklisting.

Even internationally, India's definitional framework is dated. Countries like South Korea, Indonesia, and Malaysia have evolved toward more sector-sensitive and dynamic categorisations. India, by contrast, clings to static definitions based on investment and turnover thresholds. This not only disincentivises growth but also excludes thousands of deserving units from support. The Union Budget 2025 did try to rationalise the definition, though.

44.

Category	Investment Limit	Turnover Limit
Micro Enterprises	Up to ₹2.5 crore	Up to ₹10 crore
Small Enterprises	Up to ₹25 crore	Up to ₹100 crore
Medium Enterprises	Up to ₹125 crore	Up to ₹500 crore

No Exit, No Afterlife: MSMEs Left to Bleed

A glaring policy void is the complete absence of an 'Exit Policy' for MSMEs. What happens when they fail? Who helps restructure or recover? Which institution intervenes to prevent a slow death? None. Thousands of MSMEs have gone bankrupt or shut shop post-COVID, and yet no systemic mechanism exists to rehabilitate them, support displaced workers, or even officially record their closures. It's as if failure is a personal sin, not a systemic outcome.

Conclusion: Either Lead the Sector or Let Someone Else Do It

India cannot afford to treat its MSMEs like decorative props in the policy circus. These enterprises are not just economic engines—they are social balancers, employment generators, and innovation labs. However, for them to thrive, the Ministry of MSME must itself be reimagined. It cannot continue to be a sunset home for retiring bureaucrats or a pitstop for irrelevant politicians. It needs vision, leadership, and continuity.

> In a power-cut zone, imagine a generator wired only to the VIP (Very Important Person) lounge, while workers in the main hall sweat in the dark.
>
> That's how KVIC operates. It absorbs most of the MSME budget but delivers little beyond slogans and political symbolism.

Secretaries must be given fixed tenures, and their performance evaluated based on outcomes, not survival. Ministers must be appointed based on sectoral passion and capacity, not caste calculus or coalition compulsions. KVIC must be restructured to be truly professional. And most of all, MSMEs must be heard, not just herded. If the government continues its current trajectory of slogans without substance, it won't just betray a sector—it will derail the economy itself.

The time for cosmetic reforms is over. What the MSME sector needs now is radical surgery—and for once, a doctor who doesn't walk out mid-operation.

CHAPTER 21

◆◆◆

NSIC's Marketing Brochure Economics

Abstract:

> Imagine a school where students get certificates for just enrolling—not for learning, attending, or passing exams.
>
> That's NSIC's training program. Over 1.3 lakh people were 'trained', but no one checked who got jobs, started a business, or even finished the course.

In a year where India's MSMEs continued their uphill climb through post-COVID turbulence, funding stagnation, and market saturation, the NSIC[45] *served up its annual performance report. A shiny, self-congratulatory volume that painted a picture of relentless achievement: crores of rupees facilitated, lakhs of youth trained, and a long list of MOUs signed with foreign entities. But behind this veneer lies an uncomfortable truth. There is little by way of measurable outcomes—no employment numbers validated by independent surveys, no follow-up on startup survivability, no proof of successful market linkages, and no granular data on the fallout*

45. National Small Industries Corporation

of these much-hyped incubation and international cooperation ventures. This chapter peels away the layers of NSIC's 2023–24 report to reveal a disconcerting lack of transparency, objectivity, and evidence-backed achievement.

The NSIC's 2023–24 report begins with a flourish, celebrating its alignment with the Atmanirbhar Bharat vision and MSME competitiveness. The headline figures are formidable: over ₹21,000 crore worth of tender facilitation, support to 18,000 MSMEs, training to 1.33 lakh youth, incubation for over 1,000 aspiring entrepreneurs, and participation in dozens of domestic and international exhibitions. On paper, this sounds like a success story in motion. But the trouble is that none of these figures are backed by hard, disaggregated data. No beneficiary lists, no job tracking, no case studies. The report reads more like a brochure than an accountability document.

> Suppose 1,000 people are inspired to run a marathon. But no one tracks how many started, finished, or collapsed midway.
>
> That's NSIC's incubation story. Motivating 1,392 youth sounds good—but how many actually built startups, raised funds, or created jobs?

Let's dissect this by starting with employment generation—the holy grail of any MSME-oriented intervention. The NSIC report claims to have trained over 1.33 lakh people through its skill development and incubation centres. But it offers no evidence about where these individuals landed post-training. There is no published data on how many found jobs, how many started businesses, how many are still unemployed, or worse, dropped out mid-programme. It is now standard practice among serious training institutions to conduct third-party tracer studies to assess long-term impact. The Ministry of Skill Development has already acknowledged the need for such outcome-based evaluation under the Skill India mission. Yet NSIC, in 2023–24, seems happy to measure inputs, not outcomes.

The startup support ecosystem narrative is similarly suspect. The report notes that 1,392 youth were 'motivated' through the Incubation Programme. Again, we are not told how many startups were actually founded, how many received follow-on funding, or how many were still operational by year-end. The quality of incubation is nowhere examined. What sectors were these ventures in? Were they tech-driven or traditional? Did they manage to create employment for others? How many fell through the cracks of India's brutal startup mortality curve? There are no answers. It's as if the mere act of motivation is enough to claim success. The absence of post-programme support details, mentorship mechanisms, or survival rate statistics makes the entire exercise look like a photo-op model rather than a genuine enterprise-building initiative.

Even the so-called Marketing Assistance and Consortia Tendering schemes fall into the trap of quantity over quality. NSIC proudly announces having facilitated ₹21,000 crore worth of tenders. But what proportion of these resulted in final contracts to MSMEs? How many beneficiaries were repeat clients, indicating satisfaction and growth? How many were first-time entrants, highlighting outreach success? These are fundamental indicators of marketing ecosystem maturity. But in NSIC's reporting universe, such granularity is absent. The corporation also boasts about organising and participating in dozens of trade

A teacher puts up a world map to show international exposure, but never teaches a single geography lesson.

That's NSIC's MOUs with foreign countries. Great for photo ops—flags, handshakes, framed agreements—but zero follow-up on tech transfer, exports, or joint ventures.

fairs and exhibitions, both in India and abroad. However, no follow-up information is given about orders received, buyer-seller conversions, or export deals struck. It's all activity, no outcome.

> Suppose a cooking show airs dozens of episodes—but never lets the judges taste the food or talk to the participants later.
>
> That's how NSIC reports its schemes. Activities are listed—trainings, expos, MoUs—but outcomes are missing. No follow-ups, no field impact.

This trend is especially glaring in NSIC's chest-thumping over International Cooperation. MOUs have been signed with multiple countries—Kenya, Ethiopia, Ghana, Cambodia, and several ASEAN (Association of Southeast Asian Nations) members. The optics are fantastic: Indian flags, foreign delegations, and framed agreements. But what have these MOUs actually yielded? How many Indian MSMEs have secured technology transfers or export orders? Has there been any tangible inflow of investment or upskilling? The answer lies buried under silence. None of the MOUs are accompanied by implementation timelines, performance metrics, or third-party validations. A similar pattern was observed in past CAG audit reports on MSME international collaboration mechanisms, which flagged the tendency of agencies to sign MOUs without a strategy for operational follow-through or impact assessment.

The NSIC's 2023–24 report also fails to offer any critical self-reflection. There is not one paragraph acknowledging challenges faced, schemes that underperformed, or lessons learnt. This absence of humility undermines the report's credibility. It is as if NSIC exists in a parallel universe where every scheme runs smoothly, every target is met, and every participant benefits. The reality, as multiple Parliamentary Standing Committees and CAG reports have repeatedly noted, is far murkier. Credit access remains patchy, tender processes continue to favour larger players, and real job creation has stagnated.

A school claims 100% digital attendance, but it's the teacher uploading names—not students logging in.

That's NSIC's '97.67% digital transaction' claim. Backend staff may have gone digital—but no proof that MSMEs, especially in rural areas, actually used it.

Equally troubling is the lack of demographic disaggregation. Given the current government's strong emphasis on inclusion—be it women entrepreneurs, SC/ST enterprises, or aspirational districts—NSIC should have published data segmented by region, gender, and social category. How many women were trained? How many rural entrepreneurs received marketing support? How many micro enterprises from backward districts got linked to larger supply chains? None of this data is available.

A football club displays trophies in its office while the team loses every match and fans stop showing up.

That's NSIC's glossy report. No mention of challenges, failures, or learnings. Just victory lap after victory lap—with no scoreboard.

Without such granularity, it is impossible to judge the equity or reach of NSIC's interventions.

Moreover, data integrity is weak. There is no mention of external audits, impact assessments by independent agencies, or even customer satisfaction surveys. The few 'success stories' are anecdotal and lack depth. Compare this with the DPIIT, [46]which at least attempts startup ranking exercises with peer feedback and state-level comparison matrices. The NSIC remains opaque, insulated from performance benchmarking.

46. Department for Promotion of Internal Industry and Trade

The financial statements in the report also raise flags. While the operational figures are tabulated with care, there is scant commentary on whether NSIC's internal costs are rising, whether overheads are being rationalised, or whether any surplus has been

> What if a hospital tracks how many patients walked in, but not who got better, who relapsed, or who died?
>
> That's NSIC's skill and support story. Input numbers are counted—but outcome, recovery, and success remain unmeasured.

ploughed back into scaling operations. The absence of discussion on Return on Public Investment (ROPI) makes it hard to assess efficiency. A CAG review of similar schemes in 2021–22 had flagged the tendency of PSU-type bodies like NSIC to act more as intermediaries—routing government subsidies—than as innovation leaders or entrepreneurship accelerators.

There is also no clarity on post-pandemic course correction. What lessons did NSIC draw from COVID-19 disruptions? Did it pivot towards digital marketing? Were new virtual incubation models explored? Did they address the digital divide afflicting smaller Tier III entrepreneurs? None of these strategic questions finds space in the 2023–24 report. In an era when even municipal corporations publish dashboards and performance indices, the NSIC appears stuck in a bureaucratic time warp.

Finally, let's talk about synergy—or the lack thereof. There is no reflection on how NSIC's activities align or overlap with

> What if a hospital tracks how many patients walked in, but not who got better, who relapsed, or who died?
>
> That's NSIC's skill and support story. Input numbers are counted—but outcome, recovery, and success remain unmeasured.

those of other institutions, like SIDBI, MSME-DFO, KVIC, or the multiple skilling agencies under the Skill India umbrella. Are they duplicating efforts? Are they leveraging cross-institutional data? Are they pooling expertise? Coordination among public agencies is critical for holistic impact, and yet the NSIC report is silent on this.

Conclusion

India's MSMEs do not need patronising promises. They need performance, partnerships, and proof. The NSIC's 2023–24 annual report, unfortunately, offers little of these. It is a document written for file closures and PR (Public Relations) handouts, not for serious evaluation or public scrutiny. If NSIC wants to stay relevant in a rapidly evolving startup and enterprise ecosystem, it must reform how it reports, how it measures, and how it delivers. The next report should be outcome-centric, independently audited, demographically disaggregated, and linked to national priorities like employment generation, women entrepreneurship, and export capability. Only then will NSIC's 'achievements' stop being a mirage and start becoming milestones.

> Imagine five chefs preparing the same dish in five different kitchens—with no coordination or shared recipe.
>
> That's how NSIC, SIDBI, KVIC, and MSME offices often work. No synergy, no data pooling, no shared learning. Just duplication and inefficiency.

We move on to the discussion of digital initiatives of the MSME ministry for the development of MSMEs in the following chapter.

References:

1. Comptroller and Auditor General of India, 'Performance Audit Report on Ministry of MSME – Training and Support Schemes', Report No. 18 of 2021.

2. CAG Report No. 3 of 2022, 'Functioning of National Small Industries Corporation – Marketing and Credit Schemes', presented to Parliament in March 2022.

3. Press Information Bureau, Ministry of MSME releases, 2023–24.

4. DPIIT Startup Rankings 2022 and 2023.

5. Parliamentary Standing Committee on MSMEs, 2023 Session Reports.

CHAPTER 22

◆◆◆

Digital Dreams, Hollow Platforms: MSME Champions and Udyam[47] Portal

In recent years, the Ministry of MSME has unveiled a series of digital governance initiatives, ostensibly aimed at empowering entrepreneurs, formalising the informal, and ensuring 'minimum government, maximum governance'. Two

Imagine someone proudly flashing their gym membership card at every opportunity. They tell you they've signed up for a one-year plan at a swanky fitness centre. But when you ask them how often they work out, they sheepishly admit—'Oh, I never actually go.' That, in essence, is the story of India's Udyam registration portal. The ministry proudly states that over 3 crore MSMEs are now registered. But what no one tells us is whether these units are active, functional, or even alive. Like unused gym cards, many registrations may be simply entries on a database—done to unlock a subsidy, access a loan scheme during COVID, or just tick a bureaucratic checkbox. Being 'registered' does not mean being fit for business.

---

47. Ineffectiveness of Udyam and CHAMPIONS portals has also been referred to in Chapters 10 and 19, being relevant to the context.

flagship programmes—MSME CHAMPIONS and the Udyam Registration portal—have been projected as cornerstones of this digital renaissance. Yet, beneath the dashboard gloss and promotional slogans lies a more complicated reality marked by inconsistent implementation, opaque outcome metrics, and questionable utility for the actual MSME beneficiaries.

MSME CHAMPIONS: From Tagline to Tangled Execution

Launched with much fanfare in June 2020, amidst the economic chaos unleashed by COVID-19, the MSME CHAMPIONS initiative claimed to be an end-to-end grievance redressal and handholding platform for entrepreneurs. The name was an acronym in itself—'Creation and Harmonious Application of Modern Processes for Increasing the Output and National Strength'. It promised to be a real-time, AI-enabled control room where government officials, industry experts, and technology tools would converge to solve problems, offer guidance, and create success stories.

According to the ministry, the initiative was powered by AI-driven data analytics, video conferencing facilities, and feedback loops that could track and resolve grievances lodged by MSMEs through a centralised dashboard (Source: PIB release, 1 June 2020). Over 68 MSME field offices were roped in to make this control room operative across India.

On paper, this sounded futuristic and robust. In practice, it has largely become a glorified complaint monitoring system, with very little insight into whether the grievances were substantively addressed, let alone resolved to the satisfaction of entrepreneurs. A CAG audit on grievance redressal mechanisms under various MSME schemes (Report No. 14 of 2022) noted that 'none of the sample grievances reviewed under CHAMPIONS could be tracked conclusively from complaint to resolution with verifiable documentation of redressal'.

Many complaints, once logged, merely showed a change in dashboard status from 'Pending' to 'Resolved' without any feedback or follow-up from the concerned MSME.

> Picture a frustrated resident who files a complaint about loudspeakers blaring through the night in his neighbourhood. He waits patiently, checks his phone the next day, and sees an SMS: 'Complaint closed'. But when night falls, the loudspeakers are still there—louder than ever. That's how MSME grievances are often handled under the CHAMPIONS platform. Once a complaint is logged, the system shows a change in status from 'Pending' to 'Resolved'—but there's no follow-up, no explanation, and definitely no confirmation from the entrepreneur that the problem was genuinely fixed. It's grievance redressal as a status update, not a service.

Moreover, the AI-enabled monitoring touted by the ministry has raised eyebrows in terms of its actual capability. A 2022 Lok Sabha reply by the minister of MSME admitted that the platform used 'basic analytics' but stopped short of detailing any real machine learning or decision-support functionality. The CHAMPIONS portal also lacks third-party

> A restaurant boldly claims it uses AI to take your orders. Curious, you visit, expecting a robot waiter or voice assistant. Instead, you find a regular server scribbling your order on a notepad. 'AI-enabled', he explains, 'just means our billing software has drop-down menus.' That's how the MSME CHAMPIONS portal works. Launched as an AI-driven interface promising predictive analytics and smart resolution, it mostly runs on basic keyword tagging and manual status changes. What was promised as high-tech decision support turns out to be glorified Excel tracking dressed up in fancy terms.

evaluation or beneficiary audit. No study has been published showing how many businesses were transformed due to the interventions facilitated through the portal. Without such transparency, claims of success sound more like bureaucratic self-congratulation than evidence-based governance.

Udyam Registration: A Giant Leap to Formality, or a Stumble in the Dark?

In stark contrast to CHAMPIONS' nebulous outputs, Udyam Registration was positioned as a clean digital reform with measurable goals. Launched on 1 July 2020, Udyam replaced the older, cumbersome processes of EM-I/II (Entrepreneur's Memorandum-I/II) and UAM. It promised single-window, Aadhaar-verified, PAN-linked registration of MSMEs, drawing data automatically from GSTN and ITR (Income tax Return) filings, thereby formalising enterprise identity through API integration. The idea was not just to reduce paperwork but to link registration directly to regulatory compliance and access to finance, government tenders, subsidies, and emergency credit.

> Suppose a student registers for a board exam and receives a hall ticket. But then, he never shows up to take the test. Years later, his name still appears in the 'enrolled students' list. That's the absurdity behind the Udyam portal. Once an enterprise is registered, there's no requirement to renew or validate its status. Even if it shuts down, its name remains forever in the database unless someone formally deregisters it. The system keeps counting them—giving policymakers a bloated sense of reach, even when the enterprise has quietly folded up.

Indeed, by December 2023, the portal had registered over 3 crore MSMEs, with more than 93% of them being micro enterprises (Source: Udyam Dashboard, MSME Ministry). But this striking number conceals a major problem: what does 'registration' actually indicate? Is it a genuine sign of active enterprise, or merely a form-filling exercise undertaken to qualify for collateral-free loans or COVID-related moratoriums? Independent surveys by entities such as LEAD (Leveraging Evidence for Access and Development) at Krea University and the IFC have repeatedly flagged the mismatch between MSMEs' Udyam registration status and their actual operational or financial viability. One 2022 survey in Tamil Nadu and Maharashtra revealed that 37% of registered units were inactive or non-operational at the time of the survey.

This exposes a bigger structural flaw. Udyam, while ostensibly linking enterprise data with PAN and GSTN, has no mechanism for verifying whether an enterprise is alive and kicking or merely exists on paper. There is no sunset clause or renewal requirement. Once registered, an enterprise continues to feature in the MSME count unless explicitly deregistered. This inflates the base of 'registered MSMEs' used by the ministry for policy planning, funding decisions, and even international benchmarking. In effect, it is a castle built on sand.

The usefulness of Udyam Registration as a gateway to government schemes is also debatable. An RTI (Right to Information) reply from SIDBI in 2022 noted that only a fraction—less than 6%—of Udyam-registered enterprises had accessed the CGTMSE scheme in that financial year. Similarly,

> It's like trying to apply for a driving license where your identity is on one portal, address proof on another, and health test results on a third. But none of the systems are integrated. Similarly, Udyam doesn't speak to state MSME registries, pollution control boards, or local electricity utilities. The same unit may exist under three databases, or may never get cross-verified at all. The dream of a unified, authenticated MSME ecosystem collapses in the face of this digital babel.

enrolment under marketing support initiatives like GeM or Public Procurement Policy lagged far behind, with very few handholding mechanisms provided for newly formalised enterprises to actually participate in public tenders.

> Imagine a cricket match where the scoreboard lights up every time the ball is bowled, but no one records the runs or wickets. At the end, you know how many balls were thrown—but not who won. That's how MSME portals operate. They count how many businesses were registered, how many grievances were logged, and how many calls were made. But they don't tell us how many enterprises grew, how many jobs were created, or how many MSMEs finally accessed real credit or markets. Inputs are measured obsessively; outcomes are ignored completely.

In terms of inclusion, the Udyam system's online-only, Aadhaar-PAN-dependent interface inadvertently excludes many rural, women-led, or tiny informal enterprises that still operate outside the tax/GST net. A 2023 study by the Indian School of Business (ISB) and Deutsche Gesellschaft für Internationale Zusammenarbeit (GIZ) pointed out that first-generation micro-entrepreneurs found the portal intimidating, and several faced glitches in OTP (One-Time Password) authentication, document upload, and access to grievance redressal.

The portal also does not integrate with state-level MSME databases, nor does it cross-verify Udyam data with trade license, pollution control, or electricity board registrations. This results in duplication, unverifiable claims, and even 'ghost MSMEs'. The CAG in Report No. 10 of 2023 flagged this explicitly, noting discrepancies in the beneficiary count for the PMEGP and MSE-CDP schemes when compared with Udyam data, and advised periodic audit and physical verification.

The Illusion of Outcomes: Where Is the Proof of Impact?

> Picture someone attending a one-hour cooking workshop and receiving a certificate of culinary excellence. Now imagine them applying to run a restaurant. That's what MSME CHAMPIONS does when it celebrates having 'motivated' 1,392 youth under its incubation program—without telling us what happened next. Did they start businesses? Raise capital? Survive beyond six months? The story ends with a workshop and a certificate. Impact remains a black box.

Both CHAMPIONS and Udyam embody the Indian state's new-age infatuation with dashboards and data portals. However, the obsession with inputs—number of registrations, number of grievances logged, number of video calls—has thoroughly obscured the more important question: what have these schemes tangibly achieved for the average entrepreneur? How many jobs were created? How many inactive enterprises were revived? How many informal units gained real access to formal credit and markets? On these counts, the silence is deafening.

In fact, the 2022–23 annual report of the Ministry of MSME merely lists achievements in terms of 'outputs' (registrations made, grievances received) without tracking 'outcomes', such as improved credit flow, enterprise longevity, employment growth, or export enhancement. Even internal KPIs are conspicuously absent or vaguely worded. In the case of CHAMPIONS, it is not even clear what constitutes 'success': Is it grievance closure? Is it the satisfaction of the MSME? Or is it just a change of status on a web portal?

The lack of independent third-party evaluation is perhaps the most glaring shortcoming. There has been no formal impact assessment published by NITI Aayog, nor by academic or industry research bodies, to test whether these digital tools

> What if the only way to get a voter ID was to upload your PAN and Aadhaar online, receive an OTP, and scan documents—no physical help desks, no local verification? Many senior citizens, rural voters, and first-time applicants would be left out. That's the design problem with Udyam. It assumes all entrepreneurs are tech-savvy, have smartphones, and are comfortable navigating digital forms in English. But many micro-entrepreneurs—especially women, Dalits, and rural vendors—struggle with digital-only interfaces. The very people the system aims to empower are often excluded by its design.

have actually improved MSME productivity, competitiveness, or sustainability. The NCAER (National Council of Applied Economic Research) Working Paper Series (2022) called for such outcome tracking and flagged the risk of using self-reported registration data for policy targeting without ground-level validation.

> Think of a large jigsaw puzzle dumped on a table, with no reference image on the box. That's the state of MSME digital governance. Portals are built, numbers collected, dashboards updated—but no one checks if the pieces are coming together to form a coherent picture. There's no third-party evaluation, no tracer studies, and no regular audits to ask: Are we really helping small businesses thrive? Or are we just digitising their despair?

State-Level Realities: Maharashtra and Tamil Nadu

In Maharashtra, the MSME sector is a significant contributor to the state's economy. The state has implemented various initiatives to support MSMEs, including the organisation of MSME Sammelans and exhibitions to promote competitiveness and global value chain integration. However, challenges persist in terms of access to finance, technology adoption, and market linkages.

Tamil Nadu, on the other hand, has introduced innovative measures such as the 'Smart Cards' for startups, providing access to a range of products and services at subsidised rates. The state has also focused on fostering innovation and collaboration between MSMEs and engineering colleges to enhance technological capabilities. Despite these efforts, issues related to formalisation, access to credit, and integration into larger supply chains remain areas of concern.

Conclusion: Technocracy without Touch?

The MSME CHAMPIONS initiative and the Udyam portal represent bold strides into the digital governance frontier. But ambition alone is not enough. In their current form, both initiatives run the risk of becoming expensive showcases—platforms that collect data but do not necessarily translate it into real change on the ground. If the government truly wants to make CHAMPIONS and Udyam transformative, it must move beyond ornamental metrics and dashboards and invest in third-party audits, feedback loops, offline support mechanisms, and enterprise-level follow-through.

Because in the world of small business, it is not the number of registrations that matters. It is whether the registered enterprise thrives, creates jobs, and contributes meaningfully to the economy. And that, as of today, remains a promise more than a proven fact.

Any discussion of the Ministry of MSME would be incomplete without the examination of the role and achievements of the Coir Board—an autonomous institution under the ministry, which is tasked with the promotion and development of the traditionally significant coir industry in the country. This is the focus of the next chapter.

References:

1. Ministry of MSME, Annual Report 2022–23, https://msme.gov.in/sites/default/files/MSMEENGLISHANNUALREPORT2022-23.pdf

2. Press Information Bureau (PIB) Release on Champions Portal, 1 June 2020.

3. CAG Report No. 14 of 2022 on MSME Grievance Redressal.

4. CAG Report No. 10 of 2023 on Implementation of MSME Schemes.

5. Udyam Dashboard Data, as accessed on 1 May 2024, https://udyamregistration.gov.in

6. LEAD-Krea University Survey on Udyam Uptake, 2022.

7. NCAER Working Paper on MSME Data Systems, 2022.

8. Indian School of Business and GIZ Study on MSME Formalization, 2023.

9. RTI response from SIDBI dated 22 August 2022.

10. Lok Sabha Unstarred Question No. 1128, Answered on 12 December 2022.

CHAPTER 23

◆◆◆

The Coir Board: Tradition Without Transformation

Abstract:

The Coir Board, a statutory body under India's Ministry of MSME, oversees the development of the coir industry—a traditional rural cottage sector turning coconut fibre into products. This chapter critically examines the Coir Board's performance and alignment, especially in light of its 2023–24 annual report and findings from audits by the CAG. We analyse whether the board's placement under MSME (unlike other commodity boards under commerce,

> Coir Udyami Yojana was like a new coaching class for coir entrepreneurs—promising to help thousands set up shop. But just when it began to attract attention, it shut down. Like a tuition centre that ran for two years, enrolled a few hundred students, and merged into a bigger school without assessing whether its students really improved. The scheme did help launch nearly 1,900 coir units—but no one knows how many still survive. Some may have flourished, but others faded without a trace. When government schemes come and go without long-term support or follow-up, it's hard for any grassroots industry to grow roots.

agriculture, or textiles) has hindered or helped its mission. The effectiveness of major schemes like Coir Udyami Yojana (CUY) and the umbrella Coir Vikas Yojana (CVY) is evaluated against their objectives and targets. State-specific case studies from Kerala, Tamil Nadu, and Andhra Pradesh illustrate ground-level implementation issues and employment impacts in the coir sector. The Coir Board's export promotion endeavours—including market development assistance and international branding efforts—are reviewed alongside recent export trends. We also assess modernisation initiatives in technology, training, and research linkages to gauge how far the board has spurred innovation. The discussion weighs the evidence of outcomes in rural employment and industry modernisation to question whether MSME is the appropriate administrative home for the Coir Board. Finally, recommendations are offered on realigning administrative control, instituting measurable performance indicators, and implementing reforms for greater transparency and impact.

Background and Possible Misalignment of Administrative Control

Imagine a school trying to run a successful kitchen garden program—but instead of putting it under the science or environment department, it's placed under the school's accounts department. Sure, it may still run—but without the right expertise or focus. That's the Coir Board today. It deals with agricultural fibre (coconut husk), product design, exports, and rural employment—but it sits under the MSME ministry, not under agriculture or textiles. Other boards—like Rubber and Tea—are under commerce or agriculture, where they fit more naturally. This misfit matters. Because when coir-specific issues—like fibre retting, mechanisation, or export logistics—need urgent attention, they risk being lost in a ministry chasing dozens of unrelated MSME priorities.

The Coir Board was established in 1953 under the Coir Industry Act with a mandate to promote, develop, and regulate the coir industry across India. Uniquely, the board operates under the Ministry of MSME, reflecting the coir sector's cottage industry roots. However, this administrative placement appears misaligned when compared to other commodity boards in India. Most primary commodity boards function under ministries more directly connected to their product domain or markets. For instance, the Rubber Board is under the Ministry of Commerce and Industry, as are the Coffee, Tea, Tobacco, and Spices Boards—aligning those products with trade promotion and export market access. The Central Silk Board, by contrast, reports to the Ministry of Textiles, reflecting silk's role in the textile and apparel value chain. Likewise, the Coconut Development Board—dealing with coconut cultivation and products—comes under the Ministry of Agriculture and Farmers' Welfare. Coir, which is coconut fibre, naturally straddles the agricultural and textile domains: it is an agro-based fibre used for floor coverings, mattresses, geo-textiles, and more. Placing its development board under MSME (focused broadly on small industry promotion) has long raised questions. Critics argue that situating the Coir Board outside the sectoral ministries (like textiles or agriculture) may dilute focus and accountability. Historically, commodity boards under commerce or agriculture have enjoyed clearer mandates for export promotion or crop development, respectively. The Coir Board's attachment to MSME was perhaps intended to leverage MSME schemes for the rural industry. In practice, this structure may have led to bureaucratic disconnect. The board's activities—spanning research, training, marketing, and welfare in the coir sector—must compete for attention and resources within a ministry covering all MSMEs. Meanwhile, issues specific to coir (such as agricultural raw material supply or integration into textile markets) might receive less priority than if the board were housed in a more thematically aligned ministry. The 2023–24 annual report of the Coir Board itself notes its broad remit: from scientific research to marketing to welfare. Yet the oversight framework under MSME has sometimes been lax. A CAG review of Union Government accounts found that during 2011–14, the MSME ministry released recurring grants-in-aid of ₹4,507.86 crore to bodies, including the Coir Board, without adjusting for ₹438.45 crore of unspent balances already with these institutions. This suggests a lack of rigorous financial oversight by the parent ministry. Moreover, no performance MoUs were signed with the Coir Board despite significant budgetary support exceeding ₹5 crore annually, as the former is not a PSU.

It was a different matter at least till 2006 when the Coir Board used to be with the then Ministry of Agro and Rural Industries or ARI. But the ARI and Small Scale Industries got merged into a new Ministry of MSME with the coming into effect of the MSMED Act in 2006. The little rationale that existed for the Coir Board to be with the Ministry of ARI evaporated in 2006.

In contrast, commodity boards under other ministries often have defined targets or trade-focused mandates. The misalignment in administrative control, therefore, is more than a formality—it has real implications for how the Coir Board is monitored and how effectively it can champion the coir industry's interests. The backdrop of this structural issue frames the evaluation of the board's schemes and outcomes.

Objectives and Performance of Major Coir Board Schemes

Two major schemes encapsulate the Coir Board's development efforts in recent years: the CUY and the CVY. Each had distinct objectives, and examining their actual performance sheds light on the board's effectiveness in delivering on promises.

CUY: Launched around 2014–15, CUY was a credit-linked subsidy scheme aimed at promoting entrepreneurship by setting up coir manufacturing units. The scheme provided a government subsidy (along with bank credit and beneficiary contribution) for new coir projects, with an emphasis on smaller rural units. The objective was to rejuvenate the coir industry by modernising its production base, creating employment, and encouraging young entrepreneurs into this traditional sector. In practice, CUY had a brief run and was implemented from 2015–16 to 2017–18 across nearly all coir-producing states. The Ministry of MSME reported that the scheme was

> Kerala's coir cooperatives received new spinning and defibering machines to modernise production. But many societies didn't get any training to run them. It's like gifting computers to a school with no electricity or giving smartphones to elders without showing how to use them. Machines lay idle. Funds were spent. But workers—especially women—were left out of the loop. A lot of effort was made on hardware, but the human software—training, handholding, confidence-building—lagged. The outcome? Fancy gadgets sitting in corners, unused and forgotten.

'successfully implemented' in states including Tamil Nadu, Maharashtra, and Tripura, among others. However, as part of a rationalisation of government schemes, CUY was discontinued in 2018 and merged into the broader PMEGP. This merger suggests that CUY's activities were overlapping with or could be subsumed under a larger MSME scheme, potentially indicating limited unique impact. In terms of outcomes, during its tenure, the CUY is supposed to have assisted the establishment of 1,886 coir units across the country. There is no verifiable data on how many of these units have survived, if not stabilised. This fell short of any transformative change, but may have provided a stimulus for new units, particularly in states like Tamil Nadu and Kerala. Notably, Tamil Nadu emerged as the top beneficiary under CUY—accounting for 554 units (about 29% of total units) and over ₹21.8 crore in subsidies, the largest share of any state. This also reflects Tamil Nadu's proactive coir entrepreneurs leveraging the scheme, and perhaps the state's robust coir MSME network. Kerala, the traditional home of coir, actually saw a larger number of units (849) assisted than Tamil Nadu, but drew only about ₹5.9 crore subsidy in total, indicating that most Kerala units were very small-scale with lower project costs. Other states like Andhra Pradesh (189 units) and Odisha (130 units) also appear to have participated moderately. The average subsidy per unit varied widely (Tamil Nadu's higher subsidy per unit suggests costlier, possibly more mechanised units were set up there, whereas Kerala's many units were low-cost interventions). By 2018, the government decided to integrate CUY with PMEGP, meaning new coir entrepreneurs would henceforth be supported under the general MSME umbrella scheme. The Coir Board continued to receive funds for a couple of years to settle 'spillover' cases—pending subsidies for units sanctioned earlier. In the transition period 2018–2020, an additional ~155 coir units were set up under PMEGP with Coir Board facilitation, on top of the CUY figures.

While CUY did create new enterprises, its short lifespan and merger into PMEGP hint at policy inconsistency and possibly duplicative objectives. The lack of a dedicated coir enterprise scheme after 2018 shifted the focus back into a generic scheme, raising questions about sustained support for coir-specific needs.

CVY: In contrast to CUY, the CVY is an ongoing umbrella scheme that consolidates most of the Coir Board's development activities. Launched after the restructuring of coir schemes, CVY embodies the broad objectives of coir industry advancement. According to its official charter, the scheme aims to 'revitalise the

Indian coir industry' by addressing a gamut of issues: improving raw material utilisation, providing skills training, supporting the establishment of new units and technology upgrade of existing ones, empowering women artisans, developing new products and markets, and delivering welfare measures for coir workers. In essence, CVY absorbed various components that previously might have been separate schemes.

Key components under CVY include:

Skill Upgradation and Mahila Coir Yojana (MCY): Training programmes to impart skills (especially to women) and provide subsidised spinning equipment for self-employment. Under CVY, women coir spinners can get a 75% subsidy on motorised *ratt* (spinning machine) and other equipment, reflecting a push for women's empowerment in coir.

Coir Industry Technology Upgradation Scheme (CITUS): A capital investment subsidy for coir units to modernise plant and machinery. This offers 25% of the cost of eligible equipment (up to ₹2.5 crore per unit) to encourage mechanisation and new technology adoption in coir processing.

Science & Technology (Research) Component: Funding R&D projects for process modernisation, product development (e.g., new coir composites, diversified products), and quality improvement in collaboration with research institutes.

Domestic Market Promotion (DMP): Activities to popularise coir products in India, including running showrooms, publicity, and participation in trade fairs/exhibitions domestically.

Export Market Promotion (EMP): Support for coir exporters to attend international exhibitions and buyer-seller meets, Market Development Assistance (MDA) for export marketing, opening overseas offices, and branding efforts abroad.

Trade and Industry Related Functional Support Services (TIRFSS): A catch-all for knowledge services, IT integration,

> The Coir Board sends Indian exporters to international trade fairs. Banners fly, stalls glitter, pamphlets circulate. But how many new orders are won? How many small coir producers actually get export contracts? It's a bit like a college participating in a science exhibition without mentoring its students on how to explain their ideas. Promotion without preparation. The board's own report talks of 'awareness generation', but in real terms, we don't know if these trips and subsidies led to any deals—or just added to government expense accounts.

and other support functions to help the industry (including export awards, trade facilitation, etc., possibly).

Welfare measures: Notably, a Coir Workers' Group Personal Accident Insurance scheme (which has been merged with the national PMSBY (Pradhan Mantri Suraksha Bima Yojna) insurance) to provide a safety net for the often underprivileged coir workers.

CVY essentially provides the framework for the Coir Board's activities since 2018, so measuring its performance involves looking at each sub-programme's outputs versus targets. The 2023–24 Coir Board annual report highlights some quantitative achievements. Under the Skill Upgradation & Mahila Coir training programmes, the board has been training thousands of rural women every year in coir spinning and product making. For example, in the five-year period audited by CAG in Kerala, the Coir Board is understood to have trained 5,492 women under MCY and another 7,336 workers in value-added product training, far outpacing the state government's coir training (only 613 persons trained by the state's agency in that period).

> The Coir Board trains women, promotes exports, runs showrooms, conducts research, helps cooperatives, gives subsidies, pushes for tech upgrades—and tries to do all this with limited staff and shifting funds. It's like a small team running a school, a clinic, a shop, and a research lab—all at once. The intentions are noble. The execution? Often stretched thin. Unless responsibilities are streamlined and outcomes are audited rigorously, the board may keep moving without reaching.

This indicates that the board's training outreach has been quite significant and was a bright spot, even noted by auditors. However, the outcome vs target needs scrutiny: while tens of thousands are trained nationally each year, the absorption of trainees into gainful employment or entrepreneurship is less clear. Many trained women become self-employed micro-entrepreneurs, making coir ropes or mats, but the sustainability of those livelihoods is hard to gauge without systematic follow-up data.

Under technology upgradation (CITUS), the board has had mixed results. On paper, CVY set out to modernise the antiquated coir production processes (many of which were labour-intensive and inefficient) by co-funding new machinery—from automated spinning machines (motorised or electronic *ratt*) to defibering machines (to extract coir fibre from coconut husks) and weaving equipment. The push for mechanisation was critical because low productivity had plagued the coir sector for decades.

Progress has been incremental. The Coir Board has indeed facilitated the distribution of machines: for instance, in one initiative in Kerala, 6,490 electronic spinning *ratts* were distributed to coir cooperatives between 2015–2017.

New defibering units, willowing machines, and other processing equipment were also introduced. But implementation snags often reduced the impact. A CAG performance audit in

Kerala found that even when equipment was supplied (often fully subsidised) to cooperatives, training on using those machines lagged. In a mechanisation drive, 71 mini-fibre extracting machines, 65 willowing machines, 61 screener machines, and other units were given to societies—yet due to staff shortages, the state machinery company did not train the operators, and no workers from 221 out of 355 coir societies received any training in the new machines over five years.

This resulted in many machines lying idle or underutilised at the cooperative level. The CAG audit highlighted such gaps, noting that a large section of workers remained untrained in mechanised processes, with less than 1% of the coir workforce in Kerala's cooperative sector having been trained during the mechanisation push.

These findings imply that while CVY's technology support component has provided hardware, the actual productivity gains were limited by inadequate on-ground handholding and capacity building. The Coir Board's scheme design did include both hardware and training, but coordination with state agencies and coir societies was a weak link.

In terms of financial outcomes, the annual report 2023–24 likely details the number of units assisted under CITUS and the amount disbursed, versus targets. While those figures aren't quoted here directly, a general assessment is that uptake of the tech-upgradation subsidy remained modest. Many micro-entrepreneurs and small coir units may be hesitant to invest in machinery even at 75% or 50% subsidy if market demand is uncertain. Moreover, coir production's geographic shift from Kerala to states like Tamil Nadu has meant that private firms (e.g. in Tamil Nadu, many fibre mills are private) invest in machinery on their own, outside the board's scheme, while the traditional cooperative sector in Kerala, which the board targets, is slower to modernise. The objectives of CVY—e.g., full utilisation of raw material and large-scale investment in the coir industry—remain partly unmet.

An astonishing audit statistic from Kerala showed that out of an estimated 580–590 crore coconut husks produced annually in the state, barely 1–2 crore (around 0.2%) were actually collected and used for coir. This indicates enormous raw material wastage and missed opportunities, despite CVY's goal of better raw material utilisation.

Under CVY's marketing and export promotion components (discussed in detail in a later section), the board has set targets for expanding domestic sales and increasing exports. The performance here has been a mixed bag: domestic market activities have expanded to new regions, and exports did see robust growth until 2021–22, but have since faced headwinds. MDA schemes under CVY have provided incentives to exporters and producers to participate in fairs and sell coir products in new markets, but measuring their direct impact is difficult. The board's annual report for 2023–24 emphasises intangible achievements like 'popularisation of coir in non-traditional markets' and new product awareness campaigns, which are important but not always quantifiable.

In summary, outcomes versus targets under these schemes show partial success. The CUY met its immediate target of setting up small units (nearly 1,900 units), but it was short-lived and folded into a general scheme, suggesting limited strategic impact. CVY, with its expansive mandate, has achieved outputs in training (thousands trained, equipment subsidised), research (new products and processes introduced), and marketing (fairs, showrooms, etc.), yet the ultimate targets—like doubling coir production, fully utilising raw materials, or significantly raising coir-based employment—remain works in progress. One positive under CVY is the emphasis on women's employment: about 80% of coir workers are women and schemes like MCY directly target them for skill development and entrepreneurship, contributing to rural women's income generation. However, even this could be more measurable—for instance, tracking how many trained women actually started profitable coir businesses would be a valuable metric, which is not clearly reported. The analysis of schemes thus reveals a need for stronger monitoring and clearer KPIs to truly assess the Coir Board's effectiveness.

State-Wise Case Studies: Kerala, Tamil Nadu, and Andhra Pradesh

The coir industry's landscape differs markedly across states. Kerala, Tamil Nadu, and Andhra Pradesh together account for the vast majority of coir fibre production and coir product manufacturing in India; however, their experiences highlight diverse challenges. Let us examine each as a case study to understand implementation issues on the ground and the real impact on employment.

Kerala – Tradition Amidst Challenges:

Kerala is often dubbed the cradle of the coir industry. The image of rural women in Kerala deftly hand-spinning coconut fibre into coir yarn is iconic. Coir mats and matting from the Alleppey region once dominated global markets. Even today, Kerala has a large number of coir cooperatives and workers. However, Kerala's coir sector has struggled with outdated methods, low wages, and stiff competition from other regions and substitute products. The Coir Board's presence is heavily concentrated here—its HQ is in Kochi, and it operates research institutes and training centres in the state.

Despite these efforts, Kerala's production has not kept pace with its potential. As mentioned, a vast majority of coconut husks in Kerala go unutilised for coir—only on the order of 1% are actually collected for processing—reflecting a breakdown in the raw material supply chain. Traditional methods of retting husks in water for months (to extract fibre) have given way to mechanical defibering in some areas, but mechanisation is not uniform. State-run coir development programmes in Kerala have also faced issues. According to a CAG audit of Kerala's coir and handloom sectors, many government interventions have not yielded the desired results. Working capital assistance was given to 544 coir cooperative societies in the early 2010s, but 21 of those societies (receiving ₹81.94 lakh in aid) became defunct soon after, essentially wasting the funds. This points to the weak viability of some coir cooperatives and possibly poor due diligence or support in those cases. The audit also found examples of equipment meant for coir societies lying idle: in one scheme to introduce Integrated Coir Processing Units, machines were ready for supply by the end of 2016, yet due to delays in assessing societies' infrastructure, the machines were not delivered and stood idle in factories. Such bureaucratic delays and coordination failures meant that even when funds were spent on modernisation, the benefits failed to reach workers on time.

Employment in Kerala's coir sector may have actually declined over the decades, as many younger workers turned away from the strenuous, low-paying fibre extraction and spinning jobs. The board and state have attempted to improve wages and welfare (for example, by introducing a minimum wage for coir workers and providing the Coir Workers' Group Insurance scheme). Still, mechanisation poses a double-edged sword: while it is necessary to raise productivity, it can displace traditional spinners. Kerala witnessed agitations historically against fully mechanised spinning for fear it would rob women spinners of their livelihood. The compromise has been to introduce motorised traditional spinning wheels (*ratts*) that increase output but still employ the spinner, rather than fully automated mills. The Coir Board's MCY in Kerala may have helped thousands of women obtain motorised *ratts* and training, enabling them to earn more than before. Yet, many of these women still earn meagre incomes and remain in the informal sector of the rural economy. The state's coir workforce, once numbering over 3.5

lakh, has dwindled, though precise current figures vary. The board claims that nationwide, about 7 lakh people are supported by the coir industry (with a large share in Kerala).

In Kerala, coir is no longer a top employer; however, in certain coastal pockets, it is still vital for communities. In summary, Kerala's case shows implementation issues, like idle machinery, defunct cooperatives, and slow adoption of technology. It also highlights that despite decades of Coir Board and state efforts, raising incomes and sustaining employment in coir remains difficult in a high-labour-cost state. On the positive side, Kerala has been the centre for R&D—innovations such as coir geo-textiles for soil erosion control and coir-pith compost were pioneered here by the board's research institute. This scientific strength could be leveraged further to create new industries in Kerala around value-added coir (e.g., manufacturing coir geo-textiles for infrastructure projects, which could employ local women in stitching or quality checking roles).

The case of Kerala ultimately underscores that traditional approaches had to change—and are changing slowly—but with social challenges in tow.

Tamil Nadu – Emergence of a Coir Powerhouse:

In contrast to Kerala's cooperative-driven, artisanal heritage, Tamil Nadu's coir industry has grown through a more entrepreneurial, market-driven approach. Over the past two decades, Tamil Nadu became a leading producer of coir fibre—the raw fibre extracted from husks—largely due to the widespread adoption of mechanical defibering units in districts like Coimbatore and Tiruppur. Abundant coconut cultivation in Tamil Nadu (especially in the Pollachi region) and enterprising MSMEs spurred this boom. Today, Tamil Nadu is understood to be hosting over 4,600 coir MSME units, providing employment to more than 1,50,000 people, about 80% of whom are women.

This is a remarkable scale, indicating that Tamil Nadu may now rival or even exceed Kerala in total coir employment. The state's success is attributed to higher mechanisation (hence higher productivity per worker) and better integration with modern markets (e.g., supplying coir fibre and yarn to exporters and factories). However, Tamil Nadu's coir sector faces its own 'panorama of challenges', as identified in a recent policy document. These challenges include insufficient credit support for small units, competition from synthetic fibre products, low domestic demand, quality control issues, lack of standardisation, inadequate infrastructure, and limited innovation.

Tamil Nadu now produces more coir fibre than Kerala. Andhra, too, is catching up. But in many areas, the shift is from household hand-spinning to private fibre mills. In these mills, workers often get fixed wages and few rights. The traditional coir maker—usually a woman working from home—has less space in this new industrial model. While productivity goes up, people lose flexibility and community control. The Coir Board tries to bridge the gap—but unless it adapts its schemes for this changing reality, it may end up serving a shrinking base of old-style units.

While the Coir Board's schemes (like CUY and CVY) have certainly been accessed by Tamil Nadu entrepreneurs—as evidenced by the state's leading share of CUY funds—much of Tamil Nadu's coir growth has been organic and driven by private initiative. Recognising the need for further support, the Tamil Nadu government in 2023 launched a dedicated Tamil Nadu Coir Policy and set up 'TANCOIR' (Tamil Nadu Coir Business Development Corporation), a Section 8 non-profit company under the state's MSME department, to act as a business assistance organisation for the coir sector.

This state-led initiative aims to fill gaps by providing credit facilitation, marketing support, and technology infusion specifically tailored to coir units. It represents an acknowledgement that the central Coir Board, under MSME, alone has not fully addressed the sector's needs in the state. For example, a key issue, like pollution control technology for coir retting and fibre extraction (to manage the wastewater and pith by-products), is specifically highlighted as a challenge in Tamil Nadu, requiring more innovation—something the board's R&D could focus on.

Employment impact in Tamil Nadu appears to have been positive in terms of numbers—new units may have generated jobs—but the jobs are different in nature from Kerala's traditional ones. Many are in fibre mills or curled coir rope manufacturing factories with semi-automated processes. The work tends to be less physically taxing than traditional spinning, and with machinery, productivity and wages can be higher. Yet, many workers still earn modest daily wages, and the industry remains seasonal to an extent (linked to coconut harvest cycles).

The Coir Board's presence in Tamil Nadu includes regional offices and showrooms, and it often conducts training in entrepreneurial skills. The board's export promotion programmes may have also benefited Tamil Nadu exporters (a significant number of the 1,956 registered coir exporters are based in Tamil Nadu and Kerala). Notably, Tamil Nadu companies are big exporters of coir fibre and coir pith blocks (used as garden soil substitute)—these are lower-value products than finished mats, but high volume.

The state-wise snapshot thus shows Tamil Nadu making great strides by leveraging schemes like CVY, along with its own policy push, but needing further modernisation and product diversification to move up the value chain (for instance, making more value-added matting, rubberised coir mattresses, or geo-textiles locally rather than just exporting raw fibre).

Andhra Pradesh – Potential and Niche Growth:

Andhra Pradesh, with its long coastline and coconut-growing belts (especially in the Godavari and Krishna districts), has significant coir potential. Historically, AP's coir industry was smaller than Kerala's or Tamil Nadu's, but it has been growing. By 2018–19, the coir industry in Andhra Pradesh is stated to have employed over 55,000 people, and this number likely increased as new units came up in recent years.

The Coir Board and state agencies have attempted to promote coir clusters in AP, including coir product manufacturing units in coastal rural areas. The nature of coir work in Andhra has been a mix: some traditional cottage units (often extensions of Kerala's industry, given their geographical proximity) and newer mechanised fibre extraction units akin to Tamil Nadu's model.

One notable initiative is the development of coir clusters under the SFURTI scheme in Andhra Pradesh. Through SFURTI, which the Coir Board implements for coir, among other industries, clusters in regions like West Godavari have been formed to aggregate artisans and provide them with modern common facility centres.

While a detailed CAG audit of these clusters is not available publicly, anecdotal evidence suggests varying success—some clusters have helped increase incomes by providing better machinery and direct market linkages, while others have struggled with maintenance and marketing even after project implementation. For instance, if a coir cluster set up a centralised fibre extraction and weaving facility but failed to ensure a steady coconut husk supply or to find buyers for the end products, it may underperform.

Andhra Pradesh's coir units benefited from the CUY in its brief run—189 units were assisted in AP, making it the third-highest state in CUY uptake after Kerala and Tamil Nadu. This indicates active interest among entrepreneurs in AP to start coir businesses when support is available. Many of these would be small units engaged in making coir ropes, door mats, or curled coir for mattresses.

The employment in AP's coir industry tends to be concentrated among marginalised communities in rural areas, for whom coir provides a supplementary livelihood. The employment impact here can be significant in specific locales: for example, a single coir fibre factory employing 50 workers in a village can make a big local difference. However, scaling that up has been a challenge. AP has not yet achieved the same scale of mechanised production as Tamil Nadu, nor the high-end product manufacturing that Kerala (with its matting/matting designs) has traditionally done.

Implementation issues in Andhra Pradesh include a lack of awareness and training. The Coir Board has fewer training centres in AP, so reaching artisans to educate them on new techniques or products is hard. Additionally, credit linkages are a problem—many coir entrepreneurs in AP find it difficult to get bank loans, even with subsidies, as banks perceive coir units as risky or low-profit ventures. The Coir Board's intervention via PMEGP after CUY's merger has supported some coir units in AP (the PMEGP data from 2018–20 shows that AP had 78 coir units financed during that period), but again, these are relatively small numbers for a large state.

On the positive side, Andhra's government in recent years has shown interest in promoting coir as part of rural development. Some rural SHGs were encouraged to take up coir pith composting (turning coir pith waste into organic manure) and small-scale fibre extraction. If supported well, these micro enterprises can provide supplementary income to farming families and also address waste utilisation (since coir pith is an abundant waste otherwise).

AP's case study reveals a story of untapped potential: the raw material is available, and employment need is high in rural areas, but the coir industry has yet to flourish fully due to gaps in infrastructure, training, and marketing. The Coir Board can play a catalytic role here by establishing more common facilities and aggressively marketing AP coir products (for example, promoting AP's coir doormats, which are known for quality). Without that push, AP might continue to lag behind its southern neighbours in the coir sector growth. In all three states, a common thread is that coir work provides livelihoods primarily to rural, economically weaker sections, especially women.

The Coir Board's schemes have had to adapt to very different local contexts: from heavily unionised cooperatives in Kerala to MSME clusters in Tamil Nadu to nascent SHGs in Andhra. The board's presence under MSME means it often works through DICs and state MSME departments to reach beneficiaries. Where state governments are proactive (as in Tamil Nadu recently), the outcomes are better because state schemes and institutions supplement the board's efforts. Where local institutional support is weak, the schemes sometimes flounder, as seen in Kerala with dormant cooperatives or in parts of Andhra with insufficient credit flow. These case studies underscore the need for decentralised, state-tailored strategies within the Coir Board's national programmes. They also highlight that simply measuring the number of units or people trained is not enough; one must look at how sustainable and impactful those interventions were in each state context.

Coir Export Promotion Initiatives and Performance

Export promotion is one of the core mandates of the Coir Board—in fact, it was a driving reason for the board's creation in the 1950s, when India's coir products (especially mats and mattings) were a major foreign exchange earner. Over time, the board's export promotion initiatives have included marketing delegations abroad, participation in international trade fairs, running overseas offices, and offering incentives to exporters. The 2023–24 period saw renewed emphasis on boosting coir exports, especially with the government setting ambitious targets. According to the Coir Board's latest report, India's coir and coir product exports are supposed to have reached ₹3,992 crore in fiscal year 2022–23 and then declined to ₹3,396 crore in fiscal year 2023–24.

This is a noteworthy trend: after strong growth in the late 2010s, exports peaked at around ₹4,340 crore in fiscal year 2021–22 and then fell by about 20% over the next two years. The drop could be due to a combination of global economic factors (recessionary trends reducing demand for floor coverings, for instance) and domestic issues (like raw material shortages or higher costs). The board's performance must be evaluated in this context. It has been promoting diversification in export products to reduce reliance on any single item. Traditionally, coir fibre and coir pith (cocopeat) have made up a large share of exports by volume, even though they are low-value-added products. In recent years, there's been a push to export more value-added items, like coir pith growing media, coir geo-textiles, coir rugs and carpets, coir composites, etc. MDA from the board provides financial help to exporters for things like freight or exhibition costs. The EMP component of CVY also extends assistance for sending delegations abroad or conducting market studies. The Coir Board's 2023–24 annual report likely highlights a few key initiatives in export promotion:

- Organising Buyer-Seller Meets (BSMs) internationally (in markets like the US, Europe, or Asia) to connect Indian exporters with foreign buyers.

- Participation in major trade fairs such as the International Coir Fair or relevant lifestyle product expos in target countries.

- Running the India Coir Pavilion at events to brand Indian coir.

It also mentions the establishment (or proposal thereof) of overseas offices to represent the Coir Board and help exporters.

Historically, the board had offices in locations like New York and London many decades ago, but not in recent times. There are discussions to re-open such presence, or at least to leverage Indian embassies for coir promotion.

One important initiative noted in late 2024 is the government's plan to amend the Coir Industry Act (1953) for the first time in 72 years to make it more export-oriented. The amendments aim to facilitate the creation of new value-added coir products, such as blended coir (coir mixed with other fibres like jute or rubber), to cater to modern market demands. This move is directly tied to export competitiveness—blending can create stronger or more versatile products (for example, coir+jute area rugs or coir+rubber moulded doormats) that might sell better overseas. The Act changes also propose to trim the Coir Board's size from 40 members to about 20 to improve agility and to set up dedicated export facilitation centres to guide producers on export procedures and market preferences. These policy steps, as reported in January 2025, indicate that the board and the MSME ministry recognise that exports haven't grown as fast as desired and that structural reforms are needed.

Indeed, the government has set a target to increase coir exports by 50% to reach ₹5,000 crore by 2027. Achieving this will require reversing the recent export downturn. In terms of MDA specifically, the board provides rebates or incentives on the domestic sale of coir products (to encourage exporters to develop the domestic market as well) and reimburses part of the expenses for export promotion activities. The annual report would detail the amount disbursed under MDA and how many exporters benefited. If we interpret from context, hundreds of coir exporters (out of the ~1,956 registered) likely availed MDA for attending trade fairs or sending samples abroad in 2023–24. However, quantifying how that translated into export orders is tricky. Some criticism arises that MDA spending should be tied to outcomes (like actual export growth in new markets) rather than just activity (number of fairs attended). International branding efforts of the Coir Board have modestly improved the recognition of Indian coir. The board has been promoting the eco-friendly nature of coir products as a selling point globally. As a PIB release notes, coir products have been certified with the Indian government's Eco-Mark (environmental product certification), and coir fits well in the current global trend towards sustainable, natural products. The board often uses slogans like 'Coir – Golden Fibre, Eco-Friendly Fibre' in its marketing. Yet, Indian coir doesn't enjoy the same strong geographical branding as, say, Indian carpets or Egyptian cotton. One reason is the diverse range of coir products and the fact that many are intermediate goods (coir fibre, yarn, etc.) rather than consumer-facing branded goods. A mat or doormat made of coir might just carry a private label in a store overseas, with little mention that it is from India or made of coir, unless the brand specifically highlights it. To address this, the Coir Board has initiated steps like branding Indian coir geo-textiles for civil engineering use. Coir geo-textile (a woven mat of coir fibre) has been a flagship new product—it got endorsed by the Indian Road Congress and mandated for use in a percentage of rural road projects in India.

Internationally, the board hopes to market coir geo-textiles as a natural erosion control solution. Some pilot projects have been done in countries prone to soil erosion. Indian coir's USP in the international market is its natural origin and biodegradability—unlike synthetic geo-textiles or plastic mats, coir products are organic and decompose without harming the environment. The board's challenge is to turn these attributes into a brand advantage. Possibly in 2023–24, the board has worked with India's missions abroad to hold 'Coir Buyer Conferences' or roadshows highlighting Indian coir's eco-friendly qualities.

Export performance can also be dissected by product category: Coir pith products (mostly exported to horticulture markets abroad) have grown significantly, but face competition from other peat substitutes. Coir fibre exports had actually been curtailed in some years to ensure raw material for domestic value addition, but Tamil Nadu's fibre exporters still ship large quantities to countries like China (which uses coir fibre in their mattress industry). Then there are tufted coir mats and handwoven mats, which are traditional export earners, primarily to the US and EU markets. During 2023–24, high freight costs and a sluggish home furnishings market abroad contributed to a dip in those exports. The board's international marketing wing tried to counter this by exploring new markets in Eastern Europe, Latin America, and Africa, as noted in meetings and possibly in the annual report. Another initiative often mentioned is leveraging e-commerce for exports—encouraging coir MSMEs to sell on global online marketplaces. This is still at a nascent stage, but a few exporters have started retailing products like coir doormats through Amazon's international platforms, with the Coir Board's guidance on compliance and branding. Overall, the board's performance in export growth can be summed up as follows: During the 2014–2022 period, coir exports nearly tripled from around ₹1,400 crore to over ₹4,000 crore, an achievement the board touts as evidence of effective promotion. This growth was aided by rising global demand for eco-friendly products and the entrepreneurial push of private exporters, particularly for coir pith and fibre. However, the recent slump exposes the vulnerabilities—limited product diversification and over-reliance on a few markets can quickly translate to stagnation. MDA and branding efforts are the tools at the board's disposal to combat this, but their success will depend on how strategically they are employed. The forthcoming policy changes (amended Act, smaller board, export facilitation centres) are promising if implemented earnestly, as they align the regulatory framework with export goals. The Coir Board's own narrative in 2023–24 is certainly export-focused; whether that translates to measurable gains (like penetrating a new market or launching a recognisable 'Indian Coir' brand) is what needs to be seen in subsequent years.

Modernisation Efforts: Technology, Training, and Industry-Science Linkages

Modernising a traditional industry like coir has been a continuing central theme of the Coir Board's work. Modernisation entails introducing new technology to improve efficiency, establishing training centres to upgrade skills, and forging linkages between industry and scientific research to foster innovation. The board's initiatives in these areas have had some notable successes; however, challenges remain in fully transforming the sector. On the technology front, the Coir Board's R&D wing—primarily the Central Coir Research Institute (CCRI) in Kerala and the Central Institute of Coir Technology (CICT) in Bengaluru—has developed a range of improved machines and processes over the years. According to official records, 'a lot of sophisticated machinery [was] invented by the Coir Board from fibre extraction to finished products.' These include motorised spinning *ratts*, mobile fibre extraction machines that can be taken to farms, machinery for weaving coir geo-textiles, and a technology for manufacturing 'Coir Wood'—a wood substitute made by compressing coir fibre with resins. Coir Wood is promoted as an eco-friendly alternative to timber, thus 'saving trees and forests' by using a renewable waste material. The board's research institutes are understood to have also perfected the process of making coir pith compost (often called coir waste into wealth, turning the spongy coir dust into organic manure), which helps in waste management and creates a by-product to sell. A critical area of technological linkage has been with external scientific bodies. The board is stated to have actively collaborated with CSIR (Council of Scientific and Industrial Research) labs and universities on R&D projects. For instance, joint research has been done on improving the quality of coir fibre (ret treatment to make it softer), developing fire-retardant coir composites, and testing the application of coir geo-textiles in road construction scientifically (in collaboration with engineering institutes). One outcome of such linkage is the acceptance by agencies like the Indian Roads Congress and Railways of coir geo-textiles for infrastructure uses. The real challenge is implementation and actual field use. The board's push led to standards and guidelines being issued—the Ministry of Railways, in 2022, released guidelines for using coir geo-textiles in railway embankments, and as noted, the rural roads programme, PMGSY (Pradhan Mantri Gram Sadak Yojana), now mandates a portion of roads to use coir geo-textiles. These are significant because they demonstrate modern applications of coir beyond traditional cottage products, validated by scientific and governmental bodies. The real test is to scale up production for these uses and ensure quality consistency, which is where industry-science linkage remains important (e.g., working with textile research institutes to improve the durability of coir geo-textile nets).

Training has been the other pillar of modernisation. The Coir Board runs training centres, such as the National Coir Training and Design Centre (NCT&DC) in Alappuzha, Kerala, and regional training extension centres. Through these, the board offers various courses: a popular one is the two-month training in spinning and weaving for rural youth and women, after which they can avail a spinning machine under subsidy to start micro units. Another is the Entrepreneurship Development Programme (EDP) courses that impart basic business skills to coir unit owners.

During 2023–24, hundreds of such training programmes were conducted under the Skill Upgradation component of CVY (as gleaned from past reports). The outcome in terms of modernisation is that a new generation of coir artisans and entrepreneurs is being created, gradually replacing or supplementing the ageing traditional workforce. However, the scale of training relative to need is still small. With 7 lakh workers in the industry, training a few thousand each year will take a long time to reach everyone. Moreover, many trained individuals do not have easy access to credit or machinery to put their new skills to use, something that modernisation efforts have to consider holistically. One of the Coir Board's modernisation successes is the integration of digital platforms for knowledge dissemination. The board has developed websites and mobile apps that provide information on coir processing techniques, supplier contacts, and even an e-commerce portal for coir products. Under CVY's TIRFSS component, there was mention of 'integration of various digital platforms' for the coir industry. This forward-looking move aligns with making the coir sector more accessible to youth who are tech-savvy and can bring innovation. For example, digital marketing of coir doormats on online marketplaces is a new avenue that some trained entrepreneurs are exploring, with the board occasionally facilitating onboarding to these platforms. Despite these efforts, a critical look is needed at whether modernisation has truly taken root. The evidence suggests only partial success:

Productivity: The average productivity of a coir worker has improved with motorised equipment, but overall industry productivity in India still lags behind competitors like Sri Lanka on certain metrics. In Sri Lanka, coir production is highly mechanised and factory-based. India's coir sector is in transition—pockets of high-tech and expanses of low-tech coexist. The board's goal of improving productivity and quality through modern infrastructure is ongoing; however, uneven adoption means many units still operate much as they did decades ago.

Innovation: There have been notable innovations (coir wood, coir composites, geo-textiles). Yet, not all have been commercial successes. 'Coir Wood', for instance, is promising but hasn't seen mass adoption due to cost and manufacturing complexity. The Coir Board will need to work closely with private industry to commercialise such technologies. One positive sign is that some startups and innovators have entered the coir space (like making coir-based packaging material as an eco-friendly alternative to thermocol). The board could do more to incubate such startups or facilitate venture funding, bridging the gap between lab and market.

Environmental compliance: Modernisation must also tackle issues like effluent from fibre extraction (which can be a pollutant if husks are soaked in water) and the dust from coir mills. The board has (long back) developed technology for these—e.g., a decorticating machine that doesn't require prolonged retting in water, and dust extractors for mills. However, implementation again is key; not all units use these cleaner methods unless enforced or incentivised. The board's modernisation narrative often emphasises coir's eco-friendliness (which is true in usage), but the production process itself also needs to become eco-friendlier through tech upgrades, which is part of the CVY objectives (like making industry pollution-free and leveraging eco-friendly techniques).

Human resource development: A subtler aspect of modernisation is professional management and technical expertise in the coir sector. Many coir cooperative societies and small units suffer from poor management practices. To address this, the board, in recent times, has begun workshops for cooperative managers, exposure visits, and including coir business in the curricula of MSME training institutes. This is slowly injecting more professional practices. Also, industry-science linkage helps here: by involving university researchers and students in coir projects, the sector benefits from fresh ideas and the students see coir as a field worth working in.

In conclusion, the modernisation efforts of the Coir Board have laid important groundwork. The board has tried to effectively act as a conduit between the scientific community and grassroots industry, introducing numerous new technologies and processes into the field. Training centres may have spread awareness and skills. However, the impact on the ground is still uneven, with progressive adoption in some areas and stagnation in others. It raises the question of whether the board under MSME has enough leverage and resources to drive modernisation at the required pace, or if it would do better under a different administrative setup with possibly more focused funding (for instance, under the Ministry of Textiles, coir might access broader textile technology missions). Nonetheless, modernisation remains a crucial goal because without it, the coir industry cannot attract the next generation or compete in quality and cost with alternative products.

Impact Assessment: Rural Employment and Modernisation Outcomes

After examining schemes, state experiences, exports, and modernisation initiatives, a critical question emerges: Has the Coir Board's work under the MSME ministry delivered measurable and verifiable outcomes in terms of rural employment generation and industry modernisation? The answer is nuanced—there have been some measurable achievements, but also clear shortfalls, and attribution is not always straightforward. In terms of rural employment, the Coir Board often cites that the coir industry supports over 7 lakh people in India, predominantly rural women. This figure itself is a result of decades of coir development efforts. Without the Coir Board, it is unlikely that coir would have spread beyond Kerala; today, coir activities are found in many coastal states, providing supplementary income to rural families. The board's schemes, like CVY and previously CUY/REMOT (Rejuvenation, Modernisation, and Technology Upgradation), have directly created jobs by establishing units. For example, the 1,886 units under CUY might employ, say, five to ten people each on average—translating to roughly 10,000–15,000 jobs. Under PMEGP (2018–2020), another set of coir units was financed, adding more jobs. Through training, the board has tried to enable individuals to become self-employed;

those numbers may run in the tens of thousands over the years. However, from a verifiability standpoint, there is a lack of systematic tracking of what happens to trainees or units after setup. This is where outcome measurement is weak. The board can say 'we trained X people' or 'set up Y units', but how many of those X are actually gainfully working in coir a year later, or how many of those Y units are still functional and profitable, is not rigorously reported.

Third-party evaluations would be valuable here. CAG audits and NITI Aayog's evaluation office (DMEO) were supposed to look into CVY's outcomes. The Terms of Reference for evaluating CVY explicitly mention assessing if intended outcomes were achieved and if output targets were substantially met. While the results of such an evaluation are not public yet, the necessity of it implies some uncertainty about outcomes. For rural employment, the board's impact has been incremental rather than transformational. In many coir-growing regions, coir remains a low-paid, arduous occupation that younger people avoid, suggesting that despite the board's efforts, it has not yet transformed coir into an attractive employment option. Wages have improved somewhat (e.g., due to mechanisation, a spinner can earn more per day than before, and due to state interventions like minimum wage), but still are often around the minimum wage level or below, which is not too enticing. The board did implement welfare schemes—the Coir Workers' Insurance (linked to the national PMSBY) means any coir worker can get accidental insurance coverage at a nominal cost. This is a positive social safety measure, but it doesn't directly create jobs; it does, however, show the board's recognition of the need to support the workforce's well-being. It is also important to note that coir work is often part-time or seasonal for many rural people. The DSIR (Department of Scientific & Industrial Research) once noted that about 5.5 lakh persons get employment, 'mostly part-time', in this industry. So one can argue that the board's schemes have provided additional income sources rather than full livelihoods in many cases. To deliver more substantive outcomes, coir employment needs to be year-round and better paid, which ties back to modernisation and market expansion, allowing more work and value addition per worker. When it comes to modernisation outcomes, the Coir Board certainly has some verifiable successes:

- The increase in production of coir and coir products can be one metric. In fiscal year 2023–24, India is supposed to have produced 1.89 million tonnes of coir products, slightly up from 1.87 million tonnes the previous year. Production has been rising gradually, showing that modernisation and expansion into new states may be yielding more output. But the growth is small year-on-year (just 20,000 tonnes increase), indicating that there is no dramatic jump.
- **Quality improvements:** It is harder to quantify quality, but industry reports suggest that Indian coir products have improved in quality consistency, partly due to better fibre quality control and bleaching/dyeing techniques innovated by the board. One tangible indicator is that Indian coir mats and mattings have regained some ground in European markets in recent years after quality issues had caused a decline in the early 2000s. The board's quality testing labs and coir markings (there is a 'Coir Mark' for quality similar to an ISI (Indian Standards Institution) mark) have contributed here.
- **Diversity of products:** Perhaps the most striking modernisation outcome is the diversity of coir-based products now available. A few decades ago, coir meant basically mats, ropes, and mattresses. Now, as highlighted, we have geo-textiles, garden articles, acoustic panels (coir composite boards are used as sound-proofing material), erosion control logs, etc. The board's R&D and promotional support played a key role in launching these. The popularity of some products, like coir garden pots or coir-based

doormats with printed designs, is rising in domestic and export markets. That is an outcome one can observe in trade statistics (the share of value-added products in the export basket has, in fact, increased relative to raw fibre/pith over time, according to Coir Board data).

However, modernisation in terms of industry structure (i.e., having a large, competitive industry) is still incomplete. The coir sector is fragmented—hundreds of small producers and limited big players. This makes diffusion of technology slow and scaling up difficult. If one asks, for instance, how many fully automated coir product factories exist in India capable of mass-producing standardised products, the number would be very small. In comparison, competitor countries or alternate product industries (like jute or synthetic mats) have bigger factories. The Coir Board under MSME has tried to cluster small units to achieve scale (through SFURTI and common facilities), but more investment is needed. Perhaps if coir were under a ministry that could attract larger industrial investment (commerce or textiles), there might be a push for larger integrated coir mills.

Accountability is another facet of verifiability. We saw that monitoring and reporting had gaps—e.g., utilisation certificates not disclosing all details. Without strict KPIs, it is hard to hold the board accountable for outcomes. For years, the board operated without a performance contract (MoU) with the MSME ministry, which meant that its achievements were not formally evaluated against targets. This scenario has been improving lately, with the introduction of output-outcome frameworks in government budgeting. For 2023–24, the MSME ministry likely had a results framework for the Coir Board (for example, targeting a certain export figure, a number of trainees, etc., in the Outcome Budget). If so, early indications are that some targets, like the number of coir units to be assisted or the number of exhibitions to be held, were met or exceeded, whereas targets like export growth were not met (given the export decline).

Crucially, one must consider whether keeping the Coir Board under MSME helps or hinders achieving these outcomes. The critical view is that the MSME ministry's broad focus might dilute commodity-specific strategies. Coir as a sector might benefit from the kind of focused schemes and large investments that, say, the Ministry of Textiles deploys for technical textiles or that the Department of Commerce deploys for plantation crop boards. For instance, the commerce ministry runs a comprehensive rubber development programme through the Rubber Board, which covers everything from planting subsidy to research to market promotion—similarly, coir could require an integrated approach from farm (husk collection) to factory to international market, which cuts across agriculture and trade domains.

In MSMEs, the approach tends to be scheme-based and somewhat siloed (e.g., one scheme for tech upgrade, one for marketing, etc., which we have seen). Moreover, MSME schemes often rely on beneficiaries taking initiative (like applying for a subsidy), which in a sector like coir—full of tiny rural players—can result in lower uptake due to a lack of awareness or the capacity to navigate bureaucracy.

Despite these criticisms, it's also fair to acknowledge that the Coir Board under MSME has delivered some 'measurable' outcomes: an increase in the number of coir units (the data shows continuous growth in registered coir units year over year in the last decade), steady if slow growth in production, and a sustained export presence that kept India as the world's largest coir producer-exporter. Many of these can be quantified (e.g., number of units, export value, etc.) and thus attributable in part to the board's interventions.

In verifying outcomes, nothing speaks louder than beneficiary stories: In many coir clusters, one can find women who have been trained by the board, given a spinning machine, and now earn perhaps ₹8,000–₹10,000 a month from part-time coir yarn spinning—not a lot, but it is an empowering, independent income for them. And when asked, they attribute this to the Coir Board's training centre in their area. Similarly, an exporter in Tamil Nadu who got an MDA subsidy to exhibit in Germany and secured a big order for coir rugs might credit the board for that crucial support. These qualitative outcomes are harder to aggregate, but are real. The gap lies in scaling these successes and ensuring they are not anecdotal but widespread. In conclusion, on impact: the Coir Board's tenure under MSME has yielded incremental growth in rural employment and a foundation for modernisation, but the outcomes have not been as dramatic or rapid as one might hope, given the sector's potential and decades of government support. Many planned outcomes remain only partially fulfilled—raw material utilisation is far below potential, the workforce is shrinking in some traditional areas, and technology adoption is spotty. This points to a need for rethinking strategies, improving accountability with clear KPIs (e.g., setting targets for husk utilisation rate, increasing average wages, or number of high-tech units established, and tracking them), and possibly repositioning the board for better effectiveness.

Conclusion and Way Forward

The Coir Board's journey illustrates the trials of reviving and expanding a traditional rural industry in modern times. It has been at the forefront of promoting a sector that is inherently sustainable and employment-generating, yet also beset with structural issues. This chapter highlights both achievements and shortcomings.

Going forward, several key steps can enhance the impact of the Coir Board and address the issues identified:

i. **Administrative Realignment:** A recurring theme is whether the Coir Board should continue under the MSME ministry or be placed under a more suitable ministry for its activities. Given coir's linkages, a strong case can be made for aligning it under the Ministry of Agriculture (for raw material and rural livelihoods focus), the Ministry of Textiles (for integration into the fibre/textile value chain), or even under the Department of Commerce (to leverage export infrastructure and commodity board expertise). Each option has pros and cons. Agriculture could help in ensuring that coconut husk supply is integrated into farm extension programmes—for instance, mobilising coconut farmers to sell husks could be easier if the Coir Board worked closely with the Coconut Development Board under the agri ministry. Textiles, on the other hand, could integrate coir in its natural fibre promotion and technical textiles initiatives. Commerce would emphasise export growth and could give coir representation in trade talks and marketing events globally. Any of these might offer more targeted support than MSME's generic approach. Even if a full administrative transfer is not immediately feasible, improved inter-ministerial coordination is essential—a formal mechanism where Agriculture, MSME, and commerce/textiles collaborate on coir development (for example, a joint task force on increasing husk utilisation and coir exports) could be instituted. Realignment, if done, should ensure that the Coir Board retains its identity but gains a clearer strategic direction aligned with the chosen ministry's mandate.

ii. **Measurable KPIs and Accountability:** The Coir Board must be held to clear performance indicators that align with its objectives. These KPIs could include: the annual increase in coir fibre utilisation percentage, the number of new jobs created in the coir sector (with a methodology to count sustained jobs, not just training outputs), growth in export value and number of new markets entered, reduction in processing time/cost via modernisation, etc. Each scheme under the board should have targets (e.g., CITUS should target a certain number of units upgraded and measure productivity gains there; skill training should target placements or self-employment rates of trainees). The MSME ministry (or whichever ministry in future) should sign a performance MoU with the Coir Board each year, as is done with many public agencies, detailing these targets—something that was conspicuously missing in the past. With defined metrics, it becomes easier to evaluate success and demand accountability. For example, if ₹50 crore is spent on export promotion over five years, what increase in exports resulted? If negligible, strategies must change. If the board underperforms on key metrics, there should be managerial and strategic reviews to course-correct.

iii. **Policy and Scheme Reforms:** The analysis indicates that some schemes need retooling. Now that CUY is gone, the PMEGP needs to prioritise coir units within its ambit—perhaps a sub-quota or special incentive for coir projects under PMEGP could ensure that the momentum of CUY is not lost. For CVY, feedback from the ground should shape its next phase. If CITUS uptake is low, maybe increase the subsidy or simplify the application. If many machines were idle due to a lack of training, make training a compulsory part of any machinery grant (disburse final payment only after training completion). The welfare scheme coverage should be expanded—every coir worker should be insured and perhaps covered by a contributory pension or provided access to schemes like Pradhan Mantri Shram Yogi Maandhan (a pension scheme for unorganised workers), with the board facilitating enrolments.

iv. **Enhanced Transparency:** The Coir Board should maintain transparency in its operations and finances to build trust and attract collaboration. This includes regularly publishing data on its website—for instance, the number of beneficiaries of each scheme by state, details of funds utilised (something the CAG found wanting in clear disclosure. Additionally, success stories and failures should both be openly analysed. If a particular cluster failed, the board should commission a study on why and publish those learnings to avoid repeat mistakes. Embracing digital governance (as the government is doing across sectors) can help—e.g., an online portal where coir units can apply for schemes and track status, which also gives real-time data to management on scheme progress.

v. **Focus on Impact, Not Just Activity:** It's easy for any promotional board to count activities—trainings held, exhibitions participated in, etc.—and consider the job done. The next step is to focus on the impact those activities have. Did training increase incomes? Did exhibitions result in orders? Did R&D projects get commercialised? By conducting impact evaluations (perhaps in partnership with academic institutions), the board can refine its programmes. For example, if training in one module consistently yields better livelihood outcomes than another, resources can be shifted accordingly. Impact focus will also guide new initiatives: the board might find that investing in a certain technology gives huge labour productivity improvements and thus choose to scale that up massively.

vi. **Strengthen Industry-Scientific Linkages and Commercialisation:** The Coir Board should continue to play match-maker between inventors and investors. If CCRI has developed a great new machine, the board should facilitate a private manufacturer to produce and sell it widely (beyond just board-subsidised distribution). They have done this occasionally, but it should become routine. The involvement of institutions like CSIR, IITs, agricultural universities, etc., should be deepened—possibly through MoUs—so that coir problems (like improving fibre quality or designing small-scale machineries) become research projects for students and scientists. At the same time, the board should engage with industry associations (there are coir industry associations in Kerala and Tamil Nadu) to understand market trends and where science can help. This two-way linkage will ensure that modernisation is continuous and demand-driven.

vii. **Marketing and Branding 2.0:** Given the importance of expanding markets, the board should innovate in marketing. One suggestion is to develop a unified 'Indian Coir' brand seal for quality products and aggressively promote it in both domestic and export markets–akin to how 'Silk Mark' exists for silk. Collaborating with professional marketing agencies to run campaigns highlighting coir's benefits (such as water saving, soil saving, etc., as the PIB release enumerated) can raise consumer awareness. Domestically, despite being a large coconut producer, India's per capita consumption of coir products is relatively low (many urban Indians might not own any coir product!). There's scope to push coir as fashionable and eco-friendly for home and gardening. More demand will feed back into more employment and justify modernisation investments.

In conclusion, it is evident that the Coir Board stands at a crossroads in 2024–25. It has a proud legacy of supporting a unique industry that blends tradition with sustainability. Yet, to fully realise coir's potential for rural development, the board must adapt—either by reinventing itself within the MSME ministry or by finding a new administrative home that empowers it with greater focus. The misalignment noted at the beginning—that other commodity boards sit in ministries aligned to their output—suggests that a realignment could unlock synergies (for example, coir research could tie into textile research schemes, and coir export promotion could tie into commerce's export initiatives). If administrative reform is undertaken, it should be done in a way that coir does not lose the benefits it had under MSME (such as integration with village industry schemes). Ultimately, what matters to the general public and to the rural poor is tangible improvement in livelihoods. The coir industry's expansion can provide that for many coastal communities. A modernised coir sector can also contribute to environmental goals by providing biodegradable products and utilising what would otherwise be agricultural waste (coconut husk). With climate change concerns, coir's role in things like erosion control and replacement of plastics can be amplified. These are the new horizons that the Coir Board should set its sights on. By implementing the way forward—better alignment, clear metrics, targeted reforms, and transparency—the Coir Board can ensure that five or ten years from now, we can verify a substantial jump in both rural employment (perhaps coir could employ 1 million+ people with better incomes) and modernisation (with Indian coir products being globally competitive, varied, and high quality). It is a goal worth striving for, blending the golden fibre's traditional strengths with modern efficiency and innovation.

References:

1. Coir Board – Ministry of Micro, Small & Medium Enterprises – Functions and Mandate (pib.gov.in).

2. CAG Audit of MSME Ministry (2015) – Monitoring of grants to Coir Board and others (m.economictimes.com).

3. Ministry of Commerce – Commodity Boards under Department of Commerce (Rubber Board example) (www.commerce.gov.in).

4. Central Silk Board – Administrative control under the Ministry of Textiles (x.com).

5. Coconut Development Board – Administrative control under the Ministry of Agriculture (en.wikipedia.org).

6. Lok Sabha Unstarred Question No.1865 (22 September 2020) – Coir Udyami Yojana implementation and merger (www.sansad.in).

7. Lok Sabha Q.No.1865 Annexure – State-wise units assisted under Coir Udyami Yojana (2015–2020) (www.sansad.in).

8. ni-MSME, Coir Vikas Yojana – Objectives of Coir Vikas Yojana umbrella scheme (nimsme.gov.in).

9. TICE News (September 2023) – Explanation of Coir Vikas Yojana and need for skill development (www.tice.news).

10. CAG Report No.5 of 2018 (Kerala) – Performance Audit on Coir sector in Kerala (training and mechanisation findings) (www.cag.gov.in).

11. CAG Report No.5 of 2018 (Kerala) – Husk utilisation and cooperative assistance issues (www.cag.gov.in).

12. CAG Report No.5 of 2018 (Kerala) – Delayed delivery of machines (ICPU scheme) observation (www.cag.gov.in).

13. TANCOIR (Tamil Nadu Government) – Tamil Nadu coir industry profile and challenges (2024) (www.tancoir.com).

14. Statista/Dataful – Coir industry employment in Andhra Pradesh (2019) (www.statista.com).

15. Economic Times (January 2025) – 'Measures on cards to spur coir exports' (Government plans to amend Coir Act, export targets) (m.economictimes.com).

16. Economic Times (January 2025) – Coir exports figures FY22, FY23, FY24 (m.economictimes.com).

17. Press Information Bureau (December 2022) – Coir Board achievements and data (7 lakh workers, 1956 exporters, exports crossed ₹4000 crore) (www.pib.gov.in).

18. Press Information Bureau – Coir Board R&D and new product initiatives (coir wood, geo-textiles in roads, coir pith fertiliser) (www.pib.gov.in).

19. Press Information Bureau – Environmental benefits of coir and mandates in PMGSY roads, railways, etc. (www.pib.gov.in).

20. Economic Times (May 2015) – CAG on MSME Ministry's oversight of Coir Board finances (m.economictimes.com).

SECTION V

◆◆◆

THE ROAD AHEAD: GLOBAL HEADWINDS, LOCAL CHALLENGES

As global trade wars shake India's exports and Chinese factories outpace ours, the final section charts a way forward—one where MSMEs can be both resilient and world-class.

CHAPTER 24

◆◆◆

An Industrialist Speaks: India's Manufacturing Malaise vs China

Abstract:

This chapter draws upon and critically analyses the reflections of an industrialist on India's manufacturing mindset and its comparative trajectory with China. Drawing from a 2020 opinion piece, it explores how India's industrial stagnation—especially in sectors beyond motorcycles—can be attributed not only to governmental and infrastructural bottlenecks but also to societal attitudes, corporate shortsightedness, and educational misalignments. The industrialist's personal experience in building a world-class R&D base challenges the dominant narrative that places the blame for India's economic underperformance solely on external competition or governmental failures. Integrating his insights with secondary literature on India's industrial strategy, education-to-employment mismatch, and the comparative manufacturing prowess of China, the chapter emphasises the need for a shift in national outlook and corporate vision.

Manufacturing as Mindset: The Case Made by the Industrialist

The industrialist's essay is as much a satire on India's 'anti-China WhatsApp nationalism' as it is a wake-up call to introspect on domestic failures. He opens by mocking the populist outcry against Chinese dominance in global supply chains and consumer markets, affirming that while Chinese methods and ethics are open to critique, India's position is not simply a result of China's aggression—it is also a consequence of India's complacency. Drawing from his deep industry experience, the author pivots the discussion toward a rarely acknowledged factor: the lack of seriousness within Indian companies to build genuine manufacturing capacity, talent pipelines, and global vision.

In a striking personal anecdote, the industrialist recounts his experiences in the early 2000s, trying to hire engineering graduates from reputed colleges to work on 100-cc engine R&D projects. He faced resistance not from students, but from training and placement officers who prioritised placements in IT service firms over core manufacturing roles. Even when his company offered triple the salary, the general aversion to 'shop floor' jobs was evident. This aversion, the industrialist argues, was not because of a lack of opportunities or pay, but because of a systemic devaluation of manufacturing as a respectable, aspirational career path.

This perspective is reinforced by external studies. According to a 2023 report by the India Brand Equity Foundation (IBEF), the share of manufacturing in India's GDP has stagnated around 16–17% for over a decade, despite campaigns like 'Make in India' launched in 2014. Contrast this with China, where manufacturing contributes over 28% to GDP. China trained a massive workforce in technical and vocational skills and created an ecosystem where manufacturing engineers were well-compensated, respected, and integrated into national development goals (World Bank, 2022).

Bajaj Auto and TVS (Thirukkurungudi Vengaram Sundram), he notes, bucked the trend. They invested heavily in homegrown R&D, offered competitive salaries, and redefined manufacturing careers as 'sexy' and futuristic. They built products that outcompeted not only their Chinese counterparts but also gained traction globally. The story of Bajaj's market dominance in Africa, through thoughtful product positioning between high-end Japanese motorcycles and low-quality Chinese knockoffs, exemplifies this success. Their bikes, assembled, reliable, and appropriately priced, replaced Chinese models in markets like Nigeria, where motorcycles double as taxis. The anecdote also touches on the cultural affinity that African users developed with Indian bikes, contrasting with the transactional attitude toward Chinese imports.

By 2018, India became the world's largest manufacturer of two-wheelers, overtaking China. Brands like Bajaj and TVS expanded their global footprints and even acquired prestigious European brands such as KTM (Kraftfahrzeuge Trunkenpolz Mattighofen). The industrialist points out that Chinese motorcycle manufacturers failed to penetrate these global markets not because of geopolitics, but because of subpar quality and the absence of brand credibility. Honda's decision to shift most of its R&D operations to India further validates the rise of Indian design and manufacturing excellence in this niche.

Why Not in Other Sectors?

The industrialist's lament is that this manufacturing success in two-wheelers wasn't replicated in other sectors, like electronics, pharmaceuticals, or computing. He attributes this failure to what he calls 'short-term and geographically limited vision' among Indian entrepreneurs. He contrasts the focused, long-term, high-investment approach of companies like his with the risk-averse, margin-maximising tendencies of most Indian industrialists, who prefer quick profits through trading, low-end assembly, or software outsourcing rather than capital-intensive manufacturing.

This diagnosis finds support in data published by NITI Aayog and McKinsey. For instance, McKinsey's 2021 report on India's manufacturing potential noted that India's top 25 manufacturers account for a disproportionately low share of global exports in high-tech sectors. Moreover, while India is one of the largest consumers of smartphones and electronics, over 85% of components are imported, mostly from China or Southeast Asia.

Educational Disconnect and Social Perceptions

The industrialist's critique of Indian education is blunt but accurate. He highlights that even graduates from elite institutions like IITs and NITs often lack fundamental knowledge of mechanical engineering, preferring coding careers over design or manufacturing. His decision to interview candidates in regional languages like Hindi, Tamil, and Marathi, in order to identify hidden talent, reflects a deep understanding of the social and linguistic barriers in India's education system.

This problem is mirrored in various national assessments. The Annual Employability Survey by Aspiring Minds (now SHL (Saville and Holdsworth Limited)) consistently shows that less than 20% of Indian engineering graduates are employable in core engineering roles. Furthermore, the National Employability Report (2022) shows that IT services absorb the majority of engineers, not because they are better trained for coding, but because other sectors are not hiring at scale or offering competitive salaries.

Reversing the Chinese Advantage

The industrialist's sarcastic take on Indian attitudes toward labour and entrepreneurship points to deeper socio-economic pathologies. He critiques the national hypocrisy of wanting to beat China while working nine-to-five and refusing to dirty one's hands on the factory floor. In his words, Indians want economic self-reliance without individual sacrifice, expecting the government to do what entrepreneurs and citizens refuse to.

This aligns with the insights of economists like Raghuram Rajan and Arvind Subramanian, who have often pointed out that India cannot become a manufacturing superpower without social legitimacy for industrial work. They argue that unless labour laws are liberalised, land acquisition is made smoother, and industrial culture is revitalised at the grassroots level, India's global competitiveness will remain limited to niche areas rather than broader sectors.

The industrialist's essay is more than a patriotic pep talk or a corporate success story. It is a sharp, introspective, and sometimes scathing commentary on the systemic failures that have kept India from achieving manufacturing greatness. By focusing on what worked for his company and contrasting it with what failed elsewhere, he provides a microcosmic example of what could be India's industrial future if stakeholders—corporates, policymakers, educators, and parents—embrace a mindset of long-term vision, investment in technical competence, and cultural acceptance of manufacturing as a noble pursuit.

India's rise as the largest two-wheeler manufacturer was not an accident but the result of strategic thinking, persistent effort, and a refusal to follow the herd. If similar conviction and innovation were applied across sectors, India's ambition to replace China as the factory of the world might move from slogan to reality.

References:

1. IBEF (2023). Indian Manufacturing Sector Overview. https://www.ibef.org/industry/manufacturing-india

2. World Bank (2022). China: Structural Transformation and Global Manufacturing.

3. McKinsey Global Institute (2021). Reimagining India's Manufacturing Future.

4. National Employability Report – Engineers (2022). SHL India.

5. Aspiring Minds (2021). India Skills Report.

6. Rajiv Bajaj. (2020). India and China Mindset – A Personal Take. CNBC TV18.

CHAPTER 25

◆◆◆

Comparing MSME Ecosystems Globally – India and Select Economies

Abstract:

India's regulatory thicket for setting up a small factory or MSME, as outlined in the voluminous and granular checklist (Annexure A), mirrors a bureaucratic labyrinth—tedious, overlapping, and often disjointed. From corporate registration to labour compliance, from safety audits to environmental clearances, from tax codes to licensing intricacies, entrepreneurs are faced with a dizzying and often duplicative regulatory regime. This chapter critically compares India's ease of setting up a small business with ten other economies—China, the US, Indonesia, Germany, Brazil, South Africa, Kenya, Singapore, the Philippines, and Australia—by mapping the essence of their approvals, federal structures, administrative rationalisation, and actual experience of entrepreneurs. The assessment concludes that India's quasi-federal structure, excessive procedural rigidity, and overlapping jurisdictional mandates make it one of the more complex business ecosystems for small players, despite digital interventions and reforms. The way forward lies in a deep constitutional, administrative, and legal re-imagination of industrial regulation—moving from control to facilitation, particularly at the state and district levels.

A Nation of Startups Trapped in Red Tape: India's Burdened Launchpad

To run a small factory in India, you don't just need a great idea, capital, or even the will to take risks. You need a spreadsheet of clearances, dozens of logins, multiple NOCs (No Objection Certificates), and a tolerance for Kafkaesque proceduralism. The 80-plus approvals listed in Annexure A span across at least 15 central and state departments, multiple layers of municipal, industrial, and environmental regulations, and involve simultaneous compliance with central laws, like the Factories Act, 1948, and state-specific labour rules.

What makes India uniquely tangled is its quasi-federal structure. 'Industry' and 'MSME' are subjects in the State List, but most of the crucial procedural architecture—GST, EPF, ESIC (Employees' State Insurance Corporation), and environmental laws—flows from central legislation. This results in two critical outcomes: overlapping approvals and coordination breakdowns. An MSME in Maharashtra may face a different set of procedures and timelines than one in Tamil Nadu or Assam, even for the same type of factory.

States, especially the more industrialised ones, have taken steps to simplify the process through single-window portals like Invest Punjab or Karnataka Udyog Mitra, but these are often superficial overlays on underlying manual processes. Labour inspectors still wield discretionary powers, municipalities demand separate occupancy certificates, and environmental clearances involve long delays and cost escalations, particularly for small businesses.

Contrast this with other economies.

China's Authoritarian Efficiency and Zone-Based Strategy: In China, the central government's industrial vision flows seamlessly into provincial implementation. Industrial parks come with plug-and-play infrastructure, and most approvals—

environmental, tax, labour—are fast-tracked for priority sectors. The bureaucracy is single-point and aligned with outcome delivery. Entrepreneurs don't need to chase inspectors; they are often hand-held into production.

The United States and the Local Autonomy Model: The US also follows a federal structure, but its regulatory model is vastly decentralised, with counties and cities driving most local approvals. Registering a business can often be completed in under a day. Environmental and labour compliance do exist, but they are proportional to risk and size. Critically, the tax code offers deductions and incentives, and agencies like the SBA play a facilitative, not obstructive, role.

Germany's Mittelstand Support Ecosystem: Germany's famed Mittelstand thrives because of an aligned federal-industrial strategy. Registrations are streamlined, and small manufacturers are supported through technical assistance, apprenticeships, export financing, and digital integration. The KfW (Kreditanstalt für Wiederaufbau) Bank offers special credit windows for small enterprises. Labour and environment laws are strict, but processes are digital, time-bound, and rule-bound rather than discretion-based.

Indonesia and the 'Omnibus Law' Revolution: Indonesia's 'Omnibus Law on Job Creation' of 2020 radically simplified licenses for MSMEs. It merged overlapping regulations, rationalised labour compliance, and created a risk-based licensing regime—high-risk enterprises undergo full scrutiny, while low-risk ones self-certify. This model is now a regional benchmark in Southeast Asia.

Brazil and the Cost of Complexity: Brazil, like India, struggles with overlapping federal and provincial regulatory frameworks. The 'Simples Nacional' tax regime helped consolidate taxes for small businesses, but red tape, corruption, and enforcement inconsistencies persist. It is easier to set up an MSME in Brazil than in India, but not by much.

South Africa and Kenya: Structural Simplicity, Functional Gaps: South Africa's CIPC (Companies and Intellectual Property Commission) offers a unified portal for registration, tax number, and social security in one go. However, municipal-level inefficiencies persist. Kenya has made impressive strides with eCitizen, an integrated business registration platform. Yet, physical inspections, power supply irregularities, and limited financing options act as serious deterrents.

Singapore: The Global Gold Standard: Singapore requires barely a few hours to register a business. Taxation is minimal and rational. Labour compliance is electronically integrated. Industrial estates offer world-class infrastructure. But what truly sets Singapore apart is regulatory trust—the state assumes you are compliant unless proven otherwise, the exact opposite of India's presumptive guilt model.

Philippines: Bureaucracy Meets Digital Push: Like India, the Philippines has multiple layers of approvals. But its 'Ease of Doing Business and Efficient Government Service Delivery Act of 2018' mandated three-day approval timelines for most applications. While actual compliance lags in rural areas, reforms are visible in urban zones, especially for services and IT-related ventures.

Australia's Risk-Tiered Compliance Model: Australia's system is based on enterprise size and risk profile. A home-based bakery doesn't need the same permissions as a chemical processing plant. Regulatory logic and simplicity prevail. The Australian Business Number (ABN) system consolidates tax, licensing, and business identity in one unique ID.

Critical Assessment of India's Approach: The central problem in India is the volume of micro-regulation without macro-simplification. Rationalisations such as Udyam Registration,

Digital MSME Portals, or integration with GSTN have only skimmed the surface. The long list of approvals—many of which require physical inspections, recurring renewals, and multiple NOCs—indicates a lack of trust in entrepreneurs. Environmental clearances are delayed not because of stringent laws but because of procedural opacity. Labour laws are fragmented across central and state statutes. The recent codification into four labour codes has not yet translated into simplification at the grassroots. Moreover, the absence of a unified industrial regulation authority at the district or taluka level creates a multiplicity of touchpoints.

India knows that it must reimagine its business approval ecosystem from first principles. This should start with constitutional clarity: while states retain control over industry, the Centre can work through model legislation and incentivised compliance. Second, regulatory overlaps must be eliminated. Each approval—factory license, EPF, environmental NOC—should be time-bound, digital, and risk-weighted. Third, the role of inspectors must shift from policing to facilitation. Fourth, national single-window systems must go beyond tokenism, integrating land records, clearances, tax, and compliance on a single dashboard. Fifth, MSME-specific business ombudsmen must be empowered to address harassment. And finally, a National Ease of Doing Business Council comprising states and the Centre must coordinate reform implementation.

Until India shifts from permission to promotion, from licensing to light-touch facilitation, the dream of becoming a manufacturing powerhouse will remain hamstrung—not by a lack of ambition, but by an excess of forms.

The Single Window Mirage: Paper Tigers, Digital Portals, and Entrepreneurial Fatigue

Much noise, little movement—that's the story of India's Single Window Clearance systems. Launched with grand ambition across most states under the banner of Ease of Doing Business, these digital platforms were supposed to revolutionise how entrepreneurs navigated the minefield of licenses, approvals, and inspections. The vision was compelling: consolidate multiple approvals under a single digital roof, reduce the number of touchpoints, assign nodal officers for handholding, and establish statutory timelines. In theory, the entrepreneur would click a few buttons, upload documents, track real-time status, and start production within weeks.

But in practice? The 'single window' has often been a misnomer—it is merely a glass façade masking the same rusty bureaucratic machinery behind it.

Take Maharashtra's MahaParwana portal, or Karnataka's Udyog Mitra. Both promised end-to-end digital approvals, but entrepreneurs report that key applications, like land conversion, power connection, and environmental clearances, still require offline follow-up. In Tamil Nadu, the Single Window Portal launched under the Tamil Nadu Business Facilitation Act was supposed to give investors all approvals in 30 days. But a 2023 CAG audit flagged that nearly 38% of applications had overshot deadlines, some by over three months, especially in departments like urban planning and environment.

In Gujarat, considered a poster child of industrial development, the Investor Facilitation Portal reportedly issued approvals only on paper in many cases—because field inspections and file notings still moved in silos across district, municipal, and revenue offices. The state introduced auto-approvals for low-risk categories, but local authorities often invalidated them later, citing 'review pending' or 'missing undertakings', forcing physical re-verification. In short, the single window was not backed by a single mind.

A case that made headlines in 2022 involved an MSME entrepreneur in Punjab who applied for a factory license, electricity, and consent to operate through the Invest Punjab portal. While he got acknowledgement receipts promptly, he was asked by three separate departments to 'personally visit' the respective district offices to 'facilitate processing'. The State Industry Department claimed that the portal was 'operationally sound', but in reality, backend integration had not yet taken place for a dozen core services.

The crux of the problem lies in two things: departmental silos and lack of statutory enforcement. Most Single Window Systems are front-end tech solutions built atop legacy processes. If the underlying workflow still requires manual notings, departmental approvals, and field verifications, no amount of dashboard glitter can fix the friction. Secondly, most states have not empowered the nodal agency with the authority to enforce inter-departmental timelines. So, while the portal shows 'in process', the file may be languishing on a desk in the Forest Department or with a local pollution board officer who has no obligation to obey the portal's internal deadline.

Even the Centre's National Single Window System (NSWS), launched in 2021 with much fanfare, suffers from incomplete integration. As of April 2024, only 32 Central departments and 21 states/UTs are reported to have onboarded with partial functionality. Several clearances, like land allotment, building plan approval, or fire safety, still require multiple logins and physical interaction. According to a DPIIT-commissioned report by Ernst & Young in late 2023, nearly 45% of entrepreneurs surveyed across five industrial states said the NSWS had 'marginal or no impact' on reducing delays, with only 19% able to obtain full approval digitally without a physical interface.

Then there's the accountability gap. Unlike Singapore's EnterpriseOne portal, where approvals are auto-cleared based on timelines unless red-flagged, India's portals lack the legal force to penalise delays or enforce deemed approvals in most states. This leaves the entrepreneur in a limbo—tech-enabled, yes, but not process-liberated.

So what went wrong? First, the tech was built without changing the underlying bureaucratic DNA. Second, portals were developed independently by states without ensuring data interoperability with central systems like GSTN, CPCB (Central Pollution Control Board), and land records. Third, training and ownership among lower bureaucracy were missing, making nodal officers more symbolic than systemic. Fourth, the focus was on metrics and dashboards to please investors—not on feedback loops from actual MSME users struggling on the ground.

What Can Be Done to Fix This Mess?

India must move from 'Single Window Clearance' to 'Single Window Empowerment'. Portals must be backed by statutory enforceability, API-based data exchange, and deemed approvals for low-risk activities. Departments must be made accountable for delay, with digital trails maintained and escalations routed automatically. Most importantly, the model must flip from application-driven approvals to risk-based pre-clearance, with backend mapping of industry type, location, and size to determine necessary approvals. Field inspections should follow a unified checklist—not ten different ones by ten different departments. And citizen audit mechanisms must be embedded—let the entrepreneurs rate services, upload evidence of harassment, and trigger redressal automatically.

Until then, India's Single Window system will remain what it is for most small businesses—a hall of mirrors where every 'window' leads to another door, another desk, another delay.

References:

1. Ministry of MSME, Government of India. Udyam Registration Portal. Available from: https://udyamregistration.gov.in

2. World Bank. Doing Business 2020: Comparing Business Regulation in 190 Economies. Washington, DC: World Bank Group; 2020.

3. Invest India. Ease of Doing Business: India's Reforms. Available from:

https://www.investindia.gov.in/team-india-blogs/ease-doing-business-indias-reforms

4. OECD. Regulatory Policy Outlook 2021. Paris: OECD Publishing; 2021.

5. Government of Indonesia. Omnibus Law on Job Creation (Law No. 11 of 2020).

6. KPMG. Setting up a business in Singapore. 2024.

7. Australian Government. Australian Business Register. Available from: https://www.abr.gov.au

8. SBA (US Small Business Administration). Small Business Resource Guide 2023.

9. World Economic Forum. Global Competitiveness Report 2019.

10. Government of South Africa. Companies and Intellectual Property Commission (CIPC) Portal.

11. eCitizen Kenya. Business Registration Services. Available from: https://www.ecitizen.go.ke

CHAPTER 26

◆◆◆

Trump's Tariffs and the Tirupur Test – Trade Wars and Export Shocks

Abstract:

The escalation of trade tensions between the United States and India reached a crescendo in August 2025, when President Donald Trump imposed punitive tariffs reaching 50% on Indian exports, targeting nearly two-thirds of India's $86.5 billion annual export basket to America. This chapter examines the devastating ripple effects of these tariff walls on India's MSMEs, which form the backbone of the nation's export machinery, contributing 45% of total exports and employing over 45 million people. Through compelling narratives from textile hubs in Tirupur, diamond polishing units in Surat, and chemical factories in Gujarat, this analysis reveals how trade wars fought at diplomatic tables translate into shuttered factories, unemployed workers, and broken dreams at the grassroots level. The chapter traces the journey from Trump's initial 25% tariff announcement in July 2025, ostensibly targeting India's purchase of Russian oil, to the doubling of duties that transformed Indian goods into some of the most heavily taxed imports in America. While large corporations possess the financial muscle and market diversification to weather such storms, Indian MSMEs—operating on razor-thin margins and often dependent on single market destinations—find themselves caught in an economic tempest not of their making.

The analysis projects short-term export declines of up to 70% in affected sectors, medium-term GDP erosion of 0.5–0.6 percentage points, and long-term structural shifts that could reshape India's manufacturing landscape.

The Anatomy of a Trade War

Picture this: Ramesh Patel runs a small textile unit in Tirupur, Tamil Nadu's garment hub, employing 150 workers who stitch premium cotton T-shirts for American retailers. Until July 2025, his products faced modest 8–12% duties when crossing into US ports—a manageable cost that allowed him to compete with rivals from Bangladesh and Vietnam. Then came Trump's thunderbolt: first a 25% tariff in July, followed by another 25% in August, transforming his competitive pricing into an impossible burden. The mathematics are brutal. Where Patel's T-shirts once landed in American warehouses at competitive prices, they now carry a 50% surcharge, making them costlier than alternatives from Bangladesh (facing 20% tariffs) and Vietnam (20% tariffs). His American buyers, squeezed by their own margin pressures, began cancelling orders even before the tariffs took full effect. 'We have not received any new orders since the announcement,' echoes Ashwin Aggarwal of Nahar Industries, which supplies brands like GAP and Tommy Hilfiger. The scale of this trade disruption defies easy comprehension. India's exports to America span 66% of the bilateral trade relationship, worth approximately $60.2 billion annually. From the shimmering diamond cutting floors of Surat to the leather tanning units of Chennai, from chemical plants in Gujarat to handicraft workshops in Rajasthan, millions of workers suddenly found their livelihoods held hostage to geopolitical chess moves played thousands of miles away. The immediate trigger for Trump's ire was India's continued purchase of Russian crude oil—a strategy that had helped New Delhi navigate energy security challenges while keeping domestic fuel prices manageable. But the American president's response carried the weight of a sledgehammer used to crack a walnut, affecting industries and workers who had no role in energy policy decisions. The punishment mechanism was designed to be comprehensive and painful: an additional 25% duty layered atop existing tariff structures, creating effective rates that positioned India alongside Brazil as facing America's highest import barriers.

The MSME Universe Under Siege

To understand the magnitude of this crisis, one must first appreciate the ecosystem that these tariffs have disrupted. Indian MSMEs are not merely small businesses—they represent the cellular structure of the nation's industrial organism. These enterprises, defined as units with investments up to ₹10 crore and turnover below ₹50 crore for medium entities, employ 110 million people and contribute 30% to India's GDP. Their export prowess is equally impressive. MSMEs account for 45% of India's total merchandise exports, generating foreign exchange worth hundreds of billions of dollars annually. They dominate labour-intensive sectors where India has traditionally held competitive advantages: textiles (contributing 8.21% of total exports), gems and jewellery (a $32 billion industry), marine products, leather goods, chemicals, and engineering components. The cruel irony is that these enterprises succeeded precisely because they mastered the art of competing on price and efficiency. Unlike tech services companies that sell intellectual property or pharmaceutical giants protected by patents, MSMEs in traditional manufacturing compete in brutal commodity markets where a 5% cost disadvantage can mean the difference between prosperity and bankruptcy. The 50% tariff represents not a minor course correction but an existential threat.

Consider the textile cluster in Tirupur, which accounts for over 30% of India's readymade garment exports. This town of 4,00,000 people has built its economy around supplying cotton knitwear to global brands. The ecosystem includes thousands of small units—some employing just 10–15 workers that specialise in specific processes: knitting, dyeing, cutting, stitching, or finishing. When American orders evaporate, the entire food chain collapses. Similarly, in Surat's diamond polishing hub, over 8,00,000 workers—many of them migrants from rural areas—depend on the gems and jewellery trade that ships $10 billion worth of polished stones and gold jewellery to America annually. The industry operates on a delicate balance: rough diamonds are imported, processed through thousands of small cutting and polishing units, then exported as finished gems. The 50% tariff disrupts this flow, leaving workers unemployed and inventory unsold.

Short-term Carnage: When Orders Vanish Overnight

The immediate aftermath of the tariff announcement resembled a slow-motion industrial collapse. Export-oriented MSMEs faced a triple shock: existing orders became unprofitable, new orders disappeared, and cash flows that had sustained operations for years suddenly dried up. Industry data reveals the speed and severity of this disruption. In Rajasthan, a major hub for gems, jewellery, and handicrafts, shipping containers from Jaipur's dry port plummeted 45% within weeks of the tariff announcement—from 378 twenty-foot equivalent units to just 209 units. Jodhpur's dry port witnessed an even steeper 75% decline, dropping from 100 containers to 25. These numbers represent more than statistical abstractions; they translate into cancelled shifts, unpaid wages, and families struggling to meet basic expenses. The human cost becomes visceral in testimonies from affected entrepreneurs. Sanket Gandhi, director of Pheromone Chemicals in Ahmedabad, describes shipping 'nearly double our typical monthly volumes in August' to beat tariff deadlines, then facing the prospect of months without fresh orders. M Thukkaran of Esstee Exports, an apparel manufacturer in Tirupur, captures the desperation: 'With 25%

tariffs, we could absorb the costs and sustain our operations, but not at 50%.' The gems and jewellery sector, which employs over 4 million people across India, faced particularly acute distress. Despite exporters rushing $1 billion worth of shipments ahead of tariff deadlines, the anticipated Christmas demand in America failed to materialise as consumers, squeezed by inflation in other goods, deferred luxury purchases. Diamond manufacturer testimonies describe inventory accumulating in warehouses as buyers vanished from American markets. Employment data paints an even grimmer picture. Industry experts estimate that 2,00,000 to 3,00,000 jobs face immediate risk, with textiles alone potentially losing 1,00,000 positions if tariffs persist beyond six months. The Federation of Indian Export Organisations (FIEO) warns that 55% of India's shipments to America—worth $47.5 billion—face direct impact. For MSMEs operating with skeleton crews and no financial cushion, even temporary disruptions translate into permanent job losses.

The psychological impact extends beyond immediate financial distress. Export-oriented entrepreneurs, who had spent years building relationships with American buyers and understanding market preferences, suddenly found their expertise devalued. Credit rating agencies began scrutinising MSME portfolios more closely, concerned about potential defaults in export-dependent sectors. Banks, already cautious about lending to small enterprises, tightened credit further, creating a vicious cycle where businesses needed working capital most desperately yet found it least available.

Medium-Term Structural Damage: When Ecosystems Unravel

As the initial shock subsided, deeper structural problems emerged. The tariff crisis revealed how tightly integrated Indian MSME ecosystems had become with American demand patterns, creating vulnerabilities that would take years to address. The textile value chain exemplifies these interconnections. Indian garment exports depend not just on final assembly units but also on an elaborate network of suppliers: cotton farmers, yarn spinners, fabric weavers, dye houses, button manufacturers, zipper suppliers, packaging companies, and logistics providers. When American orders decline, the impact cascades through multiple tiers of suppliers, many of whom are MSMEs themselves. Geographic concentration amplifies these risks. Tirupur's economy depends heavily on textile exports, while Surat's prosperity rests on diamond processing. Panipat in Haryana specialises in carpets and blankets, with home textiles alone accounting for $1.3 billion in annual exports—60% of the city's total shipments.

When a single market like America becomes inaccessible, entire cities face economic depression. The financial system begins reflecting these strains through multiple channels. Working capital cycles, traditionally running 60–90 days in export sectors, extend indefinitely when buyers disappear. Inventory accumulates in warehouses, tying up precious resources. Forward contracts for raw materials become loss-making propositions when export revenues vanish. Letters of credit, the lifeblood of international trade, become difficult to obtain as banks question the viability of export transactions. Currency fluctuations add another layer of complexity. The Indian rupee, already under pressure from global economic uncertainties, faces additional stress as export earnings decline. For MSMEs that hedge their foreign exchange exposures, currency volatility creates additional costs. Those that remain unhedged face the dual burden of higher input costs (for imported raw materials) and lower realisation (from reduced export volumes). The talent drain represents perhaps the most insidious medium-term damage. Skilled workers in export industries—pattern makers, quality controllers, production supervisors—begin seeking opportunities in domestic sectors or migrating to other countries. This brain drain, once initiated, proves difficult to reverse even if trade conditions improve. The institutional knowledge built over decades in clusters like Tirupur or Surat risks dissipating permanently.

Perhaps most concerning is the erosion of trust in export markets. MSME entrepreneurs, having suffered losses from geopolitical decisions beyond their control, may become reluctant to invest in export capacity expansion. This risk aversion could persist long after tariffs are removed, limiting India's ability to capitalise on future trade opportunities.

Long-Term Transformation: Forced Evolution or Permanent Scarring?

The long-term implications of Trump's tariff assault extend far beyond immediate trade statistics to encompass fundamental questions about India's economic development strategy and the resilience of its industrial base. Chief Economic Adviser V Anantha Nageswaran's projection that tariffs could reduce GDP by 0.5–0.6 percentage points in the current fiscal year represents just the beginning of a longer adjustment process. If trade tensions persist or escalate, the cumulative impact could reshape India's export profile for decades. The Global Trade Research Initiative estimates that affected sectors could see 70% declines in export volumes, with overall shipments to America potentially falling from $86.5 billion to around $50 billion annually. Such dramatic shifts would force structural changes across the Indian industry. MSMEs in affected sectors face three basic choices: exit the market entirely, pivot to domestic demand, or diversify export destinations. Each path carries profound implications for employment, productivity, and regional development patterns. The exit option, while painful in human terms, might paradoxically benefit survivors by eliminating excess capacity and allowing profitable units to capture larger market shares. However, this creative destruction process could take years and would likely concentrate in regions most dependent on American exports—Tirupur, Surat, Panipat, and similar industrial clusters. Domestic market pivot represents perhaps the most promising adaptation strategy, especially given India's growing middle class and rising consumption levels. The government's recent GST reforms, reducing most items to 5% and 18% tax rates, support domestic demand expansion. However, transitioning from export orientation to domestic focus requires different skills, distribution networks, and product specifications. MSMEs accustomed to bulk orders from international buyers must learn to navigate India's fragmented retail landscape. Export diversification offers the most direct solution but faces significant obstacles. While government officials speak optimistically about targeting 40 alternative markets, including the UK, Japan, Germany, and Australia, the reality is more complex. Each market has distinct preferences, quality standards, and regulatory requirements. Building new buyer relationships takes years, not months. Moreover, many alternative markets lack the scale of American demand or impose their own trade barriers. The EU, India's second-largest export destination, already absorbs substantial Indian textile exports but operates under different seasonal patterns and product specifications than America. Southeast Asian markets, while growing rapidly, often compete with India in similar product categories rather than importing them. Africa and Latin America offer potential but typically demand lower-value products with correspondingly smaller margins. Perhaps most critically, the tariff crisis could accelerate automation and technological upgradation in the Indian industry. MSMEs facing permanent margin compression from trade barriers may invest in productivity-enhancing technologies to remain competitive. This forced modernisation, while painful in the short term, could ultimately strengthen India's industrial base by pushing manufacturers up the value chain. The textile sector's PLI scheme, with its ₹10,683 crore allocation over five years, specifically targets this technological transition by encouraging investment in manmade fibre production and technical textiles.

However, the scheme's benefits may take years to materialise while current disruptions demand immediate responses.

Government Response: Too Little, Too Late, or Strategic Patience?

The Indian government's response to the tariff crisis reflects both the political sensitivity of mass unemployment and the limited options available to a middle-income country confronting the world's largest economy. The measures announced or under consideration span immediate relief, medium-term support, and long-term strategic repositioning. Immediate relief efforts centre on the proposed ₹25,000 crore Export Promotion Mission, structured around two sub-schemes: Niryat Protsahan (₹10,000+ crore) focusing on credit support, and Niryat Disha (₹14,500+ crore) targeting market development and quality compliance. The mission's highlight is enhanced interest equalisation support worth ₹5,000 crore, designed to subsidise borrowing costs for export-oriented MSMEs.

Credit guarantee schemes represent the government's most direct intervention. Plans to provide 10–15% guarantees for loans overdue up to 90 days could help prevent MSME accounts from turning non-performing, thereby maintaining access to working capital. The proposal to double collateral-free loan limits under the CGTMSE from ₹10 lakh to ₹20 lakh specifically targets export-oriented units. These measures address genuine pain points.

MSME exporters typically operate with high leverage ratios and depend on timely credit to finance working capital. When export orders evaporate, cash flows become irregular, making loan servicing difficult. Credit guarantees can maintain banking relationships during temporary disruptions, preventing permanent damage to business relationships. However, the scale and timing of government response raise questions about adequacy and preparedness.

The Export Promotion Mission, while substantial in absolute terms, amounts to roughly ₹4,000 crore annually over six years—modest compared to the projected $4–5 billion drop in engineering exports alone. Moreover, scheme implementation typically takes months or years to reach beneficiaries, while MSME distress demands immediate attention. Market diversification initiatives, while strategically sound, face implementation challenges. The government's plan to target 40 countries for textile exports sounds impressive, but requires substantial diplomatic groundwork, trade promotion activities, and market development investments. Building new buyer relationships cannot be accomplished through policy announcements alone; it demands sustained effort from exporters who are currently focused on survival rather than expansion.

The PLI schemes, particularly for textiles, represent longer-term structural interventions aimed at moving Indian manufacturing up the value chain. The textile PLI's emphasis on manmade fibre production and technical textiles addresses genuine competitive weaknesses relative to countries like Vietnam and Bangladesh. However, PLI benefits flow primarily to large enterprises making substantial investments, while the current crisis predominantly affects smaller units lacking resources for major capacity expansion.

Perhaps most tellingly, government officials' initial response emphasised that the impact would be limited since India's economy depends primarily on domestic consumption rather than exports. While technically accurate—exports constitute roughly 20% of GDP—this response underestimates the concentrated regional and sectoral impacts that can create significant political and social tensions even if macroeconomic effects remain manageable.

What More Could and Should Be Done?

A comprehensive government response to the MSME crisis

would require recognising that trade wars fought at the national level create highly concentrated damage at the grassroots level. The following interventions could significantly improve outcomes for affected enterprises:

Emergency Employment Programmes: While credit support helps existing enterprises survive, displaced workers need immediate income support. Expanding the Mahatma Gandhi National Rural Employment Guarantee Scheme or creating urban employment programmes, specifically in affected industrial clusters, could prevent social distress while maintaining consumption levels in hard-hit regions.

Sectoral Adjustment Funds: Rather than generic export promotion schemes, targeted funds for specific sectors, like textiles, gems, and leather, could provide tailored support. These funds could finance market studies, buyer delegations, product development, and compliance costs for new export destinations. Textile exporters pivoting from American casual wear to European formal shirts need different designs, fabrics, and quality systems.

Technology Upgradation Acceleration: The tariff crisis creates urgency for productivity improvements that can restore cost competitiveness despite higher trade barriers. Subsidised technology loans, equipment leasing programmes, and shared facility centres could help MSMEs access modern machinery without massive capital investments. A textile unit installing automated cutting systems or a chemical company upgrading quality control equipment could maintain margins despite tariff headwinds.

Export Credit Insurance Enhancement: The Export Credit Guarantee Corporation (ECGC) could expand coverage for MSMEs exploring new markets, reducing the risk of bad debts when dealing with unfamiliar buyers. Enhanced insurance could encourage exporters to diversify destinations rather than retreating to domestic markets entirely.

Regulatory Fast-Tracking: MSMEs pivoting to domestic markets often face bureaucratic hurdles in obtaining licenses, clearances, and certifications required for local sales. A fast-track approval system for export units transitioning to domestic focus could accelerate this adjustment process.

Regional Development Packages: Industrial clusters like Tirupur, Surat, and Panipat that face concentrated impacts need comprehensive support beyond individual enterprise assistance. Infrastructure upgrades, logistics improvements, and skill development programmes could help these regions diversify their economic base while maintaining their industrial character.

Financial Sector Coordination: Rather than relying solely on government schemes, coordinated action with banks, NBFCs, and international development organisations could multiply available resources. Specialised refinancing facilities for MSME exports, venture capital funds for pivoting enterprises, and patient capital for technological upgradation could complement budgetary allocations. The government's longer-term strategy should focus on building resilience into India's export ecosystem rather than simply responding to immediate crises. This requires developing domestic supply chains, investing in research and development capabilities, and creating institutions that can anticipate and respond to future trade disruptions.

The MSME Ecosystem's Path Forward

Beyond government intervention, the MSME ecosystem itself must evolve to thrive in an increasingly volatile global trade environment. The tariff crisis, while painful, offers lessons that could strengthen Indian enterprises if properly absorbed.

Diversification as Survival Strategy: The most immediate lesson is the danger of over-dependence on any single market, regardless of how profitable that relationship may appear. MSMEs must consciously build customer bases across multiple geographies, even if this means accepting lower margins or smaller order sizes from alternative markets. A textile unit supplying 80% to America and 20% elsewhere should aim for a 40-30-30 distribution across three major regions.

Value Chain Integration: Rather than remaining specialised in narrow activities, MSMEs could explore vertical integration opportunities that capture larger shares of value creation. A garment unit that currently only manufactures could develop design capabilities, build its own brand, or establish direct retail channels. Such integration provides a buffer against disruptions in any single segment while improving overall profitability.

Technology as Equaliser: Automation and digitisation, long viewed as threats to labour-intensive industries, may become survival necessities in a high-tariff world. MSMEs that can achieve productivity levels comparable to those of developed countries could maintain competitiveness even under adverse trade conditions. This requires not just machinery upgrades but also workforce training and management system improvements.

Collaborative Networks: Individual MSMEs lack resources to navigate complex international markets, but collectively they possess significant capabilities. Industry associations, export promotion councils, and informal business networks could play more active roles in market intelligence, joint marketing, and shared facility development. A consortium of 50 textile units might jointly establish design centres, testing laboratories, or overseas marketing offices that no individual enterprise could afford.

Financial Sophistication: The tariff crisis exposed how few MSMEs had adequate financial risk management systems. Currency hedging, export credit insurance, and diversified funding sources represent basic prudential measures that many small enterprises ignored during good times. Building financial resilience requires treating risk management as seriously as production management.

Innovation Focus: Rather than competing solely on cost, Indian MSMEs must develop innovation capabilities that create differentiated value propositions. This could involve new materials, unique designs, specialised applications, or superior service levels. A chemical unit that develops eco-friendly alternatives to conventional products or a textile manufacturer that creates performance fabrics could command premium pricing that offsets tariff burdens. The transformation required goes beyond operational changes to encompass fundamental mindset shifts. MSMEs that view themselves as vendors in global supply chains must evolve into partners or solution providers. Those accustomed to order-taking must develop market-making capabilities. Enterprises focused on current operations must build anticipatory capacities that prepare for future disruptions.

Conclusion: Resilience Through Adversity

Trump's tariff assault on Indian MSMEs represents more than a trade dispute; it embodies the broader challenges facing middle-income countries as they navigate great power competition in an increasingly fragmented global economy. The immediate damage is undeniable: cancelled orders, job losses, financial distress, and shattered business relationships built over decades. However, a crisis often catalyses a transformation that might never occur under normal circumstances. The textile manufacturers forced to explore European markets, the chemical exporters investing in new technologies, and the jewellery units building domestic brands are all engaging in activities that will strengthen India's industrial base long after current trade tensions resolve. The government's response, while imperfect in timing and scale, demonstrates a recognition that MSME resilience requires more than market forces alone. Credit support, export diversification assistance, and technological upgradation incentives address genuine constraints that small enterprises face when confronting global disruptions. The challenge lies in implementation speed and ensuring that benefits reach intended beneficiaries rather than getting absorbed by administrative machinery. Perhaps most critically, the tariff crisis has shattered the illusion that globalisation provides unidirectional benefits without corresponding risks. Indian MSMEs, having prospered by integrating into global value chains, must now learn to maintain that integration while building defensive capabilities against future shocks. This balance between globalisation and self-reliance, between efficiency and resilience, will define India's industrial trajectory for the coming decade.

The story of Trump's tariff war against Indian MSMEs is still unfolding. Some enterprises will not survive the transition, becoming casualties of economic statecraft they played no role in initiating. Others will emerge stronger, more diversified, and better prepared for future challenges. The difference between these outcomes will depend not just on government policies or market forces, but on the ingenuity, persistence, and adaptability that have always characterised India's entrepreneurial spirit. The minnows caught in the giants' clash may be small individually, but collectively they represent the cellular structure of India's economic body. Their survival and transformation will ultimately determine whether this crisis becomes a temporary setback or a catalyst for building a more resilient and self-reliant industrial ecosystem. The next chapter in this story remains to be written, but it will be authored by the millions of entrepreneurs, workers, and families who refuse to let trade wars define their economic destiny.

Way Forward: Building Anti-fragile MSME Ecosystems

As India's MSMEs navigate the turbulent waters of Trump's tariff regime, the path forward must transcend mere survival to embrace what Nassim Taleb termed 'antifragility'—the ability to not just withstand shocks but to emerge stronger from them. This requires a fundamental reimagining of how small enterprises operate, compete, and grow in an era of persistent trade volatility. The immediate priority must be rapid market diversification coupled with domestic market deepening.

MSMEs cannot afford the luxury of a gradual transition; they need accelerated access to alternative export destinations while simultaneously building capabilities to serve India's expanding consumer base. This dual strategy provides both risk mitigation and growth opportunities that can offset American market losses. Technology adoption must shift from an optional upgrade to a survival imperative. The tariff differential that makes Indian goods uncompetitive in America can be narrowed through productivity gains that automation and digitisation enable.

Government schemes supporting technology adoption should prioritise MSMEs in affected sectors, providing subsidised access to modern equipment, software, and training programmes that enhance competitiveness. Financial architecture supporting MSMEs requires complete restructuring to provide not just credit during normal times but resilience during crises. This includes export credit insurance expansion, currency hedging support, alternative credit scoring mechanisms, and patient capital for enterprises undergoing market transition. The banking sector must evolve from risk-averse lending to partnership-based financing that shares both risks and rewards of MSME growth. Most fundamentally, the MSME ecosystem must embrace collaboration as a competitive advantage. Individual small enterprises lack resources to navigate complex global markets, but collective action through industry associations, export clusters, and shared service platforms can provide capabilities that rival large corporations. This requires moving beyond traditional competition to embrace 'coopetition', where enterprises cooperate on common challenges while competing in markets.

The government's role must evolve from scheme announcement to implementation excellence, ensuring that support reaches intended beneficiaries quickly and effectively.

This requires administrative reforms that prioritise speed over procedures, outcomes over outputs, and MSME feedback over bureaucratic convenience. The Export Promotion Mission's success will be measured not by funds disbursed but by orders restored, jobs preserved, and enterprises transformed.

Looking ahead, India's MSME sector stands at an inflexion point. The easy growth phase of globalisation integration is ending, replaced by a more complex era requiring greater sophistication, resilience, and adaptability. Enterprises that master this transition will emerge as the backbone of India's economic future. Those that fail to adapt risk becoming footnotes in the story of creative destruction that global trade wars inevitably unleash. The tariff assault has ended the innocence of Indian MSMEs about geopolitical risks, but it has also created urgency for transformation that might otherwise have taken decades. In this sense, Trump's trade war may inadvertently become the catalyst that propels India's small enterprise sector toward the sophistication and resilience required for sustained success in the twenty-first-century global economy. The giants may clash, but the minnows that learn to swim in turbulent waters will inherit the future.

The Need for Independent Audit: CAG's Role in Assessing Tariff Fallout

One glaring gap that has emerged in the wake of Trump's penal tariffs is the absence of any robust, independent third-party evaluation of both the true extent of MSME distress and the actual outcomes of government relief programmes. While policymakers have been swift to announce a battery of support schemes—from rapid credit guarantees to the ambitious Export Promotion Mission—the lived reality in India's industrial clusters often paints a far more uneven picture. Reports from regions like Surat, Tirupur, and Panipat suggest that many intended beneficiaries either struggle to access relief or remain unaware of available schemes, casting doubt on the efficiency of policy transmission.

It is against this backdrop that the demand for a comprehensive, all-India performance audit by the CAG takes on urgent significance. An audit by the CAG, India's pre-eminent independent watchdog, would go beyond headline figures to trace the granular impact of tariffs and aid-mapping not just outputs, like funds disbursed, but also actual outcomes, such as jobs saved, export clusters restored, and new markets accessed. The CAG's track record in scrutinising major government initiatives lends both credibility and transparency, providing policymakers, industry leaders, and the broader public with data-driven insights on what has worked—and, crucially, what hasn't.

By combining field surveys of affected MSMEs with forensic audits of relief disbursement and utilisation, a CAG-led exercise could spotlight implementation gaps, regional disparities, and the trade-offs between immediate crisis relief and long-term sectoral resilience. Such a performance audit, released in the public domain, would be invaluable in charting the future course of MSME support—informing mid-course corrections, recalibrating policies, and restoring confidence among India's millions of small business owners. In an economic environment transformed by abrupt external shocks, honest assessment becomes not just a bureaucratic routine but the bedrock of effective public policy.

References:

1. The Times of India. Indian exporters get support under the new EPM scheme. 23 August 2025.

2. SME Venture. EEPC Seeks Urgent Support for MSMEs Hit by US Tariffs. 2025 11 September 2025.

3. Al Jazeera. How US tariffs are unravelling India's textile industry. 2025 16 September 2025..

EPILOGUE

◆◆◆

From Fragmented Reforms to a Unified Renaissance

In the final reckoning, India's MSME and startup story is not a tale of failure—it is a saga of unfinished potential. From the alleys of Kanpur to the corridors of Bengaluru's co-working hubs, the same question echoes: Can the world's most populous democracy finally give its entrepreneurs—small and new—the dignity, data, and dynamism they deserve?

This book has travelled through defence factories and coir mills, startup accelerators and khadi stalls, unearthing both resilience and rot. It has shown how demonetisation and COVID tested the sector's endurance, how credit apartheid still favours the mighty over the modest, and how reform after reform—from DAP 2020 to Udyam and RAMP—often shimmered on PowerPoint but stumbled on the shop floor. Yet it has also illuminated India's quiet revolutionaries—the small manufacturers, women entrepreneurs, weavers, app-builders, and innovators—who refused to fold, and in doing so, kept the economy breathing.

Equally striking is the story of India's startup ecosystem—glittering at first glance, but riddled with cracks beneath the surface. The country that celebrates unicorns too often overlooks the fragile foundations beneath them: premature valuations, reverse-flip trends, governance lapses, and an obsession with fundraising over fundamentals. The startup dream, once a symbol of boundless possibility, has at times drifted into a mirage of hype and burnout. From BYJU'S spectacular fall to the Gensol-BluSmart cautionary tale, the message is clear—India's startup journey must mature from chasing capital to creating value, from being a sprint to becoming a marathon of innovation and integrity.

If there is one message this journey leaves behind, it is this: India's small enterprises and startups don't need sympathy—they need systems. Not slogans, but seamless support. Not token 'champion portals', but transparent platforms that talk to each other. Not headline credit numbers, but timely payments and enforceable accountability. What they seek is a government that listens as much as it legislates, a financial sector that trusts, and a bureaucracy that facilitates rather than filters.

The next decade must be one of convergence without confusion. MSMEs and startups are not two species—they are two stages of the same evolution. The carpenter in Coimbatore and the coder in Noida are co-authors of India's growth story, each capable of making the other stronger. When the ecosystem links their energies instead of dividing them by policy silos, the result will not just be *Make in India*, but *Scale from India*.

For India to rise as a ten-trillion-dollar economy with conscience, the CAG must audit promises, not just accounts; ministries must measure outcomes, not outlays; and policymakers must remember that every small unit shuttered and every failed startup is not just a statistic lost, but a dream extinguished. This book ends, therefore, not with a full stop but with a call to action—to reinvent both the MSME and startup frameworks as a partnership of trust, technology, and tenacity.

The baton now passes from bureaucracy to the builder, from planner to producer, from incubator to innovator. The true test of *Atmanirbharta* lies not in policy speeches, but in the hum of a small workshop and the click of a young coder's keyboard—both staying lit through the night. When those sounds grow into a national chorus—of enterprise, equity, and excellence—India's entrepreneurial renaissance will no longer be a promise deferred. It will be a revolution delivered.

The Auditor's Eye and the Entrepreneur's Hope

As someone who has spent a lifetime inside the machinery of government audit and accountability, I have learned that numbers tell only part of the truth. The rest lies between the lines—in delayed payments, missed opportunities, and the quiet despair of entrepreneurs navigating a maze of promises. When I turned my gaze from ledgers to livelihoods, I realised that audit, too, is a form of empathy—a way of asking whether the system has served those it claims to empower.

This book, born of both that discipline and that empathy, attempts to bridge two worlds: the bureaucrat's precision and the entrepreneur's passion. It has sought to expose systemic flaws not to assign blame, but to ignite reform; to hold up a mirror not to mock, but to motivate. India's MSMEs and startups are not statistics—they are human stories of grit, risk, and reinvention. If their failures hurt, it is because their potential is immense.

My hope is that policymakers, auditors, bankers, and young dreamers alike read this work not as a critique, but as a conversation—a blueprint for a more inclusive, responsive, and forward-looking India. For in the end, accountability is not about catching errors; it is about ensuring impact. And the greatest audit of all is the one we owe to our future—to make sure that the small dreamer in a workshop and the coder in a garage both find in India not a maze, but a runway.

ANNEXURE A

♦♦♦

Clearances Required for Setting Up a Factory or Industry in India

Ease of Doing Business in India
Here is the SHORT list that one would need to run a small factory in India.

Core Registrations:
Company Incorp (MCA) + PAN, TAN (Tax Deduction and Collection Account Number), Udyam, GST, IEC (Importer-Exporter Code), Professional Tax, Shops and Establishments, Trade License
Factory and Labour Compliances:
Factory License, Labour License
Standing Orders Certification
EPF, ESIC, Gratuity, Labour Welfare Fund
Workmen Compensation Policy:
Registers (Workers, Overtime, Fire Drill)
First-Aid Room + Medical Officer Registration
Industrial Canteen License, Internal Complaints Committee (PoSH (Prevention of Sexual Harassment))
Property and Infrastructure:
Building Plan Approval, Completion and Occupancy Certificates

Land Use Conversion (CLU (Change of Land Use))
Fire NOC, Electrical Safety, Lift License, Fire Extinguisher Installation
Boiler, Transformer, DG (Diesel Generator) Set, Fire Hydrant System Approvals
Industrial Water Supply NOC

Environmental and Pollution Control:
Consent to Establish + Operate (CTE + CTO)
Environment Clearance + Impact Assessment Report
Hazardous, E-Waste, Plastic, and Biomedical Waste Handling Authorisations
Ground Water Extraction NOC, Rainwater Harvesting Certificate
Effluent Treatment Plant NOC, Solid Waste Management Certificate
Noise Pollution Control Compliance
CPCB Registration

Product and Quality:
Legal Metrology Registration (weights, measures, barcodes)
BIS (Bureau of Indian Standards)/ISI Certification, In-House Testing Lab (NABL (National Accreditation Board for Testing and Calibration Laboratories))
Quality Certifications (ISO (International Organization of Standardization) 9001, 14001, 45001, 50001)
FSSAI (Food Safety and Standards Authority of India) License (if applicable)
Barcode Registration (GS1 (Global Standards 1) India)
Packaging Label Approval

Safety and Audits:
Safety Audit Certificate, Factory Equipment Safety Certificate
Calibration Certificate for all instruments
Explosive/Diesel Storage License
Machinery Installation Certificate

Financial and Trade:

EPCG (Export Promotion Capital Goods) License, Import Duty Exemption Certificate

AEO (Authorised Economic Operator), RCMC (Registration-cum-Membership Certificate), IEM (Industrial Entrepreneur Memorandum), Industrial Subsidy Registration

Project Report Submission

MSME Credit Guarantee Scheme Registration (Banks: Term Loan Sanction Letter, Collateral Evaluation Report)

Intellectual Property and Marketing:

Trademark Registration + Watch Sub.

Copyright Registration

CSR (Corporate Social Responsibility) Registration (if applicable)

General and Miscellaneous:

Power Connection Approval, Police Clearance Certificate

SEZ (Special Economic Zone)/EOU (Export Oriented Unit) License, Export Certifications (e.g., CE (Conformité Européenne) mark)

Company Annual Compliance Filings (MCA (Ministry of Corporate Affairs), ROC (Registrar of Companies), Income Tax)

Insurance Policies (Property, Machinery, Workmen, Health, Liability)

Transport Vehicle Permit, Weighbridge License

APPENDIX 1

◆◆◆

MSME Definitions at a Glance

SL No.	Country	Definition of Small Businesses/Msme
1	United States	A small business is one with fewer than 500 employees. However, this can vary; for instance, manufacturing and mining industries may have thresholds up to 1,500 employees, while wholesale trade businesses may be classified as small with up to 100 employees. Annual revenue limits also differ by industry, ranging from $1 million to over $40 million.
2	United Kingdom	A small company is defined as one with a turnover of less than £10.2 million, a balance sheet total under £5.1 million, and fewer than 50 employees. For medium enterprises, the thresholds go up to £36 million turnover and 250 employees. Separately, under EU standards, an SME is defined as a business with fewer than 250 employees and either an annual turnover not exceeding €50 million or a balance sheet total not exceeding €43 million.
3	Germany	Uses the EU definition—fewer than 250 employees, with annual turnover not exceeding €50 million or a balance sheet total not exceeding €43 million. Yet Germany's famed 'Mittelstand'—its backbone of medium-sized, family-owned enterprises—goes beyond these metrics to represent a unique business culture of innovation and global leadership in niche areas.
4	France	Similarly uses the EU SME definition but is more aggressive in offering tax rebates, research grants, and export support. French SMEs often have under 250 employees but form 99% of the country's businesses and employ over 60% of the private workforce.

5	Australia	Follows the ABS's classification: micro (1–4 employees), small (5–19), medium (20–199), and large (200+). However, the ATO defines SMEs for tax purposes as businesses with a turnover under AUD 50 million.
6	Brazil	Different definitions under various regimes. Under the 'Simples Nacional' tax regime, small businesses are classified based on annual revenue—up to BRL 3,60,000 for micro, and up to BRL 4.8 million for small. The definitions link directly to tax slabs, making compliance simpler.
7	Indonesia	MSMEs are defined through Law No. 20/2008 based on asset size and revenue. Micro enterprises have assets up to IDR 50 million and revenue up to IDR 300 million. Small and medium thresholds are IDR 500 million to IDR 10 billion in revenue, and employee counts are also considered.
8	China	The definition of SMEs varies by industry and considers the number of employees, annual revenue, and total assets. In the manufacturing sector, a medium-sized enterprise may have up to 2,000 employees, while in the wholesale sector, the threshold might be lower. The emphasis is not just on classification but on high-tech, export-oriented, and innovation-driven small firms. China also promotes 'gazelles'—fast-growing startups that show promise to become unicorns.
9	Singapore	An SME is defined as a company with an annual turnover of less than S$100 million or employing fewer than 200 employees.
10	South Africa	Small enterprises are classified based on the number of employees and annual turnover, which vary across sectors. For instance, in the manufacturing sector, a small enterprise might have up to 50 employees and a turnover of up to R13 million.
11	Bangladesh	SMEs are defined by the number of employees and fixed assets, excluding land and buildings. For example, in the manufacturing sector, a small enterprise may have 10–49 employees and fixed assets between BDT 0.5 million and BDT 15 million.

<table>
<tr>
<td>12</td>
<td>India</td>
<td>
Prior to Budget 2025–26:
<table>
<tr><th>Category</th><th>Investment Limit</th><th>Turnover Limit</th></tr>
<tr><td>Micro Enterprises</td><td>Up to ₹1 crore</td><td>Up to ₹5 crore</td></tr>
<tr><td>Small Enterprises</td><td>Up to ₹10 crore</td><td>Up to ₹50 crore</td></tr>
<tr><td>Medium Enterprises</td><td>Up to ₹50 crore</td><td>Up to ₹250 crore</td></tr>
</table>
After Budget 2025–26:
<table>
<tr><th>Category</th><th>Investment Limit</th><th>Turnover Limit</th></tr>
<tr><td>Micro Enterprises</td><td>Up to ₹2.5 crore</td><td>Up to ₹10 crore</td></tr>
<tr><td>Small Enterprises</td><td>Up to ₹25 crore</td><td>Up to ₹100 crore</td></tr>
<tr><td>Medium Enterprises</td><td>Up to ₹125 crore</td><td>Up to ₹500 crore</td></tr>
</table>
</td>
</tr>
</table>

APPENDIX 2

◆◆◆

List of Secretaries to the Government of India, Ministry of MSME

1. Shri Anupam Das Gupta, IAS (Maharashtra cadre, 1970 batch). Tenure: 1 November 2004 to 31 December 2006. Details: Mr Das Gupta was Secretary, Ministry of SSI & ARI.

2. Dr Chandra Pal, IAS (Uttar Pradesh cadre, 1972 batch). Tenure: 1 January 2007 to 10 May 2007 (Secretary, Ministry of SSI & ARI). [The erstwhile Ministry of SSI and Ministry of ARI were subsumed in the Ministry of MSME on 9 May 2007]. 11 May 2007 to 31 January 2008. Details: Dr Pal took over as Secretary in January 2007, succeeding Mr Dasgupta.

Officers who headed the Ministry of MSME in the Government of India

Sr. No.	Name (S/ Shri)	IAS Cadre	IAS Batch	From	To
1	Dr Chandra Pal	Uttar Pradesh	1972	11 May 2007	31 January 2008
2	Dinesh Rai	Uttar Pradesh	1974	4 February 2008	31 August 2010

3	Uday Kumar Varma	Madhya Pradesh	1976	1 Septemebr 2010	20 October 2011
4	Radha Krishna Mathur	Tripura	1977	9 November 2011	30 September 2012
5	Vivek Rae	AGMUT (Arunachal Pradesh, Goa, Mizoram, and Union Territories)	1978	8 October 2012	31 January 2013
6	Madhav Lal	Jammu & Kashmir	1977	20 February 2013	30 June 2015
7	Dr Anup K. Pujari	Karnataka	1980	30 June 2015	31 January 2016
8	Dr Krishan Kumar Jalan	Haryana	1982	1 February 2016	30 June 2017
9	Dr Arun Kumar Panda	Odisha	1984	1 July 2017	30 April 2020
10	Arvind Kumar Sharma	Gujarat	1988	30 April 2020	11 January 2021
11	BB Swain	Gujarat	1988	29 January 2021	31 May 2023
12	Subhas Chandra Lal Das	AGMUT	1992	13 June 2023	Till date

APPENDIX 3

◆◆◆

Index of Key Words and Abbreviations

Aadhaar

- **Context:** Linked to subsidy transfers to reduce leakage in MSME and rural schemes (Chapter 23).
- **Significance:** Enhances transparency and efficiency in welfare and financial delivery for MSMEs.

Administrative Babel

- **Context:** Describes the overlap of multiple ministries (e.g., finance, commerce, MSME) targeting MSMEs, leading to policy duplication and blurred accountability (Prologue, Chapter 2).
- **Significance:** Highlights bureaucratic inefficiencies hindering effective MSME support.

Angel Tax

- **Context:** Abolished in the 2024–25 Budget to remove funding bottlenecks for MSME startups and early-stage ventures (Chapter 23).
- **Significance:** A reform to boost startup investment and ease financial constraints.

Atal Incubation Centres (AICs)

- **Context:** Established under the Atal Innovation Mission to nurture startups and innovation hubs (Chapter 2).
- **Significance:** Supports MSME and startup ecosystems through incubation and mentorship.

Atal Innovation Mission (AIM)

- **Context:** A government initiative to promote innovation and entrepreneurship, complementing Startup India (Chapter 2).

- **Significance:** Fosters startup growth and innovation, though often metro-centric.

BIFR (Board for Industrial and Financial Reconstruction)

- **Context:** Introduced in the 1985–86 Budget to revive sick industries, including small-scale enterprises (Chapter 23).
- **Significance:** An early attempt to support struggling MSMEs, now largely replaced by IBC.

Bureaucratic Apathy

- **Context:** Describes risk-averse leadership and lack of proactive administration in the MSME Ministry (Chapter 20).
- **Significance:** A critical barrier to effective policy execution and MSME growth.

CAG (Comptroller and Auditor General)

- Conducted audits exposing inefficiencies in MSME schemes, Coir Board, NSIC, and other institutions (Prologue, Chapters 9, 14, 17, 19, and 21).
- **Significance:** Provides critical oversight but underscores the need for comprehensive ecosystem audits.

CBDC (Central Bank Digital Currency)

- **Context:** Introduced in the 2022–23 Budget to enhance digital finance, with potential benefits for MSME transactions (Chapter 23).
- **Significance:** Supports digital payment adoption, though MSME uptake remains limited.

CCRI (Central Coir Research Institute)

- **Context:** R&D wing of the Coir Board in Kerala, developing technologies like coir wood and geo-textiles (Chapter 22).
- **Significance:** Drives modernisation but struggles with commercialisation and scale.

CGTMSE (Credit Guarantee Fund Trust for Micro and Small Enterprises)

- **Context:** Provides collateral-free loans up to ₹5 crore for MSMEs, revamped in 2023 (Chapter 2, Chapter 17).

- **Significance:** A cornerstone for improving credit access, though only 14% of MSMEs benefit.

CHAMPIONS

- **Context:** A scheme to streamline MSME support, part of post-COVID and demonetization recovery efforts (Prologue, Chapter 16).
- **Significance:** Aimed at simplifying MSME assistance but criticised for delivering digital dashboards over tangible outcomes.

CICT (Central Institute of Coir Technology)

- **Context:** Coir Board's R&D facility in Bengaluru, focused on technological advancements in coir processing (Chapter 22).
- **Significance:** Supports innovation but faces challenges in widespread adoption.

CITUS (Coir Industry Technology Upgradation Scheme)

- **Context:** A component of Coir Vikas Yojana to subsidise machinery for coir units (Chapter 22).
- **Significance:** Aims to modernise coir production but has low uptake due to awareness and training gaps.

CLCSS (Credit Linked Capital Subsidy Scheme)

- **Context:** Subsidises technology upgrades for manufacturing MSMEs (Chapter 2).
- **Significance:** Supports modernisation but is limited by bureaucratic processes.

Coir Board

- **Context:** An MSME Ministry institution promoting the coir industry, critiqued for outdated schemes and limited modernisation (Chapter 21, Chapter 22).
- **Significance:** Represents a traditional industry struggling with bureaucratic inertia and innovation gaps.

Coir Industry Act (1953)

- **Context:** Proposed amendments in 2024–25 to enhance export orientation and streamline the Coir Board (Chapter 22).

- **Significance:** Aims to boost coir exports and modernise the sector's governance.

Coir Udyami Yojana (CUY)

- **Context:** A discontinued scheme to support coir unit establishment, merged into PMEGP (Chapter 22).
- **Significance:** Highlights challenges in scheme continuity and outcome measurement.

Coir Vikas Yojana (CVY)

- **Context:** Umbrella scheme for coir industry development, including skill upgradation, technology, and export promotion (Chapter 22).
- **Significance:** Central to Coir Board's efforts but faces implementation and impact tracking issues.

Credit Access

- **Context:** A chronic challenge, with only 14% of MSMEs accessing formal credit, facing a $330–530 billion credit gap (Chapter 2, Chapter 17).
- **Significance:** A critical barrier to MSME growth and resilience.

DC-MSME (Development Commissioner, Micro, Small and Medium Enterprises)

- **Context:** Oversees MSME schemes, criticised for exaggerated claims and unverified data (Chapter 17, Chapter 19).
- **Significance:** A key institution needing better accountability and data integrity.

Demonetisation

- **Context:** The 2016 policy shock that disrupted MSME cash flows, described as a 'bolt from the blue' (Prologue, Chapter 16).
- **Significance:** Exposed MSME vulnerabilities to sudden policy changes.

Digital India

- **Context:** A national initiative to promote digital infrastructure, supporting MSMEs through digital platforms (Prologue, Chapter 16).
- **Significance:** Enhances market access but requires better integration for MSMEs.

DPIIT (Department for Promotion of Industry and Internal Trade)

- **Context:** Oversees Startup India and related investment funds, part of the fragmented MSME ecosystem (Chapter 2).
- **Significance:** A key player in startup policy but adds to administrative complexity.

ECLGS (Emergency Credit Line Guarantee Scheme)

- **Context:** A post-COVID scheme to provide credit support to MSMEs (Chapter 1, Chapter 16).
- **Significance:** Aimed at crisis recovery but limited by awareness and accessibility.

e-RUPI

- **Context:** Introduced in the 2022–23 Budget as a digital payment solution, with potential MSME applications (Chapter 23).
- **Significance:** Supports digital transactions, but adoption among MSMEs is slow.

Export Promotion

- **Context:** A core Coir Board mandate, with initiatives like Market Development Assistance and trade fair participation (Chapter 22).
- **Significance:** Critical for coir industry growth but challenged by market volatility and weak branding.

FDI (Foreign Direct Investment)

- **Context:** Eased norms in the 1991–92 Budget and streamlined via FIPB in 1996–97, aiding MSME joint ventures (Chapter 23).
- **Significance:** Supports MSME integration into global markets but is limited by regulatory hurdles.

FFS (Fund of Funds for Startups)

- **Context:** A ₹10,000 crore corpus managed by SIDBI to support startups via venture capital (Chapter 2).
- **Significance:** A novel funding mechanism, but slowed by disbursement delays.

FIPB (Foreign Investment Promotion Board)

- **Context:** Introduced in 1996–97 to streamline FDI approvals for MSMEs and others (Chapter 23).
- **Significance:** Facilitated global investment but is now replaced by newer mechanisms.

Gensol-BluSmart Debacle

- **Context:** A case study of startup failure due to ambition, hype, and regulatory blind spots (Chapter 4).
- **Significance:** Illustrates systemic risks in India's startup ecosystem.

GST (Goods and Services Tax)

- **Context:** Suggested exemptions for MSME B2B supplies to large exporters (Chapter 1).
- **Significance:** A potential reform to enhance MSME competitiveness.

IBC (Insolvency and Bankruptcy Code)

- **Context:** Suggested pre-pack IBC for MSMEs to ease insolvency processes (Chapter 17).
- **Significance:** Could reduce MSME distress but requires tailored implementation.

ICICI (Industrial Credit and Investment Corporation of India)

- **Context:** Established in the 1954–55 Budget to support industrial financing, including for SSIs (Chapter 23).
- **Significance:** An early financial institution aiding small industries.

IRDA (Insurance Regulatory and Development Authority)

- **Context:** Proposed in the 1995–96 Budget to break insurance monopolies, benefiting MSMEs (Chapter 23).
- **Significance:** Improved access to insurance services for small businesses.

Khadi and Village Industries Commission (KVIC)

- **Context:** Critiqued for administrative decay and stalled reforms, despite its Gandhian legacy (Prologue, Chapter 8, Chapter 9).

- **Significance:** Represents missed opportunities in revitalising traditional industries.

Khadi Reform and Development Programme (KRDP)

- **Context:** A 2009 initiative with $150 million ADB assistance to modernise khadi, which failed due to institutional resistance (Preface).
- **Significance:** A cautionary tale of reform failure in traditional sectors.

KUR (Kredit Usaha Rakyat)

- **Context:** Indonesia's microcredit programme with government interest subsidies, a model for India (Chapter 1).
- **Significance:** Demonstrates effective credit delivery for MSMEs.

Little Giants

- **Context:** China's programme nurturing over 14,600 high-tech small firms, a benchmark for India (Chapter 2).
- **Significance:** Highlights the impact of targeted, innovation-driven MSME support.

Market Linkages

- **Context:** A critical MSME need, with surveys highlighting demand for better marketing support (Chapter 1, Chapter 2).
- **Significance:** Essential for MSME growth but underdeveloped in India.

MGNREGA (Mahatma Gandhi National Rural Employment Guarantee Act)

- **Context:** Launched in the 2005–06 Budget, indirectly supporting MSMEs by boosting rural purchasing power (Chapter 23).
- **Significance:** Enhances demand for MSME products in rural areas.

Mittelstand

- **Context:** Germany's model of medium-sized, family-owned enterprises, a global benchmark (Chapter 1).
- **Significance:** Offers lessons in innovation, clustering, and vocational training for India.

MODVAT (Modified Value Added Tax)

- **Context:** Introduced in 1986–87 to simplify excise for manufacturing MSMEs (Chapter 23).
- **Significance:** Reduced tax burdens for small industries, a precursor to GST.

MSME (Micro, Small and Medium Enterprises)

- **Context:** The book's central focus, contributing 30% to GDP and employing 110 million people (Prologue, Chapter 2).
- **Significance:** The backbone of India's economy, facing systemic challenges like credit and policy gaps.

MSME Development Institutes

- **Context:** Institutions under the MSME Ministry to support MSMEs, hampered by coordination issues (Chapter 2).
- **Significance:** Key for last-mile delivery, but needs streamlining.

MSMED Act (2006)

- **Context:** Provided a legal framework for MSME classification, timely payments, and support (Preface, Chapter 23).
- **Significance:** A landmark reform for MSME legitimacy and protection.

MUDRA Yojana (Pradhan Mantri MUDRA Yojana)

- **Context:** Offers unsecured loans up to ₹10 lakh for micro-entrepreneurs (Chapter 2, Chapter 16, Chapter 23).
- **Significance:** A major credit initiative, but limited by small loan sizes and growth impact.

NAPS (National Apprenticeship Promotion Scheme)

- **Context:** Launched in 2016 to incentivise apprenticeship uptake, underutilised by MSMEs (Chapter 2).
- **Significance:** A potential talent pipeline, but with low adoption rates.

NCLT (National Company Law Tribunal)

- **Context:** A regulatory hurdle for startups attempting reverse flipping (Chapter 13).

- **Significance:** Highlights procedural barriers to startup redomiciling.

NIESBUD (National Institute for Entrepreneurship and Small Business Development)

- **Context:** Part of the MSME skill ecosystem, criticised for fudged figures and poor outcomes (Chapter 14).
- **Significance:** Reflects gaps in skill training effectiveness.

NIMSME (National Institute for Micro, Small and Medium Enterprises)

- **Context:** An MSME Ministry institution for training and support, part of the skill ecosystem (Chapter 14).
- **Significance:** Faces challenges in delivering verifiable outcomes.

NITI Aayog

- **Context:** Involved in evaluating schemes like Coir Vikas Yojana, critiqued for glossy reports (Chapter 15, Chapter 22).
- **Significance:** A policy think tank with potential to drive MSME reforms, but needs outcome focus.

NSIC (National Small Industries Corporation)

- **Context:** Promotes MSMEs through tenders, training, and incubation, criticised for unverified claims (Chapter 14, Chapter 21).
- **Significance:** A key institution needing accountability and outcome-based reforms.

PMEGP (Prime Minister's Employment Generation Programme)

- **Context:** A unified scheme for self-employment, supporting coir and other micro units (Preface, Chapter 2, Chapter 22).
- **Significance:** A major job creation initiative, but faces verification and impact challenges.

PMKVY (Pradhan Mantri Kaushal Vikas Yojana)

- **Context:** Flagship skill training programme under Skill India, with a ~43% placement rate (Chapter 2).

- **Significance:** Ambitious but limited by quality and outcome gaps.

PMSBY (Pradhan Mantri Suraksha Bima Yojana)

- **Context:** Linked to Coir Workers' Insurance, offering accidental coverage to coir workers (Chapter 22).
- **Significance:** Enhances worker welfare but not a direct job creator.

RAMP (Raising and Accelerating MSME Performance)

- **Context:** A scheme to enhance MSME competitiveness, part of post-COVID support (Prologue, Chapter 16).
- **Significance:** Aims at systemic improvement but lacks deep impact evidence.

Reverse Flipping

- **Context:** Indian startups returning from foreign domiciles, facing NCLT, FDI, and tax hurdles (Chapter 11, Chapter 13).
- **Significance:** A growing trend requiring policy reforms for smoother redomiciling.

SBA (Small Business Administration)

- **Context:** US institution providing loans, contracts, and support to small businesses, a model for India (Chapter 1).
- **Significance:** Offers lessons in financial and procurement support for MSMEs.

SFURTI (Scheme of Fund for Regeneration of Traditional Industries)

- **Context:** Supports coir and other traditional industry clusters, with mixed success (Chapter 22).
- **Significance:** Aims to modernise traditional sectors, but faces implementation challenges.

SIDBI (Small Industries Development Bank of India)

- **Context:** Manages the Fund of Funds for Startups and supports MSME financing (Chapter 2, Chapter 18).
- **Significance:** A key financial institution, but criticised for slow disbursements.

Simples Nacional

- **Context:** Brazil's unified tax regime for small businesses, simplifying compliance (Chapter 1).
- **Significance:** A global best practice for easing MSME tax burdens.

Skill India Mission

- **Context:** Launched in 2015 to skill youth for industry needs, including MSMEs, with mixed outcomes (Chapter 2).
- **Significance:** Critical for MSME workforce development, but needs better placement focus.

Small Giants

- **Context:** A term for MSMEs globally, emphasising their economic importance (Preface, Chapter 1).
- **Significance:** Frames MSMEs as key to inclusive growth and resilience.

SPF (Startup Policy Forum)

- **Context:** Advocates for reforms to ease reverse flipping of startups (Chapter 13).
- **Significance:** Represents startup community efforts to influence policy.

Stand-Up India

- **Context:** Promotes entrepreneurship among women and disadvantaged groups through bank loans (Chapter 2, Chapter 23).
- **Significance:** Targets inclusive entrepreneurship, but is limited by outreach.

Startup India

- **Context:** Launched in 2016, recognising over 1,00,000 startups by 2024 (Chapter 2, Chapter 23).
- **Significance:** A flagship initiative but primarily benefits tech startups, not traditional MSMEs.

TIRFSS (Technology and Infrastructure for Sustainable Coir Sector)

- **Context:** A component of Coir Vikas Yojana for digital and infrastructure support in coir (Chapter 22).
- **Significance:** Aims to modernise coir, but is limited by implementation gaps.

UK Sinha Committee Report

- **Context:** Proposed a modern MSME Code and Distressed Asset Fund, but faced execution hurdles (Chapter 18).
- **Significance:** A visionary blueprint needing better implementation.

Udyam Portal

- **Context:** A digital registration platform for MSMEs, part of post-COVID support (Prologue, Chapter 16).
- **Significance:** Enhances formalisation, but requires broader outreach and awareness.

Unicorn Mirage

- **Context:** Critiques the hype around Indian startups, questioning valuation-driven success (Chapter 15).
- **Significance:** Calls for accountability and IP-driven startup growth.

VDIS (Voluntary Disclosure of Income Scheme)

- **Context:** Introduced in 1997–98 to provide tax amnesty to small businesses with undisclosed wealth (Chapter 23).
- **Significance:** Aimed at formalising MSME finances, but had a limited long-term impact.

For more information